RADIO DIPLOMACY AND PROPAGANDA

STUDIES IN DIPLOMACY

General Editors: G. R. Berridge and John W. Young, Centre for the
Study of Diplomacy, University of Leicester

David H. Dunn
DIPLOMACY AT THE HIGHEST LEVEL: The Evolution of
International Summitry

M. J. Peterson
RECOGNITION OF GOVERNMENTS: Legal Doctrine and State
Practice, 1850–1995

Gary D. Rawnsley
RADIO DIPLOMACY AND PROPAGANDA: The BBC and VOA in
International Politics, 1956–64

Radio Diplomacy and Propaganda

The BBC and VOA in International Politics, 1956–64

Gary D. Rawnsley
Lecturer in Politics
The University of Nottingham

First published in Great Britain 1996 by
MACMILLAN PRESS LTD
Houndmills, Basingstoke, Hampshire RG21 6XS
and London
Companies and representatives
throughout the world

This book is published in the *Studies in Diplomacy* series.
General Editors: G. R. Berridge and John W. Young

A catalogue record for this book is available from the British Library

ISBN 0–333–64943–5

First published in the United States of America 1996 by
ST. MARTIN'S PRESS, INC.,
Scholarly and Reference Division,
175 Fifth Avenue,
New York, N.Y. 10010

ISBN 0–312–12972–6

Library of Congress Cataloging-in-Publication Data
Rawnsley, Gary D.
Radio diplomacy and propaganda : the BBC and VOA in international
politics, 1956–64 / Gary D. Rawnsley.
p.   cm.
Originally presented as the author's thesis (Ph.D.—University of Leeds)
Includes bibliographical references and index.
ISBN 0–312–12972–6
1. International broadcasting—Great Britain.   2. International
broadcasting—United States.   3. British Broadcasting Corporation–
–History.   4. Voice of America (Organization)—History.   5. Radio in
propaganda—Great Britain—History—20th century.   6. Radio in
propaganda—United States—History—20th century.   I. Title.
HE8697.45.G7R39   1996
384.54'0941—dc20   95–52176
                                                                        CIP

10   9   8   7   6   5   4   3   2   1
05   04   03   02   01   00   99   98   97   96

Printed in Great Britain by
Ipswich Book Co Ltd, Ipswich, Suffolk

For my parents

Contents

Acknowledgements

This book is the product of a lifelong passion for international radio broadcasting which a great many people have encouraged over the years; many more have contributed to the present volume on both an intellectual and personal level. An acknowledgement of my appreciation to them is therefore warranted.

My biggest debt of gratitude must go to the supervisor of my PhD thesis upon which this book is based – Philip M. Taylor. His advice and encouragement at every stage of this project have been invaluable, while his comments on successive drafts have always proved to be spot-on. The Institute of Communication Studies at the University of Leeds was a wonderful environment in which to work for three years; their study of the 1991 Gulf War, which began as I was preparing to start my research, was particularly exciting and stimulated much of the thinking about my own subject that has ended up in this volume.

Owen Hartley of the Institute of International Studies at Leeds has also been with me all the way. I must thank him for his confidence in me as an undergraduate and for suggesting that I do a PhD in the first place.

Owen Hartley was my examiner along with Professor John Young. Together they turned my viva into an intellectually challenging event, and provided many pertinent comments which contributed to the revisions of the manuscript. John Young's colleague at Leicester, Professor Geoff Berridge, has been a most encouraging editor, and his confidence in both me and the project itself has been reassuring.

I would like to thank Jaqueline Kavanagh and her team at the BBC Written Archive Centre, Reading, who were never too busy to give advice on source material and then run away to find it despite the relentless pressure of their internal BBC workload. If I was sometimes too demanding, then I apologise. It is with their kind permission that I reproduce selected material housed at the Centre.

The staff at the Public Records Office, Kew Gardens, were equally helpful, and again I am grateful for permission to quote from Crown Copyright material.

At the National Archives, Washington, DC, I would like to thank David Pfeifer in particular for imparting his expert knowledge of primary source material concerning and by the USIA. Also in Washington, I acknowledge the constant assistance of Martin Manning at the USIA Historical Collection, and Lola Secora of the Freedom of Information Office. Both provided an immense amount of material for which I am grateful. Michael Nelson should also be acknowledged; his own research interests have coincided with mine, and it was a pleasure to finally meet him at the 1993 Institute of Contemporary British History Summer School after months of exchanging correspondence. His advice and comments have been received with gratitude.

I would also like to thank the many people from the BBC and Foreign Office, past and present, who took the time and trouble to respond to my seemingly endless questioning: Sam Younger, the late Sir Evelyn and Lady Shuckburgh, Lord David Owen, Hamilton Duckworth, Sir Leonard Figg, Laurie Breen, Peter Sezente and John Drinkall. I should add my eternal gratitude to one former IRD operative who supplied an extraordinary amount of information (some of which lies outside the scope of the present study) but expressed a desire to remain anonymous. You know who you are, and I thank you!

I would like to acknowledge a special debt of gratitude to the Economic and Social Research Council whose generous funding allowed me to undertake the necessary research for this book.

On a more personal level I wish to thank the staff and residents of the International Student House, Washington, DC, for turning what slowly became a frustrating research trip into a most enjoyable experience. Mr and Mrs Granger of Whitton, Twickenham, also require thanking for providing me with a home from home while researching at the PRO. My wife, Ming-Yeh, tolerated my heavy workloads, as well as periods of absence, and often came second-place to my word-processor. But she was always there just when I needed her most.

But my final acknowledgement must go to my parents, Jack and Shirley Rawnsley, a source of strength without whose unremitting support and encouragement, none of this would have been possible. And they also bought me my first short-wave radio – a Russian Vega Selena 215. The rest, as they say, is history!

List of Abbreviations

ARVN	Army of the Republic of [South] Vietnam
BBC	British Broadcasting Corporation
CIA	Central Intelligence Agency
DRV	Democratic Republic of [North] Vietnam
FO	Foreign Office
FRUS	Foreign Relations of the United States Department of State
GMT	Greenwich Mean Time
GVN	Government of [South] Vietnam
IPD	Information Policy Department, Foreign Office
IRD	Information Research Department, Foreign Office
NLFSV	National Liberation Front of South Vietnam
PRO	Public Records Office, Kew Gardens, London
PWE	Political Warfare Executive
RFE	Radio Free Europe
RL	Radio Liberty
SWB	Summary of World Broadcasts
USIA	United States Information Agency
USIA HC	United States Information Agency Historical Collection, Washington, DC
USIS	United States Information Service
USNA	United States National Archives, Washington, DC
VOA	Voice of America
WAC	BBC Written Archive Centre, Caversham Park, Reading

Introduction

There are but two powers in the world, the sword and the mind. In the long run, the sword is always beaten by the mind.

Napoleon[1]

Communication between peoples widely separated in space and thought is undoubtedly the greatest weapon against the evils of misunderstanding and jealousy, and if my fundamental invention goes some way towards averting the evils of war, I shall not feel that I have lived in vain.

Guglielmo Marconi[2]

The intention of this book is to demonstrate how communications contribute to international relations. Surprisingly few scholars of international relations refer to the fundamental aspect of *any* relationship, namely communication,[3] even though such an association has long been recognised, as the two quotations reproduced above confirm. In addition they suggest that a given medium of communication possesses neutrality: it is the intention behind its use that must determine our judgement of its morality.

This book will investigate just one channel of international communication, namely radio broadcasting, and will concentrate on the work of the BBC external services and the Voice of America (VOA). The choice of these stations has not been arbitrary: primary source research has not encountered any difficulties with language; but, more important, each presents a contrasting view of its role and relationship to its government – the BBC is ostensibly independent in everything but finance, while the VOA is very much the voice of the American government. As the following discussion will suggest, however, these two stations are in fact more alike than they care to admit.

The principal arguments of this book are set against the background of four specific events in the crucial 1956–64 period of the Cold War, namely:

- The Suez Crisis
- The Hungarian Uprising
- The Cuban Missile Crisis
- The escalation of American involvement in Vietnam.

1

Individually they represent a significant stage in the development of each broadcasting service. Together they present an opportunity to ascertain the importance and contribution of international radio broadcasting to the conduct of diplomacy, conflict and conflict resolution, and to the maintenance of alliance relationships in crisis conditions.[4] However, the importance assigned to these functions has been far from equal; broadcasting to friendly audiences has, more often than not, been a subordinate consideration of programming priorities. The Voice of America in particular has been regularly criticised for having paid far more attention to perceived ideological adversaries than to America's existing and potential allies. According to this argument audiences are more selective in their reception of messages than most propaganda theory assumes; international propaganda can only reinforce, rather than change, existing opinions, while listeners avoid highly political and perhaps censored broadcasts. The critics asserted that because American propaganda perhaps made the Soviets only more defensive and inflexible, VOA should concentrate on information programming directed to audiences who hold less antagonistic political views. John Spicer Nicholls,[5] for one, was therefore most disapproving of the VOA's schedule, which does not include, for example, language services in Italian (since 1957), French to France (since 1961), German (since 1960), or Japanese (since 1970), while there is a noticeable absence of broadcasts targeted specifically at the United Kingdom.[6] This does not of course negate the fact that the UK receives (in the opinion of some, too many!) programmes from the United States via other channels, especially television which, in an age of instant satellite and cable broadcasting, is rapidly attaining pre-eminence in international communication, particularly in the developed world.

In 1962 Henry Loomis, then Director of the VOA, explained to the British Foreign Office that it was his station's established policy not to broadcast to any fully-developed friendly countries in foreign language. (As VOA would not need to broadcast in a foreign language to the United Kingdom, the absence of such a service remained unexplained.) Given its need to secure finance for new activities, the Foreign Office reasoned that VOA's 'philosophy' was 'sound' and suggested that the BBC should be urged to adopt this view, even though they would be most reluctant to do so.[7] It is more than a little ironic, then, that the North American service was the first to be abolished in 1962 for the very reason Henry Loomis had advanced.[8] John Tusa, former managing director of the external services (1986–1992), is particularly scathing of this decision. He has suggested that it ignored isolationist and parochial forces in the US, a country largely ignorant of Europe and its politics. Encouraging such sentiment by removing the North American service was, he believed, a considerable risk, given the strategic and diplomatic importance of the US to Europe during the Cold War.[9]

But this was not the first time – nor indeed would it be the last – that the BBC was pressured by the prevailing political climate into rationalising its overseas activities. The conclusions of the Hill Committee, established to review Britain's overseas information efforts in the aftermath of the Suez crisis, implied that fighting the Cold War was of decidedly more importance than broadcasting to West European allies.[10] In that year Swedish, Norwegian, Danish, Dutch, Austrian, Portuguese and Afrikaans services were abolished, while the French, Italian and American services were drastically reduced.[11] These cuts came at a time when, during the mid-1950s, the Communists were intensifying their own propaganda directed at Western Europe.[12] In light of the considerable influence of Communist parties in places like Spain, Italy and France the decision to cut down or curtail altogether various BBC and VOA European services was therefore a grave mistake, Meanwhile, services to other areas were increased; to Eastern Europe, the principal site of the Cold War at this time, and especially to Africa which, as decolonisation progressed, was to be a peripheral area of superpower confrontation.

This study will focus on the relationship between the BBC external services and the Voice of America and the propaganda objectives as devised by their governments and foreign services (and often by their intelligence services as well); and will analyse how this combination reacted to the crises which enveloped them in the 1956–64 period.

In addition, the content of broadcasts received by the monitoring services of both Britain and the United States, as recorded in the *Summaries of World Broadcasts*, will be scrutinised in considerable detail. These services act in cooperation with each other; what is monitored by the BBC at Caversham Park is usually relayed via the American Foreign Broadcast Information Service to relevant 'customers' in the US, including government departments. Departments of the British government, especially the Foreign Office, also receive monitoring reports from the BBC. Such analysis provides a means of ascertaining how the output of the BBC and VOA reacted to them. Moreover they enable us to evaluate how far the received broadcasts helped shape the government's foreign policy. As Cord Meyer, former CIA chief, has recorded, '90 per cent of what the policy-maker needs to know to make intelligent policy decisions is in the public domain.'[13] A careful analysis of this 90 per cent is then crucial to identifying the remaining 10 per cent.

The Foreign Office information services files available at the Public Records Office have provided a wealth of information about the British government and its approach to propaganda. The State Department of the United States has also been helpful in supplying relevant material, but most useful have been its series of publications entitled *Foreign Relations of the United States*.

In addition it has been necessary to analyse the internal policies of the BBC and VOA and, where available, broadcast scripts. Access to these has been provided by the BBC Written Archives Centre, the United States Information Agency Historical Collection, the United States National Archives, and of course the Voice of America itself. Such formal historical records have been supplemented wherever possible by the recollections of various BBC employees in their generous correspondence.

Writing about Radio Free Europe, Robert Holt warned the novice researcher against considering Who says What to Whom, How, Why, and With What Effect. He believed that an 'adequate consideration of "what" would demand a detailed content analysis. The problems involved would be immense. . . . It would be a brave man indeed,' he continued, 'who would attempt alone a consistent analysis of RFE's voluminous output as a study in itself, and a foolhardy one who would attempt it as a first part of a study.'[14] While the present author gratefully acknowledges this sound advice, it is nevertheless impossible to make a detailed comparison between output and government foreign policy without examining broadcasts in scripted form. Indeed it would seem that Holt himself, for all his warnings, found it necessary to adopt such a 'foolhardy' approach; he wrote that the charges against RFE during the Hungarian uprising are 'simply not supported by a study of RFE scripts'.[15]

The intention of this book is to offer a new perspective on the 1956–64 period by fusing the various academic disciplines involved – international relations, international history and international communications – and ascertain the role of international radio broadcasting as both an instrument and determinant of foreign policy. The period has of course already been well covered by scholars and continues to be the focus of academic research and reflection. In addition to relying heavily on much of this established research, this book will reveal new information provided by access to primary source material previously unavailable. Its quest for originality derives from its treatment of the material, that is, in identifying the relationship between broadcasting and international relations in a theoretical, as much as in an historical and narrative, manner.

Perhaps the best defence of this book's purpose is to be found in the pioneering work of Davison and George. Recognising that '[T]he study of international communication cuts across the established boundaries of academic disciplines', they rightly noted how political communications is always 'an auxiliary instrument of policy', which is the central argument of this book:

> It is used in conjunction with decisions or actions which may fall on the diplomatic, economic or military sphere. If we try to study a communication without reference to the decision or action of which it is an auxiliary, we may be in a position of examining a meaningless abstraction.[16]

1 Radio Diplomacy and Propaganda

Dialogue between statesmen and diplomats is at the very heart of the diplomatic process. It is an art of communication designed to exchange views towards learning what other governments aspire and object to, and then persuading them of the existence of parallel, even mutual interests.

Because the technology of global communications and its application have both grown at such an extraordinary pace, governments are no longer confined to the traditional channels of diplomatic practice. Broadcasting has emerged as a necessary and effective complement to the process, and statesmen must now be aware more than ever of public opinion – domestic and foreign – and the effects of their policy decisions upon it. Thus W.J. West's bold assertion that with the advent of the use of radio as a tool of foreign policy 'conventional diplomacy became redundant,'[1] can be dismissed; this statement is far too absolute and betrays a misunderstanding of both the theory and practice of diplomacy. However when he considers an earlier period in British history than is considered in this book, West does provide a perceptive description of the power of radio in international politics:

> Unlike previous great changes in the political state of Europe in the days before World War I, what had happened was there on the surface to be heard by everyone in the voices of the leaders themselves over countless radios all over the world. There was no time needed for understanding, analysis or debate. The actual administrative changes could take place within hours of a radio announcement.[2]

The implications of this development are of course considerable and will form the basis of later discussion. The most dangerous consequence of removing foreign policy from the élites and providing public opinion with access to the process is the possibility of greater xenophobia; by being exposed to a variety of cultures and ideologies, the differences that separate people are there on the surface for all to see, heightening their fear and suspicion of each other.[3] The reassertion of nationalism in the post-Cold War world indicates that this may be a problem which is likely to be encountered on an increasing scale.

6

As this book's chapter on the Suez crisis will demonstrate, the Arab states of the Middle East in particular have exploited such divisions in their propaganda, while radio broadcasting's ability to antagonise, irritate and offend was all too readily maximised during the Cold War.

The application of international radio broadcasting in crisis conditions has a long pedigree and pre-dates the Cold War. In fact the earliest recorded instance of an organised use of radio in foreign policy was in 1926 when Russia demanded the return of Bessarabia from Romania. Moscow was also the first to employ international radio as a tool of its foreign policy; the inauguration of Radio Moscow in 1929, first in four languages and growing to 11 by 1933, resulted from an aspiration to explain the Communist revolution to the wider world and propagandise its accomplishments. Its broadcasts definitely found an audience; in 1930 a member of the public wrote to Hugh Dalton at the British Foreign Office, expressing concern that Moscow radio had been heard broadcasting in English and 'urging revolution repeatedly'.[4] The Soviet Union can therefore be rightly considered a pioneer in the field, as other European nations with international services merely targeted expatriates scattered throughout the various empires. Britain, for example, had launched its own such Empire Service in 1932.[5]

This cosy environment was radically transformed by the rise of Fascism in Europe. In 1935, the Italians began to transmit vitriolic propaganda in Arabic against British Middle Eastern policy, compelling the BBC to establish its first foreign language service – Arabic – in 1938.

But it was the Nazis who proved particularly inventive in their use of the medium. A massive propaganda barrage certainly eased the Anschluss of Austria in March 1938. Dr Joseph Goebbels, the Nazi Minister for Propaganda and Enlightenment, arranged for 25 000 radio sets, tuned only to German frequencies, to be freely distributed throughout Austria. It this way German broadcasts enjoyed a near monopoly of information. Distributing radio receivers pre-tuned to selected frequencies was a method of transmitting propaganda subsequently developed by the allies, and was used throughout the twentieth century, especially during the Vietnam war.

But as usual the British government lagged behind its European contemporaries; it did not fully appreciate the value of foreign language broadcasting until the Munich conference of 1938.[6] On 27 September, two days before the conference convened, the BBC was asked to transmit

German, Italian and French versions of a speech to the nations by the Prime Minister, Neville Chamberlain. The objective of this exercise was to present the British case directly to the German people, but was dogged by technical failure and blunders of timing which prompted the government to secretly use the pirate station Radio Luxembourg for such activities in the future.[7] In this way the intentions of British policy were projected into Europe, and for the first time in the crisis the German people themselves were presented with the British case. The British had finally begun to use radio broadcasting as a channel of public diplomacy, albeit secretly and with the ignorance of the BBC.

PROPAGANDA

During the Cold War international radio broadcasting made by far its largest contribution to the dissemination of propaganda.[8] Propaganda is a highly emotive, often ambiguous subject with many volumes already devoted to its understanding, so here the briefest of definitions will suffice. As used in this study propaganda refers to the attempt by the government of one state to influence another to act or think in ways which are conducive to the interests of the source by whatever means are considered appropriate. Alternatively propaganda may reinforce existing convictions and attitudes, again conforming to the interests of the transmitting state. The success of this is not coincidental; if international broadcasts are politically motivated then their content and style will be the result of extensive research into the target audience. This study will present evidence, for example, that western broadcasters targeted the disaffected of the Communist systems in particular during the Cold War, so much so that their effectiveness was often restricted by a narrow Cold War mentality which tended to judge all crises by the same limiting criteria.

Such a definition of propaganda was readily accepted by Robert Holt who was scornful of the idea that the basic purpose of the United States Information Agency (USIA, the parent agency of the Voice of America), was 'to spread a proper image of the US,' 'express a point of view,' or 'to make the meanings of our actions unmistakably clear to citizens and leaders in other countries'.[9] The main purpose of the USIA, Holt believed, was to affect the policy decisions of others in such a way that American foreign policy goals would be achieved.[10] In other words, USIA was an organisation irrevocably tied to American foreign policy.

The ability of propaganda to actually change beliefs, attitudes and value systems is questionable since the manipulation of opinions, attitudes and understanding is not easily quantified. It is certain, however, that to be effective the targeted audiences must first be vulnerable to a message – either positive about the source or negative about the target's government – such as, for example, by being politically alienated from a régime. This in turn motivates them to seek out foreign propaganda which reinforces their convictions.

Lester Markel, writing in 1958 for the *New York Times Magazine*, ascribed to propaganda a neutral status, describing it as 'a method, a technique, neither moral or immoral' with 'indispensable uses' if 'employed skilfully and for good ends'.[11] In contrast the French sociologist, Jacques Ellul, judged transnational propaganda to be exclusively a weapon of war, one which actually helped to sustain the Cold War as a permanent and endemic state. But although his rejection of the neutrality of propaganda is contestable,[12] Ellul offered some pertinent comments on 'democratic propaganda' which he described as 'ineffectual' because it lacks totality. 'To the extent that a democratic propagandist has a bad conscience,' he wrote, 'he cannot do good work.'

Ellul then concluded that 'our own [democratic] propaganda is outclassed by that of totalitarian states. This means that ours does not do its job.'[13] This is less than just, a judgement which will be vigorously defended throughout the present study. Propaganda need not be as total as Ellul envisaged to be effective. K.J. Holsti accurately described the motive of propaganda as stimulating support and action, but asserted that the key to this is how the source of information is evaluated by the audience; the higher the evaluation, the more likely it is that the desired objectives of the propaganda will be realised. In this context Holsti believed the BBC to be the most respected and trusted of international broadcasting stations.[14]

This statement alone raises a number of compelling questions concerning the BBC, since such logic implies that the BBC engages in *indirect* propaganda. If it is the most effective in the terms established by Holsti, it follows that it will then be the most successful in its propaganda activities, laying to rest once and for all Ellul's criticisms of 'democratic propaganda'. Indeed during the Cold War the Soviet Union repeatedly accused the BBC of engaging in propaganda by claiming to broadcast in an objective manner and without prejudice.[15] In 1952 the BBC candidly admitted to the USIA that this was indeed its method: 'You're cheating all the time, of course,' BBC personnel told USIA's Ralph White. 'What matters is the appearance of objectivity when actually

you are not completely objective.'[16] In other words credibility, balance and truth are used to sell a political message in much the same
way as one would use overt propaganda techniques. Disguise it as news
and information and we have what Nicholas Pronay has called 'propaganda with facts'.[17] For the propagandist the most advantageous feature of operating in this way is that it can neither be proved nor disproved
as being propaganda.

Controlling the flow of propaganda has long been an anxiety for
practitioners of international relations. The first attempt to establish
the ground-rules by which the content of broadcasts could be regu-
lated was made by the League of Nations, whose members were encouraged to use radio for peaceful means, or in its own words, to
'create better mutual understanding between peoples'.[18] To this end
the League devised an International Convention concerning the Use of
Broadcasting in the Cause of Peace in 1936. This bound its signatories
to prevent the transmission of material 'which to the detriment of good
international understanding, is of such a character as to incite the population of any territory to acts incompatible with the internal order or
the security of a territory of a High Contracting Party'.[19] This was
certainly a grand and praiseworthy objective. The problem was that
only three great powers agreed to be signatories – Britain, France and
the Soviet Union. As we have seen the first two powers had already
limited their international broadcasting efforts to providing services for
their expatriates. The powers whose propaganda was of most concern
at this time, Fascist Germany and Italy, refused to sign and were therefore
not bound by its provisions. Indeed it would have been surprising had
they done so given the importance which each attached to propaganda
during this turbulent period.

After the Second World War, yet another attempt was made to control international propaganda. The Charter of the United Nations declared that the legal duty of a state required it to 'refrain from spreading
subversive propaganda hostile to the government of a foreign country
in times of peace'.[20] In addition the General Assembly adopted the so-
called 'Essentials for Peace' Resolution in 1949 which called on all
nations 'to refrain from any threats or acts, direct or indirect, aimed at
impairing the freedom, independence or integrity of any state, or at
fomenting civil strife and vetting the will of the people in any state'.[21]
In these terms propaganda can be considered a violation of territorial
sovereignty.

Yet provocative propaganda and incitement have not been completely
outlawed. Rather, their regulation has been placed at the discretion of

the individual member states themselves; they are not enforceable by the collective will of the UN. One only has to look to the political inefficiency of both the League of Nations and the UN to discover possible reasons why they consistently failed to regulate the flow of international propaganda. When states considered the League or UN to be operating in their favour they would gladly work through their framework, but readily ignored them when it suited them to do so. Now when they wish to object to broadcasts targeted at them, states have a whole body of international legislation they can refer to. For example, should they wish to declare the legality of the free flow of information across international frontiers, they can cite the Universal Declaration of Human Rights (1948), the decisions of the International Telecommunications Union, and the Helsinki Accords. In short, a state can find whatever it may require to justify its actions in international law. During the 1950s the United States invoked the Declaration of Human Rights when it appealed to the United Nations against Soviet jamming of the Voice of America. But the Soviet Union also protested against American broadcasts, referring to both a 1936 Geneva resolution and Resolution 841 passed by the UN General Assembly in 1954 which condemned broadcasts designed to 'incite the population of any territory to acts incompatible with internal order'.[22]

Such legal ambiguity has inevitably prompted states to find other means of controlling the flow of propaganda, with jamming of incoming radio signals being the most common (but perhaps also the most expensive). Jamming has itself been used as an instrument of international relations; the subject of frequent diplomatic negotiations during the Cold War, its intensity has reflected the political climate at any one time.[23]

Yet broadcasting remains a most powerful medium, despite all of these problems associated with the control of international radio propaganda. 'In at least two aspects,' wrote Terence H. Qualter,

> radio is superior to all its predecessors. It is immediate and its is universal, being bound by neither time nor space. There is no perceptible time-lag between broadcast and reception. A radio message circles the globe in an instant. It is universal; the only unstoppable medium. Radio can ignore frontiers and boundaries, for jamming and banning are rarely fully effective and may even be counterproductive. Radio can penetrate where it is officially not wanted. This makes it pre-eminent as an instrument of international propaganda.[24]

International propaganda is synonymous with 'public diplomacy'; it is specifically targeted at a mass audience, based on the supposition that public opinion can exert a considerable influence on its governments and state systems. 'Media diplomacy' is more selective and aims to influence the government or régime directly, offering the professional diplomat an alternative channel of communication, and negotiation.

This book is concerned with both public diplomacy and media diplomacy; the difference seems to be wholly dependent on both the intention of the broadcaster and the interpretation of his or her message by the recipient.

THE BBC AND VOICE OF AMERICA: A BRIEF HISTORY

It is unnecessary to chronicle the histories of the BBC external services and the Voice of America in detail. Many excellent accounts already exist and are listed in the bibliography. Here a general overview will suffice to illustrate how both stations have functioned, the principles (or lack of them) that have guided their activities, and to allow a brief comparison of their experiences.

The crisis years of 1956–64 represent a series of crucial turning points in the development of the BBC and VOA. In 1956 alone, the BBC had to confront the challenges posed by the unfortunate coincidence of the Suez crisis with the Hungarian uprising, scathing government criticism, and the tremors of a full-scale inquiry and review with far-reaching implications for its activities – all at the same time! Meanwhile the Voice of America faced its own problems: reflecting the shifting priorities in American foreign policy; persuading the politicians of its worth and power; and coming to terms with the growing realisation of the need to involve propagandists in the foreign policy process. Furthermore VOA was increasingly becoming an instrument of 'psychological warfare' as military involvement in Vietnam escalated.

Both stations claim they have achieved a degree of credibility and a great deal of popularity by broadcasting in a truthful and objective manner, and as accurately as possible. The BBC external services can trace the origins of this reputation as far back as 1932, to their inception as the Empire Service. The idea that the BBC's overseas broadcasts should simply replicate the government line of the day was forcefully rejected as inconsistent with BBC ethics. This has prevailed as a source of tension with the government since the idea of broadcasting in foreign languages was first discussed. The BBC resisted Foreign Office demands that it counter the propaganda emanating from the Fascist

Italian station at Bari.[25] The debate came to a head during the inaugural transmission of the Arabic service in 1938 when it reported how a Palestinian had been executed on the orders of a British military court. As Asa Briggs has commented: 'Only the BBC would have jeopardized the start . . . by telling the truth in a bold factual way'.[26] This observation reads more as a eulogy to the BBC than a criticism, but the episode was nevertheless an omen. As the chapter on the Suez crisis vividly demonstrates this was not the last time that the BBC's independence was to conflict with government interests.[27] Yet by 'telling the truth in a bold factual way' the BBC established a precedent for its broadcasts during World War Two. The reputation of the station as an objective, accurate and reliable source of news and information was considerably enhanced at this time, especially when it told of allied defeats as well as victories; often the BBC acknowledged more ally losses than axis propaganda!

Donald Browne has wondered whether the prevailing credibility of the BBC can be attributed to this reputation, particularly during the Second World War, or whether it may also have been intimately bound-up with 'Britain's diminishing role in world politics, so that listeners might regard the BBC as better able to broadcast accurate and complete information because Britain has less of a stake in major events'.[28] This is without a doubt an interesting, though somewhat flawed, hypothesis: although it is reasonable to describe the Suez crisis as a milestone in British foreign affairs, the argument that it reduced Britain's role and stake in world politics simply cannot be sustained. The history of foreign policy since 1956 verifies that Britain, while no longer a major power, has certainly continued to remain a major global player with the capacity to exert formidable influence on the world stage. Despite its retreat from Empire and disengagement from many areas of the globe, its diplomatic relations, its military potential and role within various international organisations – after all it remains a member of the UN Security Council – indicate that Great Britain retains the ability to command a recognised status within international affairs.

In contrast American international broadcasting was established purely as a wartime expedient. Unlike the BBC it had no experience of independent peacetime broadcasting to fall back on once the Second World War ended. Nevertheless from the outset, VOA did endeavour to imitate the objectivity that had made the BBC such a reputable service. Its first transmission, heard in February 1942 just two months after the bombing of Pearl Harbour, opened with the promise: 'Daily at this time we shall speak to you about America and the war. The news may be good or bad. We shall tell you the truth.'[29] Yet VOA's lack of peacetime experience proved to be problematic during the early post-war years; many within the American establishment were not prepared to allow propaganda – which they naively regarded simply as a war-time necessity – to impinge upon foreign policy in times of peace. However the Korean War, Stalinism in Eastern Europe and the developing Cold War together prompted a change of heart, and the information effort was made an integral part of the 'Campaign of Truth' launched by President Harry Truman in 1950.[30] Now other difficulties were created, as the professional journalistic aspirations and principles of VOA were often compromised by foreign policy objectives. The 1948 Smith–Mundt Act, which had established VOA as part of the State Department's international information programme, only exacerbated the problem. It has thus always been used and recognised as an instrument of US foreign policy. As its name suggests the Voice of America is the official voice of the government; it is state funded and receives its policy directives from the USIA, itself directly responsible to the President. Its history is the history of the alternation between Cold War and détente, reflected vividly in its output and the policies and philosophies of its long line of politically-appointed directors, which together determined the position VOA would adopt.

During the first Cold War, 1946–53, the main target area was Europe where VOA reinforced the political decision to 'contain' Communism. This initially involved the creation of a 'ring' of transmitters around the Soviet Union, a strategy brought to an inglorious conclusion by the paranoid McCarthy investigations into VOA and a subsequent cut in appropriations.[31] The fiery rhetoric of the now infamous NSC-68 justified US efforts to curb Soviet expansion and induce the destruction of the Soviet system from within.[32]

In this way the overt propaganda of the VOA and its parent agency, the USIA, was complemented by various covert economic, political and psychological warfare programmes designed to foment internal rebellion behind the Iron Curtain. Such an approach, discredited in 1956 during the Hungarian uprising, confirmed VOA's position on the front-line of the Cold War, but in the process it lost many neutral and potential pro-Western listeners. Since that time striking a balance proved most difficult. A 1953 USIA report, for example, cautioned that the 'Free' world considered America's repeated denunciation of Communism to be 'additional evidence that we are wholly preoccupied with our Cold War against the USSR, that we are fanatical in our crusade against Communism,' and warned that 'the more belligerent they think we are, the more they retreat into neutralism'. This was not to deny, however, the importance of generating a fear of Soviet aggression among audiences: 'To gain allies who will help us to deter or defeat Soviet aggression,' the report continued, 'it is essential for us to create or reinforce in our listeners a vivid awareness of the danger of Soviet aggression, and what it would mean *to them* if this aggression is not deterred or defeated.' [Original emphasis].[33]

By 1961 the so-called 'Second Wave' of decolonisation was well under way and the Soviets were pursuing their 'peaceful co-existence' as their latest objective. In this new climate Congress appropriated increasing amounts of funds to VOA to enable it to check the growing Chinese and Soviet propaganda (and therefore, it was felt, political influence) in developing areas. One can quite easily deduce from this how the output and shape of VOA has been directly related to, indeed determined by, the dictates of American foreign policy in the atmosphere of the Cold War. This relationship prompted Carl Rowan, director of USIA (1964–5), to freely concede that he saw limits to VOA's objectivity, particularly in crisis situations. VOA commentaries, he said, 'express opinion, and it is the official opinion of the United States government. . . . When there is a crisis . . . we simply cannot afford to have the intentions and objectives of the US government misunderstood by other governments.'[34]

Laurien Alexandre offered a similar observation, noting that when a particular story is 'critical to the outcome of US government efforts, the VOA becomes a malleable vehicle in the government's efforts'.[35] Alexandre then cautioned that the VOA can be 'only as objective, fair and balanced as the state which it represents' – hollow words indeed when one considers some of the more distasteful and questionable activities in which the US has engaged as part of its foreign policy process.[36] For this reason there must be a consistency between words and deeds. This was recognised in 1953 by a report on overseas information programmes prepared by the Senate's Committee on Foreign Relations under the Chairmanship of Senator Bourke Hickenlooper. This report, memorable for its strikingly perceptive understanding of the propaganda process, concluded that:

> The US is judged abroad by its actions more than by words. Words may help a people to understand action, but they are no substitute for policy. Thus a vigorous and clear-cut foreign policy enunciated badly and simply by the highest ranking officials of the US can do as much or more than large appropriations for information.[37]

But only three years later such advice was ignored by American propagandists who were clearly seeking to take advantage of the uprising in Hungary.

The Hickenlooper report then recognised the need to integrate communications into the foreign policy process, and advocated that the Director of USIA 'offer suggestions as to the possible effects on public opinion of a proposed move, in terms of method, substance and timing. Lack of liaison in this matter,' it said, 'can be very harmful to the national interest.'[38] These were wise words, but the ideas underpinning them only finally came to fruition in 1961 when they were reiterated by President Kennedy.

The activities of the BBC external services have been similarly subjected to a series of political considerations and influences. These are enshrined in various official documents with the Licence and Agreement and the 1946 White Paper on Broadcasting being the two most important.[39] These stipulate that in addition to the BBC having to accept information from the Foreign Office regarding conditions in, and official policies towards, targeted areas, the Foreign Office is also able to determine the languages of BBC broadcasts, which geographical areas they will broadcast to, and for how long. Specific political crises therefore provided the rationale for establishing, among others, the Pashto (in 1981 after the Soviet invasion of Afghanistan), Ukrainian (in 1992 following the break-up of the Soviet Union), and the Croatian language services.

The Treasury is also indirectly involved in the activities of the BBC. By controlling the grant-in-aid it has the potential to exert enormous pressure on the BBC, as the Suez episode vividly demonstrates. Because of their individual departmental interests and perspectives, and the occasional bureaucratic rivalry, the Treasury and the Foreign Office are frequently in opposition to each other regarding the BBC; the former naturally seeks ways to reduce expenditure and make savings, while the latter remains the champion of the BBC external services and the important role they play in promoting British interests overseas.[40]

While this description of the close relationship between the BBC and the government may cause alarm, it is reasonable to argue that some such control over international radio broadcasting is quite necessary. After all, the areas of international relations and foreign policy are simply too large, often complex, and certainly too important, to grant the stations the complete and unlimited independence they aspire to. This has been the cause of an acute identity crisis for the VOA; coping with the tensions between Cold War and détente, and coming to terms with the unrelenting struggle which pits the standards of professional journalism against the dictates of political expediency, have posed their own problems for the station. The very existence of the VOA Charter is testimony to this; although it was not enshrined in US law until 1976, its formulation can be traced back to 1960. There-after it served as an enunciation of the VOA's guiding principles, but was also a constant reminder of its own quest for an identity.[41]

The relationship between the BBC and the British government has inevitably passed through several painful stages, and these are re-corded in the following pages. Yet on the whole it has been a striking success; initial apprehensions on both sides have been ironed out, if not altogether resolved, and a mutual understanding with the British government has ensured that the BBC has never experienced its own identity crisis with the same intensity as the VOA (except marginally at the time of Suez and even then, as the following chapter will testify, with a number of significant qualifications). Nevertheless, the Utopian advocates of complete BBC autonomy are misguided and not only fail to appreciate the (admittedly limited) control already exercised over the BBC by the government and Foreign Office, but also ignore the valuable service provided by international radio broadcasting to the often complex and invariably sensitive foreign relationships of any given state.

2 The Suez Crisis, 1956: The Lion's Whisper

INTRODUCTION

The Suez crisis of 1956 marked the most serious challenge to British interests since the conclusion of the Second World War. It was characterised by a series of events shrouded in secrecy and clouded by disinformation, a foreign policy scarred by the efforts of a complicated interstate collaboration, and fatal military and diplomatic blundering which turned the crisis into a débâcle. The true purpose, effects and significance of the Suez episode remain the subject of excited academic debate, made even more spirited by the recent access to formerly confidential files and documents.[1] David Sanders has described the Suez crisis as a traumatic but valuable experience for British foreign policy. Since the Second World War Britain had laboured under the pretension of still being a Great Power with its military commitments and diplomacy over-extended. It took the shock of the Suez crisis to break that illusion.[2]

As this chapter will illustrate, the Suez crisis could not have occurred at a more fortunate time for the BBC. After seeking a role comparable to that which enhanced their value and reputation during the Second World War, the Suez crisis provided the background to, if not the reason for, a reappraisal of the organisation and role of the BBC external services and their relationship to the government's foreign policy.

BBC–GOVERNMENT RELATIONS, PRE-SUEZ

In the aftermath of the Second World War, the Labour government made a concerted effort to reduce the BBC's overseas operations, especially its European services. A number of reasons could be advanced in support of these cuts. Without a doubt economy was the most important; not only was the government in the process of rebuilding Britain after the war, but it was also trying to fulfil its socialist manifesto, in particular the establishment of the welfare system. All of this required enormous sums of finance. Other factors also made a reduction in services to Europe seem rational. Many native Europeans who had been employed by the BBC during the war, or who had broadcast to their home countries as 'governments in-exile,' returned to the liberated continent; and there was a need for a reconstruction of British domestic broadcasting which again needed financing, but it also required the external services to give up many of the medium-wave and long-wave frequencies they had used during the war. All of these considerations were of course rooted in the fact that the emergency itself had ended; there was no longer any perceived reason why services should be retained at their previous peak levels. So efforts to cut BBC operations were based primarily on domestic factors but ultimately impinged on foreign policy. The British soon realised that they would have to hold the line against Russia, at least until the US could be brought in to shoulder some of the burden.[3] Then in January 1948 the Cabinet decided that 'anti-Communist publicity' should launch a 'systematic attack' on Communist propaganda.[4] In other words the Attlee government was committed to a foreign policy that should have recognised the importance of international broadcasting by the BBC to its achievement, and even appeared to accept this in 1946 when it demanded that the BBC begin services in the Russian language. The error of this was that such expansion should not have involved a trade-off between West European language services and Russian; both had a valuable role to play after the war. But as the international situation quickly deteriorated with the blockade of Berlin (1948), the signing of the NATO treaty (1949) which institutionalised the Cold War, and the outbreak of the Korean War (1950), external broadcasting became the price paid for an expansion and eventual over-extension of Britain's military capabilities. According to the Chancellor of the Exchequer, Hugh Gaitskell, Britain could no longer afford such 'frills' as international broadcasting, and he believed that 'propaganda could be sacrificed without serious effect'.[5] These were certainly remarkable and naive words under the circumstances; Gaitskell clearly underestimated the value of the BBC at times of crisis, though as Chancellor he did have other priorities. In fact he later conceded the 'importance of broadcasting to the Iron Curtain countries,' but added he was 'also aware of the importance of economy in public expenditure'.[6] Others however saw no dichotomy in accommodating both economy and the need to maintain the external services. In 1950 Sir Robert Bruce Lockhart, former director of the Political Warfare Executive, remarked that the upkeep of the BBC external services cost no more than a small cruiser, but in their effectiveness they were comparable to a whole battle-fleet.[7]

Labour governments were not the only ones concerned with this issue. While in Opposition the Conservative party had savagely criticised the government's cuts in the BBC. For example in February 1951 R.A. Butler described broadcasting as 'one of the most vital [instruments] that we can use in our general defence arrangement,'[8] while Major Tufton Beamish declared that 'every farthing spent' on the European services 'would be a gilt-edged investment'.[9] Once they were elected to office themselves in 1952 however, the Conservatives made no effort to increase government finance to facilitate expansion, instead freezing the grant-in-aid at previous levels. It was not until the Drogheda Committee's review of British overseas information efforts was presented to the government in July 1953 that the relationship between the BBC and the overall government strategy in foreign policy was finally recognised and defined. This report identified three fundamental objectives for British information activities abroad: (i) The support of British foreign policy; (ii) the preservation and strengthening of Commonwealth and Empire ties; and (iii) the promotion of trade and the protection of overseas investment.

The Drogheda report also rejected proposals which had been advanced in 1950, suggesting that the output of the Arabic service should be reduced to just $1\frac{1}{2}$ hours per day.[10] By the middle of the 1950s British policy was the focus of intense hostility in the Middle East, prompting the Drogheda committee to accept the importance of supporting and defending those policies by retaining an efficient Arabic-language service.[11] The often scathing propaganda emanating from Egypt's Voice of the Arabs radio station made its own contribution to this judgement.

EGYPTIAN RADIO: AN IRRITANT

The domestic service of Cairo Radio, broadcasting its own fiery brand of anti-British (including anti-BBC) propaganda to Egyptian audiences, was firmly established by the end of the 1940s. Since Nasser did not attain power until 1952, it is therefore difficult to credit him alone with the visionary use of propaganda all too often assigned to him as a pioneer, and which reminded so many of Goebbels' Nazi propaganda.[12] If one was to believe the *Daily Mail* however, such a comparison was not without foundation; in 1956 the newspaper reported that Nasser was being advised by ex-Nazi propagandists, four of whom were named in a letter to the Prime Minister, Anthony Eden.[13] But since no reply to this letter was recorded its accuracy remains difficult to determine.

Nevertheless Nasser must certainly be credited with recognising the value of radio propaganda in the achievement of his policy objectives. Under his direction an international service, the Voice of the Arabs, was established on 4 July 1953. By 1957 the service was transmitting for seven hours daily in 16 languages including Arabic. The very name of the station indicates Nasser's vision of its purpose, but also reveals his perception of Egypt's importance. Clearly he believed that he led a nation at the forefront of Middle Eastern politics, the pre-eminent Arab state, and thought that its international radio station should reflect this status. In his eyes, and often in the eyes of its audience, the Voice of the Arabs spoke for the entire Arab world.

The Voice of the Arabs had two distinct functions: to broadcast propaganda and (pseudo-) diplomatic messages to overseas audiences; and, by broadcasting to Egypt's regional neighbours, to manipulate Arab sensitivities by appealing to cultural, religious and fraternal bonds – in short, to establish an Arab nationalism to strengthen and further the interests of the Egyptian state. Hence the Voice of the Arabs portrayed struggle in the most passionate symbolism – of Arabdom versus the West, Imperialism versus Liberty, Islam versus Evil – and this is exactly what its Arab audiences wanted to hear.

As Hamilton Duckworth, in his own words a 'comparatively junior member' of the BBC Arabic service during Suez and later its Head (1976–81), has since said, it is 'idle to suppose that Britain or anybody else could have initiated or produced a broadcast remotely similar'.[14] Nevertheless the BBC did make a considerable effort to compete with the Voice of the Arabs on comparable terms by operating in its own individual way.

It is clear that broadcasts by the Voice of the Arabs, and to a lesser extent Cairo Radio, contributed to the shaping of British policy towards the Middle East. During the Suez crisis itself P.F. Grey, the Assistant Under-Secretary at the Foreign Office, suggested that British propaganda should demonstrate how Britain had been attacked by Egypt 'in word and deed' for years. The British response to the situation, he said, derived from the fact that 'it is beyond human nature to abstain from reacting to this kind of thing indefinitely'.[15] At the very least this mounting collection of hostile propaganda must have been an irritant to British policy-makers. Eden certainly accepted it as such, and it was partly responsible for his personal dislike – if not paranoia – of Nasser. During the Buraimi dispute of 1955 for example, Eden is said to have described Egyptian propaganda which supported Saudi Arabia against Britain as 'gross impertinence by those people who are likely to be attacked and destroyed by Israel before long. I hope we give them no help.'[16] In July he wrote to the Foreign Secretary, Selwyn Lloyd: 'This kind of thing is really intolerable. Egyptians get steadily worse. They should be told "No more arms deliveries while this goes on".'[17] Anthony Nutting, the Minister of State at the Foreign Office who resigned during the Suez crisis, has recorded in his memoirs how as 'every such broadcast boomed forth from the Voice of the Arabs transmitter the British government desperately tried to tighten its grip upon those countries where its writ still ran'.[18] This was especially the case in the most sensitive areas – Sudan and Cyprus – where Egyptian propaganda encouraged insurrection against the 'imperialist' British, while in Kenya it openly supported the Mau Mau.

Despite facing such a massive onslaught however, the Information Policy Department within the Foreign Office declined from expressing too much concern with Egyptian broadcasts for fear that this would merely confirm the worth and influence of Nasser's propaganda machine. In adopting this approach the British observed one of the cardinal rules of effective propaganda, namely keep one's own propaganda positive and avoid refuting the claims made by the opposition so that the original message is not spread further amongst those who may not have initially received it. Refutation can also make one's own propaganda appear weak and defensive, and therefore one's position vulnerable.

THE BAGHDAD PACT AND GENERAL GLUBB

While Britain was seeking ways to ensure that neither its position nor its own propaganda appeared vulnerable, Egypt turned its attention towards Jordan. The Baghdad Pact, and the possibility that Jordan might become a member of it, were especially sensitive subjects both from a political and a propaganda perspective. Nasser viewed the Pact as an attempt to isolate Egypt and frustrate his aspirations of Arab solidarity. The Egyptian leader was not the only one with such opinions: the Pact had been ostensibly designed as a western defensive system based on the northern tier of regional states, but the possibility that it might be an anti-Nasser alliance of states was not ignored. Eden, aware of rumours (and no doubt strengthened by monitoring reports of Egyptian radio broadcasts) of Egyptian ambitions to challenge British influence in the area, concurred and set about securing Jordan's membership to the Pact. But the prospect of membership only destabilised Jordan and intensified Jordanian public hostility towards both its own government and the Pact. In January 1955 the new Prime Minister of Jordan, Samir al-Rifai, came to power promising that his government would not participate or link up with any new alliances. But such potent signals of Jordan's internal political situation were largely ignored in favour of a widespread belief that Egyptian radio propaganda had contributed to Jordan's decision. This was certainly the view of the American State Department which believed that Egyptian radio agitation against Jordan was 'detrimental to the west'.[19]

Propaganda against the Baghdad Pact provided a new focus for Arab nationalism since it could easily be presented as yet one more example of western imperialism. As a BBC monitoring report of December 1955 recognised, 'this struggle . . . would strengthen Arab unity, while Arab unity itself would strengthen the struggle against colonialism'.[20] Such anti-Pact broadcasts carried little diplomatic value, but the magnitude of their venom was often quite extraordinary. The anti-Israel theme was particularly effective and attractive for Arab audiences. Indeed in February 1955 Nasser alleged that a Voice of America broadcast had explicitly linked the Baghdad Pact to the security of Israel.[21] Nasser conceded that 'some of the strong feeling which existed today in the Arab countries, and particularly in Egypt, against the western powers . . . resulted directly from their [Egyptian] propaganda effort'. He was resolute however, that such an effort was 'essential to [Egyptian] security at a time when the Baghdad Pact threatened to isolate them from the rest of the world'.[22]

British propaganda about the Baghdad Pact was primarily the responsibility of the Information Research Department (IRD), the propaganda arm of the Foreign Office,[23] and this was perhaps a mistake. The IRD maintained a strong relationship with the BBC throughout its history until being closed down in 1977 by David Owen, then Foreign Secretary.[24] The BBC was one of many clients in the media world which knowingly benefited from the material it supplied, provided it was neither quoted directly, nor attributed to the government as being official policy. IRD was always prepared to praise the BBC external services who used the material as necessary, dependent on editorial policy rather than the dictates of the IRD; indeed the BBC has been described by one former operative as being 'in a class by itself' – a non-official, but authoritative source of factual information from a British vantage point, and considerate of the interests of British foreign policy.[25] So in his opinion the BBC was IRD's most important client. But there were many problems with IRD, principally that it had been established in 1947 as an anti-Communist propaganda organisation. It therefore conformed to the prevailing Cold War belief that anything which was contrary to the interests of the west could be attributed to the Communists. In other words IRD was regarded as something of a panacea. But in the more complex crises such as Suez, it was ineffective to package everything up in Cold War rhetoric. For example as the Soviets began their encroachment into the Middle East in 1955, IRD found itself on familiar ground and despatched to embassies such IRD-prepared material as 'Shore Leave – Soviet Style', 'Confused Soviet Ethics', 'Raising Inhuman Beings' and 'The Colonialism of Anti-Colonialists'.[26] Even IRD's treatment of the Baghdad Pact, on the surface a laudable example of its ability to project British policies and ideas, fell victim to the organisation's Cold War heritage. In March 1956 IRD developed several specific themes of direct concern to the Arabs which might promote the economic and strategic benefits of membership. However the link with Communism was soon re-established, despite the fact that Arabs were much more concerned with western imperialism. The IRD suggested that Arabs be warned, overtly and covertly, of the dangers of co-operating with Communists, while the onerous nature of Communism's own style of colonialism should be described to them.[27]

By way of compensation IRD must be granted some tolerance in this matter. Soviet and Communist propaganda was vehement in its condemnation of the Baghdad Pact which it equated with capitalist expansion and imperialism. Such 'colonial' issues could not therefore be considered outside the Cold War context, and so had to be refuted by anti-Communist, as much as pro-British, propaganda.

The imperialist theme was taken up by the BBC which vociferously rejected accusations that British policy could be considered in such terms. Commentators in the Arabic service recounted how various treaties and colonies in the Middle East had already been rescinded.[28] Broadcasts also suggested that the Pact could provide the basis not only for partnership and co-operation within the Arab world itself, but also between Arab states and the west.

On the whole such a favourable projection of the Baghdad Pact was achieved by one series transmitted on the Arabic service which, by virtue of the fact that it was the most popular programme, stands out as important and influential. This was *Question and Answer*, a programme which encouraged its listeners to write in with questions to be answered by experts. Its launch in 1946 had discouraged political subjects, but demand from Arab correspondents that political issues be addressed proved so overwhelming that the programme was renamed *Political Question and Answer*. Peter Partner has noted that this change of format 'asked for considerable political courage on the part of the service' and that 'most of the questions . . . were of a kind likely to be quite unwelcome to the Foreign Office; they were, indeed, exactly the political questions which British official policy did not want to hear'.[29] The fact that it continued to be broadcast throughout the Suez crisis is certainly a tribute to the independence of the Arabic service. But that independence cannot be proven beyond reasonable doubt. While questions posed by listeners undoubtedly reflected the concerns of the Arab audience, the answers provided by the independent commentators used by the BBC Arabic service reveal a remarkable consistency with government policy. Whether this was intentional or coincidental is never made explicit in the archives.[30]

The questions themselves were varied in content. One asked: 'Is it true that this [Baghdad] Pact has aggressive ends? What can be said in favour of this Pact as an economic means to help develop the Middle East and the participating countries?'[31] Another wondered: 'What is the Baghdad Pact . . . [does it] guarantee the frontiers of Israel?' As we have seen, the BBC was already prepared with the necessary IRD guidance to answer such questions. For example the audience was told how members of the Pact were enjoying the fruits of expanded trade and were sharing their information and expertise on such common problems as health, education, pest control and the care of pilgrims.[32] Yet there is nothing in the official record to suggest that the Baghdad Pact had any of these somewhat idealist objectives. A later assertion that there was an explicit link between the Pact and the aims of the Arab League is particularly bewildering, not least because the League discouraged its members from joining outside alliances. BBC broadcasts therefore appear to have been directly engaged in promoting the Baghdad Pact by distorting both its aims and the benefits of membership. The station's claims of independence, objectivity and accuracy on this issue at least are therefore questionable.

However despite such a valiant advertising campaign by the BBC, Jordan chose not to join the Baghdad Pact. This decision was based primarily on internal political considerations, but General Sir John (Pasha) Glubb, commander of the Arab Legion in Jordan, was in no doubt as to whom should be blamed. 'Egypt', he thundered in November 1955, 'has stolen the public of Jordan and turned it against its own government.'[33] Of course Egypt gladly agreed with this assessment. Glubb had made the mistake that Britain had so far tried so hard to avoid, namely giving Egyptian propaganda more credit than it warranted for decisions that were in fact beyond its control. Now smelling the fruits of one success, Egypt's propaganda was relentless and maintained its stream of anti-Pact rhetoric. In a broadcast on 23 December 1955 for example, Egyptian radio celebrated Jordan's decision in what can be considered to be a message intended for Britain. It described Jordan's rejection of the Pact as an act of Arab nationalism, and warned Britain that it would no longer be able to use its financial grant 'as one of the weapons used to exert pressure on Jordan'. The broadcast declared that to consolidate unity, other Arab States were willing to replace Britain as the main source of Jordan's finance, and that an agreement between Egypt, Syria and Saudi Arabia to aid Jordan had been reached 'in principle'.[34] Jordan however, offered repeated assurances that its government had not received any such offer of financial aid. A report on Damascus Radio that King Hussein had agreed to remove General Glubb and place the Jordanian army under Arab command was also vigorously refuted, although there is evidence that the King had already expressed a wish to see this 'Emperor of Jordan' dismissed.[35] This, together with events in the not too distant future when Glubb was finally relieved of his command, betrayed Jordan's assurances to be hypocrisy.

Another Jordanian broadcast, directed this time at Jordan's neighbours, contained a statement by Jordan's Premier. This affirmed that although membership of the Baghdad Pact had been rejected, 'it is not the policy of the government to participate in a link-up with any new alliances. We shall go on working to strengthen solidarity and the consolidation of cordial and fraternal bonds with all Arab states equally.'[36] Again this can be interpreted as a message of assurance to Britain as much as a statement of intentions to the Middle East.

The British were also anxious to counter the propaganda of the proposed Egyptian–Saudi–Syrian Pact. The Voice of the Arabs maintained that this alliance would 'prevent the enemies of the Arabs from perpetrating provocative acts against their inhabitants, whose liberties are being violated as a result of antiquated treaties concluded between unequal parties and obviously under duress'.[37] This provoked A.C.I. Samuel of the Foreign Office Eastern Department to record:

> Since our position, not only in Aden ... but also in the Persian Gulf depends on these 'old treaties,' I hope that it will be possible for our propagandists to find some way of defending them. ... I should have thought that it can be shown that in almost all cases the

Arab rulers concerned had asked for the treaties, and there was no question of duress. It might also be possible to find in the Koran suitable quotations against those who break their word. . . .

Research may disclose that some of the treaties concerned *were* signed under duress. For instance Egyptians used to argue with much justification that the 1936 Treaty was signed when British troops were in occupation of Cairo. If this is so our publicity will obviously have to sheer off that particular point. [Original emphasis][38]

So while British propagandists insisted on defending their position by referring to the historical record, they were equally prepared to sweep aside the more questionable aspects of that same history when it suited their purpose.

The Glubb Affair

On 11 January 1956, Nasser had assured Sir Humphrey Trevelyan, the British Ambassador in Cairo, that Egyptian propaganda would no longer incite the Jordanians, and that all the usual anti-British propaganda would be suspended. Nasser added however, that such propaganda would resume if circumstances changed. This was a warning that Egyptian propaganda was indelibly tied to British policy in the Middle East. The incitement of the Jordanians did indeed stop, but criticism of British policy persisted.

On 22 February 1956, prior to leaving for a tour of the Middle East, Selwyn Lloyd told his Cabinet colleagues that he intended to 'take a firm line' on propaganda in his discussions with Nasser. 'It was not to be expected,' he said, 'that, if Egypt showed such hostility towards us, we should continue to treat her as a friendly state and, for example, to giver her financial assistance towards the construction of the Aswan High Dam.' He promised that he would make it absolutely clear to Nasser that 'Egypt could not expect further help from us unless she changed her policy towards us'.[39] Lloyd arrived in Cairo on 1 March 1956, and immediately his discussions with Nasser seemed to make considerable progress; together they considered the possibility that hostile Egyptian propaganda might be terminated in return for freezing the membership of the Baghdad Pact and the revival of the Arab Collective Security Pact. Then, after dinner that evening, Lloyd received word that General Glubb had been dismissed from his command of the Arab Legion in Jordan, and all the progress Lloyd had made with Nasser fell by the wayside.

Egyptian propaganda against Glubb had been unremitting and often violent, and the allegations made against him were wide-ranging. Glubb was accused of having been in competition for power with the Jordanian government and having organised plots against the Arabs; other broadcasts were more specific and described him as being responsible for the 'imperialist' Broadcasting Station of the Arabs in Amman, and having directed 'with his own hand the poisonous dagger with which the imperialists stabbed Palestine' in 1948. 'Glubb must go,' Arabs were repeatedly told. 'It is a question of your freedom and unity.' The Jordanian people were encouraged by the Voice of the Arabs to rise up and purge their army of 'Glubb and his followers'.[40]

The Foreign Office insisted that Glubb was not dismissed on the orders of Egypt, but rather had been the victim of a personal dispute with King Hussein.[41] However, this large collection of anti-Glubb propaganda inevitably convinced Eden and Lloyd that Nasser was responsible for Jordan's decision. Lloyd has recorded how 'agents of Nasser or the Saudis' had imported into Jordan 'any magazine or newspaper saying that Glubb was the real ruler . . . Steps were taken', he said, 'to ensure that the King saw them all over the place.'[42] Eden even reached the rather melodramatic conclusion that 'the world was not big enough to hold both him [Eden] and Nasser,' and thus at a stroke he personalised the whole Suez crisis.[43]

King Hussein's decision to dismiss Glubb apparently came as quite a surprise to western policy-makers, especially since Jordan had been assuring Britain for months that the idea was not being given any serious consideration. To express its intention to abide by Treaty commitments despite the dismissal of Glubb, as well as try to temper the British government's inevitable anger, Jordan now made extensive use of its broadcasting facilities as a tool of diplomacy. Jordan Radio, for example, broadcast a communiqué by the Royal Cabinet which said that 'Jordan and Britain are bound by the Treaty of Alliance and Friendship of 1948 and that Jordan repeats its pledges and adheres to the commitments stipulated in the Treaty,' while another declared Jordan's desire to maintain friendly relations with Britain.[44] The Foreign Office, which was encouraging an Iraq–Jordan axis to isolate and pacify Nasser, advised against responding sharply to Glubb's dismissal. It is not impossible that such appeals, broadcast by Jordan at this potentially disruptive moment, influenced Foreign Office thinking.

The BBC also seems to have accepted the prevailing views of the Foreign Office concerning its own treatment of Jordan. Throughout 1955 and 1956 broadcasts reiterated Britain's obligations under the

Anglo-Jordan/Iraq Treaties which promised intervention in the event of an attack by Israel.[45] Even on the eve of the termination of the Anglo-Jordanian Treaty in 1957, such themes continued to be addressed. In a BBC General News Talk, Elisabeth Barker detailed the assistance given to Jordan since 1948 which, she added, would not have been forthcoming from other Arab states. Barker then wondered whether relations between Jordan and Britain would be preserved following the end of the Treaty, or if Egyptian propaganda would 'push the rulers of Jordan into some unnecessary and futile anti-British gesture?'[46] It was not surprising that Sir Alec Kirkbride, an adviser to King Hussein's grandfather, King Abdullah, should express similar sentiments in a 'Topic of Today' broadcast in November 1956.[47] He was convinced that Jordanians wished to retain their links with Britain, but feared they would be frustrated in this endeavour by their vulnerability to Egyptian propaganda. Addressing the British Cabinet on 9 March 1956, Kirkbride had maintained that the dismissal of Glubb was purely personal and was 'not designed to disrupt Jordan's relations with the UK'. Indeed the King and Prime Minister of Jordan were, he said, 'most seriously disturbed at the possibility that a lasting breach might . . . be created in the relations between the two countries'.[48]

After leaving Cairo on 2 March 1956, Lloyd made his way first to Bahrain, where he was greeted by stone-throwing demonstrators, and then moved on to Aden. Reporting to the Department of State on Lloyd's visit to Aden, officials at the American embassy in Israel described him as being

> somewhat disillusioned with Nasser following what he thought was a very satisfactory conversation with him in Cairo recently, as Nasser's promise to abandon anti-UK propaganda had been stepped up. . . . This adds support to conviction . . . that Nasser is prepared to witness further deterioration in relations with the west stemming from west's reaction to propaganda attacks and his military activities.[49]

On 30 March J.H.A. Watson, Head of the Foreign Office African Department, expressed his joy that following protestations by the British Ambassador in Egypt there was 'considerable moderation' in Egyptian radio propaganda directed to the Persian Gulf and East Africa. He contested that it would 'now be more difficult for them to go back to attacks of the old type'.[50] However, had Watson read a report prepared by British embassy staff in Cairo which described the working of the Egyptian propaganda machine, he may have been less cheerful. This pointed out that 'when Nasser calls off a campaign, what he intends is that news and comment should return to normal, not that there should be absolute silence on the subject. The normal here inevitably means the customary clichés about imperialism in general, and more specific stuff, for example about Glubb or Buraimi, where the occasion presents itself in the form of a news item.'[51] Indeed between April and June 1956, BBC monitors did record a lull in direct anti-British propaganda originating from Egypt. However, as the report prepared by the embassy in Cairo had warned, the campaign had not been suspended; rather its focus had been altered. Egyptian broadcasts continued to provide coverage of events in other colonies, such as British executions of nationalists in Kenya and the demonstrations in Aden.

The Foreign Office aimed for a realignment of policy in order to counter Egyptian behaviour, detach Saudi Arabia from Egypt,[52] and strengthen support for the Baghdad Pact.[53] To offset some of the more adverse effects of propaganda the US State Department proposed stronger action, including jamming Egyptian radio broadcasts. By April 1956, this was judged to be so urgent that the Americans discussed offering the necessary jamming facilities to other countries, while Iraqi propaganda in particular was strengthened as a counterweight to that emanating from Egypt.[54]

So the political fall-out from the Glubb affair was considerable and its repercussions were a concern for British and American policy-makers alike. But the key question remains to be answered – was Egyptian propaganda entirely responsible for this turn of events? In his 1969 study of the Suez crisis, Kennett Love stated that 'the actual removal of Glubb . . . was so far beyond Egypt's wildest hopes that it was never considered among the objectives of the propaganda campaign, even though the campaign included exhortations for Glubb's expulsion'.[55] In the light of available evidence this must be forcefully repudiated. The BBC monitoring reports for this period suggest that while Nasser *may* have been unaware of Glubb's actual dismissal, he was certainly instrumental, via the power of his radio propaganda, in *encouraging* King Hussein to remove him from command of the Arab Legion. In other words the Glubb affair, together with Jordan's decision not to join the Baghdad Pact, attest to the (limited) power of propaganda. No amount of Egyptian invective could have persuaded Jordan to take either decision had there not already been a latent willingness to agree with its content, or had it not been combined with an intensive *political* campaign.

With his own perspective on the world Glubb inevitably disagreed. Convinced of the responsibility of Egyptian propaganda, he penned

that 'Britain is being driven from the Middle East by words – words
to which with British impassivity she refuses to reply.' Glubb spoke
frequently of the need for a propaganda war with Cairo, but conceded
that this should be based on truth and accuracy for he believed that
'truth is fatal to dictators and racketeers'.[56]

The BBC of course, had already refused to simply counter Nasser's
propaganda. Gordon Waterfield wrote that while a campaign of counter-
propaganda may have sounded attractive given the mood of the time,
'it would not have been at all a sensible policy. To have started any
kind of radio war with Cairo,' he said, 'would have been ... good
propaganda for Nasser. . . . Once a foreign station starts to abuse anything Arab they close their ranks.'[57] During the Suez crisis Waterfield
was Head of the Eastern Service, and so he also had managerial concerns; in particular the native Arab staff of the BBC were in a most
precarious position. Following the nationalisation of the Suez canal in
July 1956 Nasser was revered as a hero throughout the Arab world
and, wrote Waterfield, 'no foreign station would have been able to
retain a competent Arab broadcasting staff if they had been expected
to broadcast abuse of Nasser'.[58] For these reasons the BBC never believed itself to be in direct competition with the Voice of the Arabs.
Hamilton Duckworth is of the opinion that it would have been both
'astonishing and quite out of character' for the BBC to have imitated
the methods of the Egyptian station.[59] A BBC report which reviewed
the crisis in December 1956 was therefore able to note that 'the staff
of the Arabic service had behaved extremely well. There were a few
murmurs at first about the tough nature of the statements which our
Arabs were called on to broadcast,' it read, 'but these died down after
a careful explanation to all concerned.'[60] Considering the heightened
natural emotions the Arabic staff must undoubtedly have felt during
the crisis, this is certainly an admirable appraisal, and stands as a tribute to the professionalism of the BBC.

One example will serve to illustrate however, that not everyone shared
these sentiments. In November 1956 a complaint reached the Foreign
Office; the British embassy in Kuwait reported that 'a reliable observer,' intriguingly identified only as 'a British subject ex-Palestinian
with BBC experience,' had judged Arabic service news readers and
commentators to be 'slanting their material'. Coverage of a speech by
Hugh Gaitskell, then leader of the Opposition Labour party, was described as having been 'reported with force and conviction', while Eden's
3 November speech was 'sabotaged by deliberate under emphasis and
by subtle use of deprecating tones'.[61] P.F. Grey, asked the Director of

External Broadcasting, J.B. Clark, to investigate the matter, and suggested he provide the Foreign Office Arabists with recordings for checking. Grey was told by Clark that they never recorded their broadcasts, and that 'they [the BBC] had this danger in mind and that he was sure our informant had got the wrong impression'.[62] Clark's investigations demonstrated how the 'Arabic speaking European staff were very alive to this danger, though they were short in numbers. In one case where suspicion existed the recording was played back and pronounced satisfactory. The opinion of . . . [the] Arabic programme organiser was that the Arabic staff were not playing them false, although their emotions were naturally affected.'[63]

Asa Briggs has been lavish in his praise of Clark, describing him as 'the doughty and experienced advocate of BBC independence'. In Briggs's opinion, 'there has been no single individual inside the BBC who has done more to establish its reputation both for reason and integrity'.[64] But Grey was unconvinced by Clark's verdict. 'I remain very suspicious of the BBC in this', wrote Grey, 'if only because Mr. J.B. Clark's initial reaction was one of shocked surprise that anything could be wrong; also his statement that there were no recordings, whereas he later admitted that one broadcast had been run over again and checked. Taxed with this he said that news bulletins were never recorded and talks only if they were to be repeated.'[65] The dispute was resolved after the embassy's informant reported that the bias had stopped. He attributed this to a change of news readers, but the Foreign Office replied that 'BBC news readers have not, repeat not, been changed.'[66]

The Voice of America was similarly troubled by its language staff during the crisis. According to Oren Stephens, author in 1957 of an official USIA report, this was because of the 'divided loyalties' of foreign language staff 'which,' he said, 'inevitably lead to emotional instability. In cases where their heart is in their homeland emigrés often express a personal and non-American point of view.'[67] Stephens discovered however, that this was not the only problem; in an effort to prove their loyalty, other foreign staff were often overzealous in their praise of America. This would have had a rather negative effect on an Arab audience which was already resentful of what it perceived as a growing cultural imperialism. Stephens concluded that 'these two related problems of languages and emotionalism are well illustrated in the Voice's broadcasts during the height of the Suez crisis'.[68]

In 1945 Noel Newsome, the Fleet Street journalist and wartime director of European broadcasts, criticised the fact that 'the lion was now whispering' whereas during the war it had roared.[69] This perhaps was a fitting description of the BBC's activities during the Suez crisis. The stand adopted by the BBC, based on its guiding principles of objectivity, accuracy and impartiality, was quite understandable. It remains, however, that the BBC could have done more in response to Egyptian broadcasts without necessarily compromising either its own position or its reputation.

During its first transmission of the day on 4 March 1956, the Voice of the Arabs broadcast 13 separate programmes, most of which were of ten to 15 minutes' duration. In comparison the BBC Arabic service was on air for just over 29 minutes and a further 30 minutes following a respite of half an hour. The Arabic service then disappeared altogether until 1700 GMT, leaving the whole day free to the Voice of the Arabs. Now international radio broadcasting, especially by short-wave, is susceptible to a variety of natural and technological constraints which necessarily limit the times of broadcasts, frequencies used and overall reception quality. The trick however is to use effectively what little time is available, and the BBC Arabic service failed to do this. During its first transmission of the day broadcasts comprised the chimes of Big Ben, readings from the Koran, the news and closing announcements. At the same time Cairo was broadcasting such politically relevant programmes as *Arab Struggle*, *Arab Idea*, and *Sudan Corner*, all interspersed with Arabic and Sudanese music, religious talks and texts. Such Egyptian broadcasts were designed to attract listeners and form Arab political opinion, which the BBC countered only with a rendition of objective news.

Little changed during the BBC's second transmission. Although audiences were now able to hear such topical programmes as *Tunisia Today*, *On the Margin of the News* and, of course, the ever popular *Question and Answer*, they were also able to listen to *Variety: Nights of Gladness*, and *Your Favourite Singer*, in addition to the news and *English by Radio*.

But we should not be overly harsh on the BBC for broadcasting what on the surface appear as having trivial programming priorities; one should be aware that by offering a variety of programmes and entertainment the BBC enticed an audience, bored with the relentless preaching of their own radio services, to listen in. The credibility of the BBC was also at stake; had nothing but news and political comment been broadcast, the station would have been perceived as nothing more than a vehicle for propaganda. Striking a balance between the two proved an exceptionally difficult task, but it seems that the BBC rose to the occasion.[70]

The criticisms are also tempered somewhat by a reading of a short resumé on Arabic service programming prepared by Gordon Waterfield in July 1956 for Leonard Figg of IRD.[71] This illustrated how in addition to the news, a commentary of five minutes' duration each day (doubled in length at the end of September 1956) restated the British viewpoint. The schedule also included *Mirror of the West, Arab News Letter* and *Political Question and Answer*. There was also *Topic of Today* and *World of Today* in which, Waterfield described, 'an expert discusses the background to a current political theme to counter political ignorance and misconception.'[72]

One of the most sensitive programmes in this schedule was *Arab Affairs in the British Press*. This was to be the target of Foreign Office criticism until 1962 by which time D.L. Stewart of IPD was convinced that although the BBC must reflect British opinion, newspaper commentaries are written for a specific section of the British public, and not for translation. They can 'only appear,' he said, 'as interference in the internal affairs of that country, usually at the best patronising, often intolerably offensive'.[73]

These heavyweight political programmes were then complemented by a series devoted to projecting *British Thought and the British Way of Life*. These were subject to 'similar criteria of objectivity' as the news bulletins,[74] and were intended to reflect British opinion on the issues of the day. Yet P.F. Grey seems to have confused British with official opinion, a mistake commonly made at the time: 'As regards the commentaries,' he wrote in November 1956, 'I had seen none that had in any sense appealed to the Arabs to understand what the government's intentions were, and only one which specifically attempted to expound the views of the government.'[75] As the following narrative will demonstrate this was complete nonsense. Deliberately or not commentaries, prepared by 'independent experts', did indeed follow the official line throughout the Suez crisis.

By way of contrast, the Voice of America responded to the crisis immediately and certainly with much more zeal than the BBC. It maximised its 13 hour expansion in Arabic and transmitted American views, opinions and policies. On reflection however, the USIA was unsure of how successful this operation had been. Oren Stephens believed: 'In fast moving events when policy lines are fluid, we sometimes express personal rather than official opinions. In several instances we were trying to do too much with too little, particularly in terms of staffing, thus lowering the effectiveness of the material.'[76] News bulletins were described as having been 'thrown together,' and often suffered from important omissions. One historian of the Voice of America, R.W. Pirsein, summarised the conclusions of the report in striking terms; VOA, he said, 'covered the Suez crisis with a pro-Arab bias. Certain commentaries were in bad taste and actually violated policy.'[77] A number of prevailing considerations throw doubt on Pirsein's verdict, however: the dominance of the Jewish lobby in the United States, American anxiety of Communist encroachment in the Middle East, Arab hostility towards the US, and the ostensibly special relationship with Britain all combine to make Pirsein's conclusions quite remarkable. Even though the US were most critical of Britain's handling of the Suez crisis, there is insufficient evidence to affirm a pro-Arab bias. This suggests that Pirsein's words can mean only one of two things; either he was simply mistaken in his judgement of bias in VOA output, or there was a breakdown of the relationship between VOA and the State Department. If the latter explanation is accurate, then it indicates that VOA has not quite always operated as the official voice of the American government.

ARMS DEALS

While the Baghdad Pact, Jordan and the Glubb affair were all demanding attention, British foreign policy was further pressured when the Soviet Union began to supply arms to Egypt.[78] But it remains uncertain how the Soviets had originally offered their co-operation. According to one Arab source the offer of free military assistance had first been made in Arabic over Radio Moscow on 10 August 1955, the text of which Nasser had obtained. The Foreign Broadcast Information Service (FBIS), the American equivalent of the BBC monitoring service, contested this. Nevertheless Nasser certainly believed such an offer had been made, and one source even claimed that Israel Radio had picked up this portion of the Soviet broadcast and used it in its own transmissions.[79] A further report on this matter was later filed by the CIA, and its relevant passages are worth quoting in full for their somewhat startling revelations:

> A report that Radio Moscow had broadcast in Arabic to the Near East an offer of free military assistance to Egypt appears to be in error. The latest Egyptian claims are that Radio Israel made the statement on 10 August, and that this statement was picked up by an Egyptian monitoring station and, as a result of haste and carelessness,

was passed to the press as having been broadcast by the Soviets in Arabic, and with the paragraph concerning military aid deleted. These reports and similar ones all apparently originate with Egyptians. They may be exaggerated in order to bring pressure on the US to satisfy Egypt's military needs on favourable terms. The fact that no western monitors intercepted any such broadcast, coupled with the lack of motivation of the USSR to broach an offer of such magnitude and portent in this manner, raises the possibility of deception which we are still trying to confirm.[80]

The whole episode was therefore muddied by claim, counter-claim and deception, but once this report is placed in context, it is seen to be consistent with the unfolding diplomatic situation. From February to September 1955, Egypt had repeatedly asked the US for arms. These demands become more urgent as Israel concluded its own arms deal with France and stepped up its raids into Gaza. On 19 May 1955, the Soviet Ambassador in Cairo, Daniel Solod, told Nasser that his government were willing to sell arms to Egypt. Before accepting, Nasser again tried to secure American arms and used the Soviet offer as a means of pressure; surely, he thought, the Americans would rather supply their own arms than allow the Soviets to gain a foothold in Egypt. However the Americans continued to vacillate. Meanwhile Israeli raids became more frequent and more severe. Nasser could wait no longer, and so he finally accepted the Soviet offer in October 1955. The quoted CIA report suggested that the offer was part of a sophisticated Egyptian deception, but this is unlikely. Presumably it was intended to be a form of pressure to secure American arms. However the Egyptian plan backfired; the Soviets had made an offer but it had been made privately rather than via a Radio Moscow broadcast, and so the Americans felt no pressure whatsoever.

The British inevitably pursued traditional Cold War themes to publicly express their derision with the arms deal and suggested to the Arab world that the path which Nasser had chosen, would only lead to further Soviet penetration in the region.[81] In this way the arms deal could be portrayed as characteristic of gradual Soviet encroachment, threatening Nasser's ideals of Arab independence and nationalism.

The arms deal was a favourite topic of letters received by the BBC's *Political Question and Answer*, and the standard reply echoed the official propaganda line: that the British recognised the sovereignty of Arab states, but preferred them not to secure arms in this way since it might encourage a renewed Middle East arms race.[82] This was a considered judgement. One reason why the west had not provided Egypt with arms was that the Americans and British were together seeking an Arab–Israeli settlement. However it was most unlikely that the Arabs would have accepted what they considered to be such hollow words of assurance from the BBC. For them such claims were merely further confirmation that the British were intent on retaining their imperialist position in the Middle East, and that British anxiety derived solely from the fact it had been the Soviet bloc which had supplied the arms.

These points were addressed by the BBC throughout the end of 1955 and into 1956, a period when the Arabic service often appears to have been a part of a sophisticated propaganda strategy against the Soviet bloc. Given the strong Bush House–IRD relationship at this time, and the latter's preoccupation with Communism, this is not at all impossible. Together they waged an offensive against the Soviet Union designed to discredit Soviet policy in Egyptian eyes. For example, in a BBC *Topic of Today* programme broadcast in November 1956, Roy Defrates asked: 'Why did the Soviet Union prefer to lend Egypt £150 million for arms rather than for the High Dam?' According to Defrates, the Soviet Foreign Minister, Dimitri Shepilov, 'with a strange disregard for Egypt's tragic population problem,' had described the Dam as 'not an urgent matter':

> Russia [said Defrates] . . . does not feel she will realise her aims in the Middle East by providing finance for constructive purposes. [Egypt] has been playing the Soviet game and becoming an instrument in the Middle East of Soviet policy.[83]

By the time this was broadcast Britain and the US had withdrawn from financing the High Dam, and were therefore guilty themselves of failing to help alleviate 'Egypt's tragic population problem'. But it is not surprising that this was conveniently ignored in favour of discrediting Soviet policy.

A similar conclusion might be reached concerning propaganda disseminated in November 1956; D.P.H. Wright, an Assistant Under-Secretary at the Foreign Office, reported the scarcity of economic evidence to label Nasser a Russian puppet: 'If it is true,' he noted, 'that the stockpile of Russian and Czech arms in Egypt is in excess of Egyptian requirements then he might be branded a Russian tool.' But, he warned, it would 'be dangerous to make too much of this in our propaganda, given our own arms stockpile in Egypt'.[84]

Not surprisingly Egyptian broadcasts devoted considerable airtime to the assistance provided by the Communist bloc, and frequently reported on the progress of their joint projects. The Sudan Programme on 2 February 1956, for instance, reported that the Czech arms had reached the front and that training in their use was complete.[85] It cannot be doubted that such broadcasts not only acted as irritants to the British, but also spurred them on to retaliate in some way; collectively they were a strike at the very people who had refused to supply arms, and thus made way for the Communist encroachment that BBC broadcasts were now so forcefully criticising.

THE ASWAN DAM DECISION

Egypt continued to conduct its diplomacy, as well as its propaganda, by radio. Broadcasts voiced repeated assurances that, provided Egyptian sovereignty and Arab nationalism were respected, Egypt remained prepared to navigate a neutral course between the two blocs. For this to be achieved, it was crucial that all traces of imperialism vanished from Egypt, including the British occupation of the Suez canal zone.

Under the terms of a Treaty agreed between Britain and Egypt in 1954, British forces were required to leave the Suez canal zone within 20 months of its signing, leaving behind only a civilian garrison.[86] The IPD told the BBC that its intended public line on the withdrawal was that it 'had been carried out according to the terms of the Anglo-Egyptian agreement and the handover of the base to the contractors had been completed smoothly and without incident'.[87] The completion of evacuation in June 1956 was greeted in Egypt with jubilation, and the occasion was inevitably celebrated by Egyptian radio, once more seizing the opportunity to rub salt in the deepening British wound. The coverage of the celebration parade in Cairo was described as 'offensive' but 'expected' by the Foreign Office which of course tried to play down the significance of the evacuation and temper the Egyptian feeling of triumph.[88] This was not easy, particularly when no less a figure than Winston Churchill had described the terms of the 1954 Treaty as requiring Britain to 'scuttle' from the Middle East.[89]

Cairo Radio's coverage included a speech by Nasser, now President of Egypt, in which he announced to the world that his country was 'prepared to be in good relations with everyone and to co-operate with everyone, provided that this shall not be at the expense of nationalism, Arabism or any Arab country'. This was followed by an explicit diplomatic message, monitored by the BBC at Caversham and reported to the Foreign Office, which described how Britain had 'fulfilled her obligations under the Evacuation Agreement. Britain had 80,000 troops in the canal zone. They have all left.' Thus Egypt now had 'no aggressive aims' against Britain. 'On the contrary,' said the broadcast, 'we want to befriend everyone and co-operate with everybody.'[90]

Similar sentiments were expressed in a review of an article in the prominent Egyptian newspaper, *Al-Akhbar*, entitled 'Two Messages to the American and British People.' At first it stretched a hand of friendship to the US, but went on to warn that Egypt had 'an account with the USA too; she assisted Zionism, adopted Israel and forgot the problem of the Arab refugees'.[91] So in one broadcast Cairo managed to combine ostensibly friendly diplomacy with a stern and chilling warning.

Despite their tone these broadcasts give an impression of lukewarm relations between Egypt and the west; and while W. Scott Lucas believes that 'the rapprochement was an illusion,' this was far from being Nasser's fault.[92] In April 1956 reports had flooded into the State Department relating how Nasser believed that the US was turning against him, and now required reassurance of their positive co-operation. In reply the State Department suggested he 'consider means of demonstrating desire for friendly relations,' including making a 'public statement . . . broadcast to Egypt and the Arab world expressing his determination to maintain Egyptian independence and recognizing desirability of friendly co-operation with Free World,' combined with the 'cessation [of] anti-west press and radio attacks directed against the Baghdad Pact'.[93] As Nasser's speeches testify he readily complied with the first wish at least, while the fall in the volume of anti-western propaganda broadcast between April and June 1956 has already been documented. Nevertheless Britain and the US continued with their long-term political strategy of weakening and isolating Nasser, culminating they hoped in his eventual downfall. Integral to this scheme was their 'promise' to finance construction of the High Dam at Aswan which provided them with considerable leverage over Nasser. But the promise was not worth the paper it wasn't written on! In March 1956 the US had already decided to pull out of this commitment, but chose not to tell the Egyptians until July so their hidden agenda would not be jeopardised.[94]

The British remained cautious, recognising that withdrawal from the promise risked providing both Nasser and the Soviet Union with a propaganda victory. Nevertheless suggestions were made as to how the affair should be handled in public, especially if Britain decided to follow the American lead and revoke their support. In addition, the possible political gains of doing so had to be clarified:

We might take the initiative and *make public our withdrawal*. [Original emphasis] This would encourage friendly governments in the Middle East; and force Nasser either to turn to Russia, thus making unmistakably plain his Russian connections, or go without his dam. It might also encourage the opposition to Nasser of elements in Egypt who do not wish to quarrel with the west. Against this we should be revealing prematurely our hostility to Nasser and not only risk an intensification of his anti-western activities (from which the UK would be the first and most severe sufferer), but also shake the confidence of many Egyptians and other Arabs in our good intentions towards them, and prejudice our chances of reverting to our offer with a more friendly government.[95]

The British were thus clearly aware of the importance of public opinion in framing political decisions; the Americans were not as advanced in this field, and did not begin to discuss such matters seriously at high levels until after the Bay of Pigs invasion in 1961. Instead State Department officials accurately predicted that Nasser would be tempted to begin a propaganda campaign designed to discredit the US in light of its 'broken promise,' but seemed to accept this as inevitable.[96]

It is no surprise that Cairo received the decision by the US (announced 19 July 1956) and Britain (announced 20 July 1956) to withdraw from financing the Aswan Dam with considerable anger. Both powers were derided as being 'united in greed and avarice and the urge to marshal the forces of aggression and evil' in order to foil Nasser's plans to 'raise the living standard of Egypt's millions'.[97] The withdrawal was denounced as nothing less than a plot designed to 'induce Egypt to deviate from the path of peace, stop campaigning against military blocs and agree to bow down at the feet of Zionism'.[98] Egypt promised that the High Dam would nevertheless 'be constructed for the benefit of the people of the whole area, whether America wants it or not'.[99]

Over the next three days, attacks on the decision gathered momentum, and Egyptian broadcasts reached new heights of venomous rhetoric. Attacks focused on the US, and while Egypt continued to promise it would still build the Dam, the possibility of Soviet aid was little discussed. On 22 July 1956, the main Arabic transmission reported an apparent Soviet willingness to provide finance if requested to do so, but completely ignored Shepilov's remarks in Moscow that the Dam was not a priority for the Soviet Union.[100] The State Department noted that the Soviet 'offer' of finance had been celebrated more by Egyptian than Soviet propaganda, 'and has been employed in a typical Egyptian fashion to frighten the west into making a swift and favourable arrangement on the project'.[101] The arms deal had taught the US that Egyptian propaganda would use Soviet 'offers' as a form of pressure in its foreign policy to induce favourable American responses. The Egyptian broadcasts were received and reported by the BBC monitoring service, and therefore acted as a relay of Egyptian intentions. Despite such broadcasts, and despite the fact that the Soviets did eventually finance the Dam's construction, the US Secretary of State, John Foster Dulles, continued to believe that the Russian offers of 1955–6 were merely bluffs.[102] Indeed, he planned to make propaganda capital of his own from the predicted Soviet response. According to Dulles, American withdrawal from the project had left Nasser 'in a hell of a tight spot and no matter what he does can be used to American advantage.' He continued:

> If he turns to the Russians now and they say 'No', this will undermine the whole fabric of recent Soviet economic carpet-bagging all over the world. . . . If the Soviets agree to give Nasser his dam, then we are working on plans to lay it on thick in the satellite countries as to why their living conditions are so miserable with the Soviets dishing out millions to Egypt.[103]

By using propaganda in this way Dulles revealed just how short-sighted he actually was. He failed to realise that American propaganda could have been employed in a much more constructive fashion to achieve greater results; but the propaganda had to be linked with an entirely different policy. Had the US supplied the finance for the construction of the Aswan Dam, American policy could have been projected as benevolent. However Dulles was blinkered by his preoccupation with fighting a crusade against the Soviet Union and Communism. By conducting his diplomacy on the basis of 'You are either with us, or against us,' without accepting the possibility of a third way, Dulles must therefore bear some of the responsibility for pushing Egypt into the arms of the Soviet Union.

NATIONALISATION

Crisis point was finally reached on 26 July 1956, the day Nasser made his now infamous speech in which he declared the Suez Canal nationalised. There is no indication of how the British or American governments first heard this news; since it was carried by the Voice of the Arabs, the speech was certainly monitored by the BBC. Although it was included in its daily *Summary of World Broadcasts*,[104] it is likely that a report was made available to officials both in Washington and London perhaps, given the speed and accuracy of monitors, within moments of the broadcast ending. It is equally probable that diplomatic sources in Egypt and the Middle East also sent word to their capitals.[105]

The speech, heralded by the sound of the Egyptian national anthem, liberation songs and martial music, and lasting two and a half hours, was largely a review of 'imperialistic efforts to thwart Egyptian independence'.[106] According to the American embassy in Cairo Nasser was 'by turns sarcastic, condescending and occasionally facetious'.[107] He was, however, resolute that former shareholders in the Suez Canal Company would be compensated, and that ships would still be able to freely navigate through the Canal. These were themes that were to be repeated time and again throughout the crisis, and were designed as a spirited defence of Egypt's action. However the speech also had an unintended effect; the west was given an unprecedented opportunity to hurl Nasser's words back at him and criticise Egypt's refusal to allow free passage of Israeli shipping. This short-sightedness of Egyptian propaganda in turn exposed Nasser's decrees and policies as hypocritical. In one of the first commentaries on the nationalisation broadcast by the BBC, Guy Wint of the *Manchester Guardian* newspaper asserted that:

> In the nature of the world today there are certain cases where a national government, even though sovereign, is bound to regard itself as circumscribed by the consideration of the vital interests of the world. The Suez canal is such a case.... The argument is that Egypt has only nationalised the canal; that is, it has declared the ownership to belong to Egypt. It has not closed the canal to shipping and says that it will not do so. Here is the crux of the matter. For in fact the canal was already closed by Egypt to certain categories of shipping. Because an exception was made – for whatever reason – there was a blow to confidence.[108]

Herbert Hoover, the US Under Secretary of State, described Nasser's speech as 'sustained invective in the most violent terms against the United States ... containing many inaccuracies,' and he advocated that these be revealed and challenged in public.[109] In fact, Hoover told the Egyptian Ambassador to Washington on 29 July 1956, that his government had been 'shocked by many intemperate, inaccurate and misleading statements regarding the US . . . particularly in [Nasser's] . . . speech,' and he observed that such propaganda was 'entirely inconsistent with the friendly relations between the two nations'.[110] In this way Hoover has provided a further demonstration of how a state's foreign relations could be affected by international radio broadcasting.

The British Cabinet acknowledged the weakness of trying to brand the nationalisation as illegal.[111] Yet this minor technicality was ignored for propaganda purposes; Douglas Dodds-Parker, Deputy Under-Secretary at the Foreign Office, noted as late as 28 September 1956 that 'the legal position was so unclear that we have been unwilling to risk stating it officially'.[112] Instead propaganda concentrated on the economic effects of the nationalisation which were clearly outlined in a Treasury 'Secret Paper' dated 24 October 1956. The fact that this is in the possession of the BBC suggests that the Corporation was prominent in applying its recommendations, and is further confirmation that the BBC was considered to be an effective agent of propaganda. The difficulties that Nasser would face in running the Canal, the futility of his economic plans, and the adverse effects of nationalisation on Asian as well as western interests, were all themes to be emphasised in future broadcasts.[113] The BBC's role in this is implied by a report penned by J.B. Clark dated 27 November 1956, which described the 'sustained effort' undertaken by the BBC to 'highlight the dangerous irresponsibility of Nasser's behaviour'.[114] Such an approach was taken in a *Topic of Today* programme, broadcast on the Arabic service by Guy Wint. Whether Nasser was right or wrong to nationalise the canal was not, in his opinion, the crucial issue: 'The central fact', said Wint, 'is that Egypt, one of the most prominent of the underdeveloped countries, is scaring away those who are most anxious to promote international co-operation'. Wint contested that Nasser had 'thereby done a disservice not only to Egypt but to all countries which hope to associate foreign capital in their development schemes'.[115] The objective of such broadcasts was to demonise Nasser and harness public opinion against his actions, particularly among the increasingly influential Afro-Asian bloc. Talks and commentaries therefore increasingly used scare tactics, and focused on the detrimental consequences that nationalisation would have on the economies and development strategies of the Third World.[116] For many, including the Middle East states themselves, this was a nightmare scenario. The small Persian Gulf sheikhdoms, described as 'miniature welfare states,' were told they would suffer from a loss of revenue as reductions in oil exports took hold; severed oil pipelines would affect the economies of Iran, Saudi Arabia and Iraq, while Egypt itself would find its canal dues reduced, its assets frozen, and new development projects postponed, all topped by an enormous balance of payments deficit.[117] Edward Hodgkin, a columnist for *The Times* and a prominent commentator on the Arabic service, pursued this theme with vigour even as late as March 1957. He contrasted the situation in Britain – a mere public annoyance with the imposition of oil and petrol rationing – with Egypt where not only revenues from ships using the Canal were lost ('revenues,' he reminded his listeners, 'which President Nasser once said in a rash moment would be sufficient for building the High Dam'), but there had also been a marked increase in unemployment 'among the many thousands whose employment depended on the canal traffic. . . . So,' Hodgkin concluded, 'it is in Egypt's own interest that the canal should be open to traffic once again as soon as possible.'[118]

It is ironic, however, that British propaganda did eventually have to acknowledge that Nasser had shown remarkable restraint. Had he carried out his threats and promises, all of which would have had severe repercussions on the world's economy, propaganda would have had an easy time; it could simply have used these as evidence of Nasser's tyranny. Precisely because he did not carry out his various threats and promises – he had not attempted to hold up shipping dues, had allowed foreign staff to leave despite threats of imprisonment, had not seized the company's assets, was not having to spend most of his revenue on maintaining and improving the Canal rather than constructing the Dam, and had not delayed or hindered ships in their passage through the Canal – British propaganda had to portray this as a climb-down. This was considered 'useful when opinion [was] hardening towards the belief he has scored more points than the west'.[119] Staff at Britain's embassy in Teheran reported that 'Nasser's first highly scrupulous plan is being subordinated to short-term tactics and it might well be claimed that this was due to the firm attitude adopted by Britain, France and the canal users.'[120] This was the propaganda line; in reality, Nasser was constrained more by the need to retain the support of world opinion.

SOVIET PROPAGANDA

In response to the Suez crisis, Radio Moscow expanded its number of Arabic broadcasts from four to five per day; the number of wavelengths (both short and mediumwave) also increased with each transmission.[121]

Soviet broadcasts followed an interesting if predictable course. They expressed support for Egypt and denounced western actions (especially after the Anglo-French invasion), but they relied mainly on Arab sources for information.[122] Hence comment and analysis closely followed, indeed in many instances reproduced, Arab broadcasts themselves. Soviet broadcasts because of their pro-Egyptian and anti-Imperialist position 'achieved a new respectability' among Arabs.[123] However a 1962 USIA report doubted that Radio Moscow had made such an impact in the Middle East, describing it as 'quite dull and monotonous'. Moreover it had used too little original Arabic and had failed to target Arab audiences with any degree of sophistication; USIA thus found the BBC to be the preferred option among Arab listeners.[124] Radio Moscow's output and style altered little over the years until Mikhail Gorbachev, *glasnost* and *perestroika* stimulated a new Soviet world perspective. Today Radio Moscow sounds nothing like the Radio Moscow of old.[125] So although the above USIA report was written after the Suez crisis, it still provides an incisive indication of how Moscow's programmes were received by their Arab audiences.

As the Suez crisis unfolded Soviet propaganda intensified its hostility, so much so that the State Department described it as 'psychological warfare of extensive character'.[126] The United States were extremely concerned that this Soviet propaganda be countered, naively fearing that it would be readily translated into political influence. The mounting reports that Soviet volunteers were prepared to fight on behalf of Egypt were particularly distressing, although Carsten Holbraad contests this threat was itself propaganda.[127] Apart from this instance the Soviet Union was careful not to implicate itself or give any firm offer of direct military assistance to Egypt. The Joint Intelligence Committee in London correctly predicted that 'although the Soviet Union will probably seek to win Arab sympathies by propaganda, economic assistance, strong diplomatic support, offers of arms and possible volunteers,' all of which were prominent themes of its broadcasting strategy, 'they themselves will not wish to become involved in fighting outside the United Nations framework'.[128]

On 5 November 1956, by which time Britain, France and Israel were militarily engaged in Egypt, Soviet broadcasts momentarily deviated from this established pattern. Dimitri Shepilov, the Soviet Foreign Minister, submitted a draft resolution to the Chairman of the UN Security Council which demanded that the three 'aggressors' withdraw their forces from Egypt. Moreover the resolution announced that the Soviet government was ready 'to make its contribution to the curbing of aggression and restoring peace by despatching the necessary air and naval forces to Egypt'.[129] Not only did Soviet broadcasts make the content of this resolution public, but in an unprecedented act of public diplomacy Radio Moscow transmitted personal messages from the Soviet Premier, Nikolai Bulganin to Eden, Guy Mollet (Prime Minister of France) and Ben-Gurion (Prime Minister of Israel), *before* they officially reached their intended recipients by conventional diplomatic channels. These contained 'constructive proposals . . . [to achieve [a] peaceful settlement [by]. . . combined efforts and co-operation'.[130] Thus 5 November 1956 marks a significant stage in the development of international radio broadcasting as a tool of diplomacy; broadcasting what previously would have been considered private diplomatic communications now became a regular method of conducting Soviet foreign policy.

But the statements also contained their fair share of threats. Eden for example was warned that the USSR was 'fully determined to crush the aggressors and restore peace in the Middle East through the use of force. We hope at this critical juncture you will display due prudence and draw the correct conclusions from this.'[131] Again this must be contextualised if its implications are to be understood; as these events were unfolding the Soviet Union was involved in violently crushing a revolution on its own doorstep in Hungary. This was not lost on officials at the State Department who interpreted such messages as merely an attempt to divert attention away from these Soviet atrocities.[132]

Such warnings were treated with contempt by western propaganda, which again sought to discredit Soviet policy. David Mitchell of the BBC told Egyptians that they were mistaken if they believed that the Soviet Union would go to war; it was a simple fact that the USSR had no vital interests in the Middle East to warrant such action. Equally they had been misled to believe that the threat of Russian intervention had motivated the French and British to seek a cease-fire and withdraw their troops.[133] The credit for this, Mitchell asserted, had to go to the combined efforts of the US and UN.[134]

Meanwhile Soviet propaganda turned on the Americans which, the USIA documented, described the US as responsible for the crisis: 'The fairly objective Soviet reporting of the US role at the beginning of UN discussions was *not* carried to Arab audiences.'[135]

Some comment on this Soviet propaganda is required. Theories of communication repeatedly stress that it is the *intention* of broadcasts which is most important. Transmissions emanating from the Voice of the Arabs, although designed to be received abroad, were intended to be nothing more than propaganda (although the fact that the broadcasts were monitored and reported suggests that diplomatic messages can be read into even the most violent propaganda). The most important aspect of any broadcast which determines its effectiveness is its credibility, or at least the *perception* of credibility. This is achieved in both the long and short terms by deed supporting word. On this basis Egypt's threats were not credible, but simple rhetoric since Egypt had neither the capability nor the will to carry out its threats. We can thus dismiss General Glubb's often repeated assertion that Britain was driven from the Middle East by words, because they failed to be backed up by concerted action.

On the other hand, broadcasts from the Soviet Union, while inevitably employing many of the propaganda techniques common to all international radio programming, were intended to be of a more diplomatic nature, commensurate with the size, power and influence of the Soviet Union at this time. For this reason, and because the British government chose to perceive the messages in this way, Soviet broadcasts appeared the most effective and credible; whether their threats were designed as bluffs or not is relatively unimportant. This was a relationship of power, best described by means of an analogy with a bank robbery. Should the bank-teller know that the gun being wielded by the robber is not real, then the threat he poses is rendered obsolete; the power of the robber in relation to the teller, that is, his power to influence his perception (of the threat) and his response (to give him the money) is weakened.[136] During the Cold War the threat of military action by a superpower, with the attendant risk that it might have escalated to nuclear confrontation, acted in a similar way, just as it did at the time of the Suez crisis. All evidence therefore suggests that the prospect of unilateral action by the Soviet Union contributed to the decision made by the involved parties to bring about a favourable settlement. Historians have debated at length the intention of the Soviet threats and whether they were in fact taken seriously.[137] Gabriel Partos dismissed the threats as a 'publicity stunt,' noting how Moscow's meagre nuclear deterrent was easily outclassed by America's strategies force.[138] The opinions of the actors involved, however, were divided. Khrushchev of course believed in the power of his threat, recording that 'the three aggressors, they knew that we weren't playing games with public opinion. They took us very seriously.'[139] Meanwhile Eden's memoirs tell us that he had 'considered that the threats ... need not be taken literally,' while the French Foreign Minister, listing four factors that compelled the allies to cease hostilities, placed the threat of Russian intervention last.[140] It obviously all depends on whose memoirs one is reading!

Whether the threats were bluffs can not be readily ascertained, but it cannot be denied that the risk of ignoring them, or alternatively calling their bluff, considerably outweighed any advantage to be gained from continuing an aggressive policy against Egypt; they at least contributed to the policy options available, and to the decision-making process itself.

THE LONDON CONFERENCE

On 8 August 1956, Eden outlined the case against Nasser in a BBC broadcast. Lloyd followed him to the microphone on 14 August, and both statements were relayed in Arabic by the BBC.[141] Eden's in particular was received with hostility in the Arab world. One letter from a group of men on the Trucial Coast was typical of the reaction registered by the BBC: 'Evil to you, you old Sir Anthony Eden, for attacking Gamal Abdul Nasser ... When you attack Gamal, you attack all the Arabs.'[142] American Secretary of State Dulles was also the focus of such personal resentment. Egyptian propaganda criticised his idea that the Suez Canal could be internationalised by a conference of its users. Adopting a personalised tone, broadcasts asked 'Mr Dulles' why he did not call a conference on the future of the Panama Canal, Gibraltar, Aden and Singapore; or, wondered the Voice of the Arabs, was such treatment reserved solely for Egypt?[143] Dulles tried to temper such criticism by confirming that the US would irrevocably remain detached from colonialist forces, an announcement that the Voice of the Arabs described as momentous but insufficient; in accordance with their tradition of anti-colonialism, said the station, the US were duty bound to actively side with small states struggling for liberation.[144] Such direct appeals to individuals and nations, latching on to their values and traditions and thereby humanising a crisis or conflict, were not uncommon. While their effects are difficult to quantify they provide further confirmation that personal diplomatic messages were indeed sent through the airwaves.

Meanwhile, 24 countries were invited to Lancaster House in London to convene what became known as the London Conference. Delegations from 22 countries gathered on 16 August 1956 (Egypt and Greece refused to attend). The premise of the Conference was that its participants would agree to international supervision of the Suez Canal, and this would then be presented to Nasser for his acceptance. Force was considered to be an option of final resort which if used would require the full support of world opinion; Dulles warned the Foreign Office that without it, 'we could not associate ourselves in a military undertaking. . . . We believe,' he said, 'that Nasser can be forced to disgorge by means other than military. Some form of organised effort to create a favourable world opinion is required.'[145]

Both the BBC and VOA had a crucial role to play in supporting and projecting the objectives of the Conference, thus illustrating their growing importance as channels of diplomatic communication. The participants agreed to the proposals on 23 August 1956, and in September J.B. Clark was able to report that, government criticisms of the BBC notwithstanding, 'Mr. Dodds-Parker . . . has expressed appreciation of the vigorous line which has been taken'.[146]

The BBC and Voice of America were certainly assisted by Nasser's refusal to attend which provided them with a momentous propaganda coup. Now he could really be portrayed as the villain, apparently unwilling to find a peaceful settlement to the crisis, ignoring the norms of diplomatic behaviour and heightening the tension to ever more dangerous levels. Such a line must have seemed justified once Egyptian broadcasts issued their first threats of force. On 10 August 1956, a press review of the Egyptian newspaper *Al-Ahram* commented on Eden's broadcast (providing further evidence of its reception), and warned that should Britain use force, oil arteries throughout the whole Arab world would be severed, thus hastening the expiry of what it labelled 'the decrepit empire'.[147] The next day the now familiar voice of Ahmed Sa'id, Director of the Voice of the Arabs and often its most outspoken commentator, used similar threatening language and declared that Egypt was prepared to meet force with force.[148] Such broadcasts had very clear objectives; they were certainly issued as threats but they also hinted at the existence of an Arab unity that would find strength in western-backed hostilities against Egypt.

In comparison to the coverage of the London Conference by the Voice of the Arabs, which amounted to little more than a consistent stream of invective against the west, the BBC was calm, moderate and inevitably less dynamic. It was considered necessary, for example, to broadcast Arabic translations of speeches made by Dulles and Lloyd at the conference in their entirety. Rationalising this decision, J.B. Clark said that 'it was rightly anticipated that only distorted versions of the speeches would be available to newspaper readers in Egypt and other parts of the Arab world'.[149] In other words the BBC assumed the crucial role of providing a summary of 'the truth' – or at least the British version of it – to an audience which would otherwise have been denied the full picture of events. In addition Clark had felt it was essential that broadcasts provide a 'forceful presentation' of the British point of view as presented at the conference to Asian audiences.[150] It was in fact yet another example of the BBC engaging in 'public diplomacy'.

But now the BBC had to begin explaining and justifying the outcome of the London Conference. For example in a BBC *Political Question and Answer* programme, Edward Hodgkin said the Conference had confirmed how Nasser did not have the firm support of world opinion; many eastern countries had in fact agreed that the Canal was too important to be left to the control of just one government. Hodgkin reiterated that neither Egypt's sovereignty over the Canal, nor their legal right to nationalise it, had ever been questioned; the priority was the satisfactory running of the Canal on behalf of its owners and users and this had been verified by the very convening of the Conference which Egypt had refused to attend.[151]

Broadcasts nevertheless affirmed that the west remained intent on reaching a negotiated settlement, and had thus despatched a five-power delegation, led by the Australian Prime Minister, Robert Menzies, to meet with Nasser and present to him the Conference's proposals.

For Britain at least, the failure of the Menzies Committee was a foregone conclusion; Britain had based its plans on Nasser's inevitable rejection of its proposals ever since the idea of the Conference had been discussed. Britain's foresight was in fact corroborated by reports of monitored Egyptian radio broadcasts which violently attacked the proposals agreed to at the conference.

The Americans had also been aware that the possibility of failure vastly outweighed the chance of success. On 22 August, that is before Menzies's meeting with Nasser, the State Department had speculated that Soviet propaganda would contribute to Nasser's decision of whether to accept his terms: 'Moscow Radio is still of a character making it hard for the Egyptian government to do anything but give a complete rejection.'[152] Similarly at a meeting of the National Security Council on 30 August, Dulles accused the Soviet Union of having been 'playing a very reckless game in its efforts to induce Nasser to reject the plan'. The minutes of the meeting note that 'at the very time that . . . Dulles was personally trying to gain the co-operation of . . . Shepilov at [the London Conference] the Soviet radio was viciously attacking the US plan as an example of western imperialism and colonialism. Such attacks had continued without interruption ever since'.[153] Thus viewing the world from their red-and-white Cold War perspective, the US believed they knew very well who to blame for Nasser's rejection of the Menzies Committee on 5 September.

So another London Conference was convened to discuss the options now open. Dulles presented his idea of a Suez Canal Users Association (SCUA) which would provide pilots for ships using the Canal and receive all its dues. Under its terms the users, running the Canal from a ship moored at each end, could enforce their rights in the event of Egyptian interference or non-co-operation. Again Nasser rejected any such idea. By describing it as no less than a declaration of war against Egypt, and in declaring how British action ultimately threatened the peace of the whole world,[154] Egyptian propaganda magnified the issue to exploit the global fear of disturbing the international peace and status quo. This was a constantly used broadcasting device and a highly effective form of propaganda in times of diplomatic crisis, particularly in the Cold War climate.[155]

To retain the support of the US and Canada, it was crucial that the British introduce the *idea* of recourse to the UN, even though the organisation was to be virtually excluded from the practical politics. In this way Britain could be seen to be actively searching for a peaceful settlement. Moreover American and Canadian anti-colonialism needed to be placated; this required evidence that any settlement would not wound Egyptian pride and that the rule of law would prevail. In this way British broadcasts, involved in maintaining alliance relationships at a potentially critical time, reflected a sensitivity to their values and ideals in much the same way that propaganda to the Arabs sought to appeal to their culture, religion and way of life.[156]

However, other American sensitivities – a dislike of overt aggression and an intense hatred of anything anti-American – were also deliberately targeted. The British delegation at the UN asked the Foreign Office for evidence of the Egyptian army having been mobilised once the canal was nationalised, since this sort of thing was deemed 'likely to impress American public opinion.' In addition the delegation requested extracts of the 'more poisonous Cairo wireless broadcasts, especially those which are unpleasant to the Americans as well'.[157] This provides further confirmation that international radio broadcasting could be used to help a state create conditions for a favourable diplomatic position.

CONSPIRACY AND WAR

If it was clear by this time that Egypt was unwilling to accept any of the western-sponsored proposals, it was equally obvious that Egyptians suspected the English, French and Israelis of hatching a plot against them. Yet for a long time it seemed that the discussed conspiracy would come to nothing. Initially the Israelis were opposed to the idea that their invasion of Egypt should be the pretext for Anglo-French military 'policing' operations. Even Egyptian intelligence believed the Israelis would not involve themselves in any scheme against Egypt simply over the Suez Canal.[158] However on 24 October, during a secret meeting at Sèvres in the suburbs of Paris, Britain, France and Israel reached agreement. The carefully devised strategy that became known as the 'Sèvres Protocol' called for an Israeli assault to begin on 29 October; an Anglo-French ultimatum would then be issued to both sides on the 30th, and its rejection by Egypt (indicating Israel did not have to fulfil its requirements) would signal the beginning of the allied bombing campaign on 31 October.

As the triumvirate were finalising their plans in secret, the Voice of the Arabs insinuated that Egypt was aware of Israel's involvement in an 'imperialist' plot. The station recalled how the western powers had reacted swiftly to Egypt's nationalisation of the Suez Canal but had done next to nothing about Israel's 10 October attack on Qalqilya in Jordan despite the Anglo-Jordan Treaty. Then five days later, a Foreign Office blunder allegedly revealed the plan's existence, handing the Voice of the Arabs a major propaganda coup. Commenting on the transfer of Iraqi forces to Jordan, the Egyptian station said: 'A British Foreign Office spokesman disclosed the objects of this plot when he said yesterday that the Iraqi forces which may enter Jordan need not frighten Israel, and his government had convinced Israel of this fact. Any force which enters Jordan with the consent of Israel can only be there in the interests of Israel itself. [He] made the plot transparent when he emphasised that the Iraqi forces likely to enter Jordan would be very small in number and would not go beyond the East Bank which is far from Israeli borders.'[159] While Egyptians had misread the signs and overestimated the role of Iraq,[160] they were nevertheless sure that some sort of military action was imminent.

According to the British Ambassador in Baghdad, Sir Michael Wright, the BBC had implied collusion by its presentation and coverage of the opening of hostilities. On 31 October he demanded that the BBC Overseas Service immediately and repeatedly broadcast that Israel was being urged to withdraw and comply with the ultimatum; and as British and French bombing of Egypt began on 3 November his requests became more urgent. He said that the BBC's reports of Allied military communiqués concerning Egyptian airforce losses, together with Israel's claim to victory, 'could not suggest more clearly that Israel and Britain are in collusion if [it] had been calculated to do so'.[161] The Foreign Office files are littered with memoranda from Sir Michael criticising the BBC for its coverage of Israel's part in the aggression. His communications not only demonstrate the inadvisability of keeping important overseas missions unaware of what is going on, but also the naivety of the Ambassador himself. They also suggest one of two things: either the BBC was acting in compliance with the government's secret strategy, or the pace of events on the ground had overtaken the preparation of official, media and public support. As there is no evidence which indicates the BBC was knowledgeable about the plan (and this, of course, does not rule out the possibility that they did know about it), the second explanation is likely to be the most accurate. Such judgement is not assisted in any way by the fact that right up until the outbreak of hostilities on 31 October, the BBC had continued to assure its audience that force would be used only as a last resort. After all this was the official line taken by the British government, not only in its propaganda but also in its discussions with the US, at the UN, and in the House of Commons. However events on the ground were gathering momentum and proceeding at such a pace that allied propaganda could not keep up. The British ignored the discrepancy between policy and propaganda; maintaining tight security was judged to be a much more important consideration.

To demonstrate this Sir Michael Wright, on 4 November, disapproved of BBC news which concentrated on the continuing bombing raids, and he described this as the 'worst thing possible. . . . Could we not follow up today the Prime Minister's statement,' he asked, 'by announcement of a blockade or some naval measure off the Israeli coast until ceasefire takes place and Israel forces withdraw?. . . Even a statement in a few hours time such as "British naval forces off the coast of Israel". . . would be of utmost assistance pending something further'.[162] As this communication was received in Whitehall, a British frigate shot down an Israeli aircraft which had interfered with its patrol. The news was quickly distributed to IPD, the Foreign Office News Department and all overseas missions. Sir Michael registered his 'hope that Overseas and Arabic services of the BBC will make immediate and maximum use of this news, will play it up prominently and repeatedly, and will not imply in any way that either interference with us or our reply were a mistake. Overseas broadcast at 4.30 am [made] no mention of it,' he said. 'Their selection of news is most unhelpful.' To temper such implicit accusations that the BBC was in some way involved in the collusion with Israel, an indistinguishable Foreign Office signature minuted in reply to Sir Michael, 'the news was carried in the General Overseas Service on four separate bulletins, apart from use in the Arabic service'.[163]

The evacuation of British and French nationals from the Middle East, and especially from Jordan and Egypt, was another worry. The State Department was nervous about how such moves might be interpreted by Arab opinion which was already anticipating conflict. Evacuation may have only served to indicate that the situation had deteriorated so much that the lives of nationals were judged to be in danger. The risk was that it could then have been a self-fulfilling prophecy. The BBC and VOA have always made a point of supplementing official embassy warnings by broadcasting Foreign Office and State Department appeals to their respective nationals, advising them to leave areas considered dangerous. It is unclear what effect these broadcasts actually have; they may serve to heighten tension by anticipating what may not in fact be inevitable, or perhaps they provide enemy propaganda the pretext for launching a fresh campaign highlighting the imminent dangerous situation. But whether such warnings emanated from the BBC during the Suez crisis, or were issued directly by the British embassy, they were at least definitely heard.[164]

As the situation deteriorated, relations between the BBC and the government plummeted to an all-time low. Selwyn Lloyd invited suggestions as to how greater control over Middle and Far East broadcasts might be secured 'against the background that the BBC was thought to attach too much importance to impartiality'. The most prominent idea was the appointment of an officer to work in liaison between the Foreign Office and the BBC to 'ensure that the external services of the BBC conformed to the Government's policy requirements'.[165] Appointed to the job was J.L.B. Titchener – 'Titchener of Tartoum'[166] – a Foreign Office official who at the time was stationed in Teheran. While awaiting his arrival back in London, the post was temporarily filled on 2 November 1956 by Duncan Wilson who, it is said, had many friends at the BBC.[167] A report written by J.B. Clark reveals not only what the officer considered his work to be, but how the BBC thought of him:

... he said his first task was to examine the nature of the intended news and associated output ... That postulated a handling of news in a manner which ... would not expose the sharp division of opinion in the country and in Parliament on current Government policy. It was clear that this would involve giving special prominence to Governmental statements ... and whittling down to the point of suppression Opposition speeches. ... every item was open to his inspection, though he had no editorial function whatsoever. But suggestions were made on the undesirability of news items ranging from the views of the Opposition to communiqués issued from GHQ in Cyprus on the bombing of military installations in Egypt.[168]

In short the Liaison Officer was an instrument of news management, selection and censorship; although Clark's wording is inevitably loaded to present an unfavourable picture of the appointment, it would have been unnecessary had its functions been otherwise. In its defence the BBC attached an Appendix to a vitally important report written in 1961[169] in which the Foreign Office described its relationship with the BBC. In its entirety the report vindicates both the work and position of the BBC, declaring that programmes were prepared 'in the national interest with a high degree of responsibility,' and recognising that their work had achieved a 'high standard of performance'. The report defined at length the relationship between the BBC and the Foreign Office, and thus indicates those areas abused by the latter during the Suez crisis. The Foreign Office was already in almost continuous contact with the BBC without the need for a Liaison Officer. Indeed there was 'direct and consistent contact at all levels, and *it has not been found necessary to establish special machinery for this purpose*' [emphasis added]. The Foreign Office acknowledged that the 'scripts of foreign language material with a political content are available as necessary to the appropriate sections of the Information Policy Department *after* broadcasting'[170] [emphasis added]. Daily contact was maintained between the Heads of the BBC language services and the regional desks of the Foreign Office Information Departments, while the BBC's diplomatic correspondents had their own established link with the News Department:

The Foreign Office conveys through this channel special information, background and guidance, whether initiated in Whitehall or received from HM Missions abroad, who maintain a service of special 'guidance' telegrams designed particularly for the BBC external services. In addition telegrams below 'secret' grading ... are seen by certain officials of the external services.[171]

The mechanics of the relationship were already well defined, and no refinement was really necessary. Again the relationship between the BBC external services and foreign policy was accepted. The government's behaviour towards the BBC during the Suez crisis however, demonstrated one significant factor; when its objectives coincided with those of the BBC – especially concerning the Cold War and the crusade against Communism – the government failed to appreciate that the BBC best fulfilled its role as an instrument of foreign policy by being editorially independent, objective and impartial. The government, concerned only with the short term, also ignored the fact that the BBC must operate on a long-term basis, building up audiences and a reputation over many years. The BBC could not be expected to alter its policies according to short-term crisis circumstances, then revert to its original policies once the crisis had been averted. Clearly there was room for improvement in the government–BBC relationship at this time.

On 29 October Earl Mountbatten had written to the Prime Minister's Press Secretary, William Clark: 'I don't envy your job in the next few days; this will be the hardest war to justify ever.'[172] But justified it had to be and the burden of that task fell to the BBC. The Arabic service consistently projected the official line that Israel had invaded Egypt with the objective of destroying the terrorist fedayeen bases in the Sinai, and described the ultimatum as having been issued to prevent war from spreading and becoming a 'full scale war involving the whole Middle East and,' it said, 'perhaps even the whole world'.[173] Thus once again propaganda, this time British in origin, exaggerated the issue to one of global significance.

As late as April 1957 the BBC continued to answer charges stemming from the conspiracy; broadcasts still vigorously defended British policy and forcefully denied accusations that Israel was favoured over the Arabs. Had not the ultimatum been issued to both Egypt and Israel? Had not Britain threatened to attack Israel if Jordan was attacked? Had not Britain evacuated the Suez Canal base before being legally obliged to? Sudanese independence had been granted, Libyan independence supported and the treaties with Iraq and Jordan ended before they expired because Iraq and Jordan wanted them ended.[174] British policy was painted as white as it could be. Thus it is a little unnerving to find C.C.B. Stewart actually defending British colonial history in 'economically backward and politically chaotic territories'. He believed that they should 'abandon [their] hysterical devotion to the outworn dogma of absolute sovereignty'.[175] Mercifully this was written in 1957. Had Stewart placed these thoughts on paper sooner, and had they been adopted as part of a propaganda strategy, the result would no doubt have been disastrous for British foreign policy.

So in much the same way that the BBC had sold the Baghdad Pact, it now urged its Arab audiences to adopt British-style democracy: 'Policy in Britain,' said one broadcast, 'even at a time of heightened anxiety, is being debated in a thoroughly democratic way. Ever since the crisis began the discussion ... has been carried on in a thoroughly open way – in the newspapers, in Parliament, and in every household ... there are no secret councils. All is open.'

This allowed the BBC to contrast the British situation with the complete absence of democratic consultation within Egypt. In fact there had been no debate on the Suez crisis within Egypt at all, and no point of view expressed or opinion aired which deviated from the official line.[176] Such broadcasts were intended to separate the Egyptian people from their rulers in the hope that they might be persuaded they were being misinformed or shielded from certain truths by their government. It was a strategy designed to stir up an (often latent) opposition within the country and thus weaken the government to the advantage of the transmitting state. For example Egyptian propaganda, 'designed more to strengthen the morale of the home front than to give an accurate picture of what was going on',[177] frequently exaggerated the numbers of dead and wounded British soldiers. But this did not encourage credibility; the BBC reported that the total of British casualties was 21 killed and 112 wounded, and only one aeroplane had been lost. These, it was concluded, were figures that were 'never officially told the Egyptian public'.[178]

Yet despite such insistence on telling the Egyptians 'the truth' and depicting debate and dissension as the essence of democracy, many felt that the BBC was more of a hindrance than a help at a time when strength through unity should have been projected. From within IPD, C.C.B. Stewart launched an uncharacteristically fierce tirade against the external services in September 1956. The main thrust of his criticism was that 'the British point of view does not seem to be presented forcefully enough. There is too much hedging, ambiguity and over-subtlety'. Stewart did concede that the Arabic service had represented the British case 'pretty well', but warned that if 'the temperature of the Suez crisis were to fall I expect this service to become critical of some aspects of HMG's policy'.[179] What Stewart and his fellow critics failed to appreciate was that the BBC was not critical of the government's policies *per se*, but rather reflected the division of opinion within the country as a whole so that any defence of policies would appear credible. It was essential to broadcast the facts as they were, for in democratic broadcasting truth is the most effective form of propaganda. Even General Glubb recognised this. The issue came to a head when William Clark requested that the BBC should edit Hugh Gaitskell's broadcast of 4 November 1956, and that 'in repeating it on sound radio some of the more inflammatory portions should not be given on the Arabic service'.[180] The BBC flatly refused, and its internal review, written in 1961, defended its stand: 'For the BBC [external services] to have omitted the main Opposition views would have damaged its own value without vindicating the Government. The essential thing was to give criticisms squarely; and gaining credit for honesty, to lead the listener on to an appreciation of the situation which the Government felt had forced its hand.'[181] P.F. Grey, forever a critic of the BBC, interpreted the Licence and Agreement as requiring the BBC 'to frame the Overseas broadcasts in the national interest and . . . in the present critical and exceptional circumstances it was not in the national interest to broadcast news bulletins and editorial round-ups which gave the impression of national disunity'. Grey emphasised that he was not advocating that the BBC suppress the truth, but 'thought it only reasonable . . . that it should exercise some discretion and some selection'. He concluded that 'it will be a long time before the BBC is of much positive help to us in the crisis unless things take a turn for the better and they can report more favourable news'. In particular Grey was dismissive of the BBC practice of reporting the same news in the same way in all language services, as well as the Home service. He believed that all news is by nature selective and that 'there was nothing inherently wrong in making up a special bulletin for the benefit of the Arab world.' He hinted at the type of treatment he expected when he revealed he 'did not always tell the whole of the news even to my wife, if she and I had had a heavy day, and I hoped that there would be better news tomorrow'.[182] This certainly reveals Grey's lack of skill as a propagandist. The BBC's Hamilton Duckworth has since said that 'part of the external services business must always be to reflect the policy of the government of the day. It would be absurd if this were not so.' But Duckworth maintains that by broadcasting the views of both the Government and the Opposition 'they accurately reflected opinion in Britain and gave a true account of British political nature'.[183]

So the combination of truth and accuracy ensured that the BBC retained the confidence of its audience. This has recently been confirmed by John Drinkall, an IRD operative stationed in Cairo during the crisis; recalling how the BBC announced in advance which Egyptian targets would be bombed by the RAF, he has testified that the 'Egyptians so trusted the accuracy of the BBC and RAF that they used to drive out to watch the spectacle!'[184]

Voice of America broadcasts reflected at this time the vague and vacillating American policy which occupied the grey hinterland of being neither right nor wrong. They never questioned the fact that the invasion was an aggressive act against Egypt, but neither was Egypt's responsibility in provoking the crisis overlooked. However, the military campaign certainly assisted VOA in its task of propagating American policy: 'We had an opportunity to make the point that such issues should be resolved without the use of force,' wrote Oren Stephens in 1957. 'We could take a stand against aggression. We could underscore our traditional belief... in liberty, national independence and international co-operation'.[185] By projecting the US during the Suez crisis as a peace-loving nation, devoted to self-determination and resisting aggression, the VOA ensured that America was in a favourable position *vis-à-vis* world opinion once the crisis was over.

The British and French military operations were complemented by a concerted psychological offensive against Egypt. This was described as a 'systematic and graded application of pressure... on certain carefully selected economic and military targets,' among which was Cairo Radio, described by Keith Kyle as 'arguably the most important target of all'.[186] In a fatal error of judgement it was decided that it would not be attacked until later on in the campaign because of the prospect of killing civilians. In every war during the twentieth century, this has been a common concern of democratic military planners. Killing civilians has always provided the enemy with good propaganda, and as Mountbatten had already pointed out, Suez was already difficult enough to justify. The Egypt Committee duly instructed General Keightley to issue a warning before the attack in an effort to avoid civilian casualties.[187] Whitehall however was unaware that the transmitters were not located in Cairo after all, but rather were in the desert. So while selected strategic targets in the city were bombed, Cairo Radio was able to sustain its volume of propaganda output and urge the Arabs to take up arms against the 'aggressors'. Even when the transmitters had finally been taken out by allied bombers, Cairo Radio made every effort to continue operating. Apparently Nasser was due to make an important speech on 2 November, the day that the transmitters were destroyed. However, Ahmed Sa'id was determined the speech be broadcast. He therefore recorded and broadcast it less than two hours after the bombing on a transmitter stored for shipment; loudspeakers in the streets informed the audience of the new frequencies. The transmitter was far weaker than the previous shortwave transmitter, but was of sufficient strength for British and American monitors in Cyprus to hear its broadcasts. The staff of the Egyptian State Broadcasting Offices remained at their station day and night for the duration of the war. A number of broadcasters were stuck in other Arab capitals where they had gone before the war began to cover other news stories; in the event they were provided with facilities to transmit for the Voice of the Arabs. Kennett Love, who has recounted this story, believed that their 'improvised programmes gave an air of indomitability to the Egyptian image,' and concluded that because the Arabs were 'more dependent than westerners on radio for news and amusement, the Egyptians made extraordinary efforts to remain on the air'.[188] Clearly the Voice of the Arabs would continue to make a most valiant attempt to win the propaganda war.

CEASE-FIRE AND AFTERMATH

After only seven days of military activity, the British government was forced to seek a cease-fire on 6 November 1956. The devaluation of sterling, together with the impossibility of raising a loan from either the United States or the International Monetary Fund, imposed severe economic pressure on Britain. More importantly Israel and Egypt had accepted the terms of an unconditional cease-fire offered by the UN Secretary-General, Dag Hammarskjöld. More than any other factor this forced Britain's hand. As Keith Kyle has written, perceptively recognising the need to maintain a consistency between policy and propaganda, 'self-respect required that Britain at least try to act consistently with her story. Israel and Egypt had stopped fighting; the UN Secretary-General of the UN was raising an international force; the ostensible reason for the landing was over.'[189]

The BBC now turned to defending both the military campaign itself and the British decision to stop. In this context the tone of broadcasts changed only slightly, but still noticeably. In answering the question, 'Did the United Nations stop the fighting in Egypt?' N. Leadbitter's views aligned with those of the government, and he explained how they would reject any suggestion their action had been aggressive. 'The Prime Minister has repeatedly described the Anglo–French action as a police one,' he said, 'with the sole intention of stopping the spread of hostilities.' He described how the UN had stopped the war before it contaminated the whole region and that UN forces would remain in

Egypt 'until mutual confidence is restored. . . .[UN action] is important as an experiment to maintain international law and justice'.[190] Partner derided Leadbitter for 'trying to have his Suez cake and eat it with UN icing', but such opinions were consistent with the official line.[191] In a similar way Partner discussed a broadcast by Edward Hodgkin transmitted after the cease-fire. Labelling it as 'a model of discretion, though far from the British line,' Partner believed its pro-UN content 'would not have given much pleasure to Conservative hawks at this time'.[192] Why did this marked change in BBC broadcasts occur? Obviously with the immediate end of the crisis and the 'defeat' of the government line the BBC felt more liberated to broadcast as it had always done and had tried to do over the preceding few months – that is with objectivity. Yet far from overtly criticising the government such broadcasts sought only to celebrate the peace, analyse the situation objectively and accurately, and express hope for a new era in international relations based on a more active United Nations.

Equally it was now time for the Voice of the Arabs to gloat, but add that Egypt would continue to fight any aggression. This was not the end of the battle, it warned; rather it was only the beginning of the eradication of imperialism from the Arab East.[193] Propaganda highlighted the cultural more than the political consequences of the invasion, and so the Anglo-French forces were charged not only with colluding with Israel and defying the UN, but also with desecrating mosques.[194] In this way the 'aggressor' states became the victim of a sophisticated propaganda campaign carefully orchestrated to heighten Arab wrath against them by appealing to the anger inherent in every Arab when his culture is violated. This encouraged Britain's Lord Privy Seal, R.A. Butler, to propose that 'the baseless propaganda which the Egyptian government were disseminating about alleged atrocities by the Anglo-French troops in Port Said' be forcefully denied.[195] The Postmaster General, Dr Charles Hill, was sent to Port Said to investigate these allegations of atrocities. Upon his return he reported to the Cabinet that he had discovered 'slight' physical destruction, 'except in a few areas where stiff resistance had to be overcome'.[196]

Soon Egyptian broadcasts abandoned their reliance on emotional themes for their propaganda, and instead assumed a much more direct diplomatic function. On 1 November Cairo Radio had already announced that Egypt was severing all diplomatic relations with Britain and France.[197] Public diplomacy therefore ensured that the British knew of this a full two hours before the Ambassador to Egypt, Sir Humphrey Trevelyan, was officially informed of the break through the traditional private channels. Then on 1 January 1957, the Voice of the Arabs broadcast Nasser's abrogation of the Anglo-Egyptian Treaty, along with reports that the British bases referred to in the 1954 treaty had been liquidated and were now 'mere history'.[198] Perhaps no other message so evoked the spirit of the crisis and signalled the beginning of the end of British influence in the Middle East.

The Eisenhower Doctrine

As the immediate crisis reached its conclusion both the Voice of the Arabs and Soviet radio shifted their attention towards the United States. Both denounced the Americans as hypocritical in their alleged attempt to dominate Middle Eastern affairs and supplant the colonialism of the French and British with their own brand of imperialist power. This was less than just. Throughout the crisis the Americans were vociferous in their opposition to imperialism in any form, and had rejected the use of force to settle the dispute. For example on 2 October 1956, Dulles had told a press conference that 'the US cannot be expected to identify 100 per cent . . . with the colonial powers . . . any areas encroaching in some manner on the problem of so-called colonialism find the US playing a somewhat independent role'.[199] The Voice of the Arabs eagerly seized on this as an opportunity to portray their fight against imperialism as justified, with Dulles's words echoed to indicate American support. This theme was then picked up by the BBC, particularly by Bickham Sweet-Escott.[200] In a *Survey of the Middle East* broadcast in the General Overseas Service in December 1956, he said that the Russians had 'made great progress' in exploiting the break in Anglo-American relations to penetrate the Middle East. He thus applauded President Eisenhower's declaration that 'the United States would view with the utmost gravity any threat to the territorial integrity or the political independence of Turkey, Persia, Pakistan and Iraq'. Eisenhower had 'asserted in unmistakable terms and for the first time the interest of the US in the Middle East . . . And, above all, it has given a clear warning to Moscow that there is a point beyond which the US will not tolerate the Soviet penetration of the Middle East.'[201] In this way the painful birth of the Eisenhower Doctrine was recorded.

As Sweet-Escott had intimated this Doctrine promised US military action in support of the political independence of Middle Eastern states if they requested aid 'against overt armed aggression from any nation controlled by International Communism'.[202] It was, however, harshly criticised as being 'aggressive'. The Voice of the Arabs said that the

Arabs themselves were able to fill the so-called 'power vacuum' that the Doctrine was designed to seal.[203] It was also the subject of considerable attack by Radio Moscow – understandably so given that the Doctrine was designed more as a means to contain the Soviet Union in the advent of British and French withdrawal rather than a serious attempt to secure a stable new order for the Middle East. In what Thomas Sorenson has termed 'a classic example of propaganda of the deed,' the popularity of the US soared among developing countries during the crisis precisely because it was viewed as having applied equal standards to its allies as to other less amenable powers.[204] However the USIA predicted that the Doctrine would meet with public hostility in the Middle East, but since the opinion of the USIA was never officially sought by American statesmen until after the 1961 Bay of Pigs invasion, efforts to sell the Doctrine were largely unsuccessful.

Egyptian broadcasts made further attempts to split the Atlantic Alliance by focusing on the possibility that America might provide its allies with assistance before Britain and France withdrew their forces; one warned the US that this would suggest they were 'participating in their aggression . . . in the collusion . . . Beware America! Any aid from you to the aggressors would make your participation more grave than all the crime which they have committed.'[205]

Nevertheless the British made every effort to encourage the Americans to begin supplying them with oil again, so on 1 December the US started fresh negotiations with the Chancellor of the Exchequer and Prime Minister in waiting, Harold Macmillan. Lloyd's announcement in the Commons on 3 December that troops would withdraw from Egypt by mid-December provided that an effective UN force was in place, was also decisive. Lloyd mentioned no specific date in order to avoid providing the Arabs with ammunition for their inevitable celebratory propaganda.[206] Consequently American oil was flowing again to Britain within 72 hours, and by 22 December Britain had received a US-backed loan and additional aid, all to the derision of the Voice of the Arabs.

So, despite the conclusion of the immediate Suez crisis the Voice of the Arabs sustained its noisy and virulent attack on the US, Britain, and of course Israel. In January 1957 British policy in Aden and its dispute with Yemen over the protectorate intensified, and so Egyptian propaganda now veered towards criticising Anglo-Yemeni relations. In language echoing that of previous years, a Colonial Office press release stated that 'interference from the Yemen has been aggravated in recent times by propaganda emanating from the radio at Cairo and also from Yemen itself. Present Egyptian policy encourages the aggressive attitude towards Aden and the Aden Protectorate of the Yemen government.[207] 1957 also witnessed the inauguration of Cairo's 'Voice of Free Africa' service which, much to the chagrin of the colonial powers, concentrated its invective and incitement on British and French Africa. The reception of these African transmissions were described as good and were said to have the 'greatest potential influence' on listeners 'vulnerable to Islamic propaganda.'[208] Egyptian radio had clearly survived the Suez crisis to continue to irritate and aggravate the British government. The crisis had, in fact, bestowed the Voice of the Arabs with a new integrity; because Israel refused to withdraw from the territory it had captured during its military campaign in the Sinai desert, Egypt encouraged the Palestinian fedayeen to intensify their terrorist offensive against Israel. By being able to precipitate action, albeit against a traditional enemy, the credibility of Egyptian propaganda was considerably enhanced. This was however due less to its appeal or its popularity, than to the political failure of the Anglo-French–Israeli conspiracy against Egypt.

REFLECTIONS

The Suez crisis left the position of the BBC in some doubt. Yet rather than demanding a whole new relationship with the government, the crisis merely clarified the existing one; the BBC had admirably maintained its stand in the most adverse of circumstances and had proved that it would not tolerate any government which found itself in political hot water walking all over it.

The Cabinet minutes for September 1956 record how Eden 'continued to be dissatisfied with the conduct of the overseas services of the BBC'.[209] The reason is left to speculation since nothing so much as a hint is offered by the minutes. It now seems that Eden's concern with the BBC was long-standing. When on a tour of the Middle East as Secretary of State for War in November 1940, he cabled, 'Wherever I go I hear complaints of BBC announcements both in English and Arabic. They are continually putting out rumours obviously emanating from enemy sources ... In general BBC announcements show lack of virility and incisiveness.'[210] However, Evelyn Shuckburgh, Eden's Private Secretary, never 'heard or believed that Eden had a very real dislike of the BBC external services'.[211] Indeed Eden was Foreign Secretary when the Arabic service was established in 1938 and remained a champion of its role.[212] His distrust of the BBC was therefore rooted in specific circumstances – the way the Arabic service had operated at particular moments during the Second World War and the Suez crisis – and did not derive from any deep-seated personal resentment of the external services in general or the Arabic service in particular.

As we have seen the BBC was subjected to a variety of pressures from the government – the appointment of a Liaison Officer, threats of a cut in the grant-in-aid, verbal and written criticism, and questioning of its integrity – all in a concerted, some would say paranoid, effort to exercise some semblance of management over its output. It was all very unnecessary; the BBC's reputation was, and remains, based on its reputation for objectivity and accuracy, and this is what makes it such a successful agency of propaganda. At the same time the external services did reflect if not actually defend the government position on Suez, and used in broadcasts many of the propaganda themes suggested by the Foreign Office.

It is possible to suggest the impact which VOA and BBC broadcasts had during the other crises scrutinised in this book. For the period of the Suez crisis however, we are not in a position to even speculate. Even the audience research,[213] usually an insufficient guide but an indication of listenership nevertheless, is unavailable. This is unfortunate. The British viewpoint – government and public – was presented and the government's actions explained, all within the agenda set by the government itself rather than by the media. But the overall impact of the propaganda campaign cannot be gauged precisely because the role assumed by the BBC during the crisis was as a channel for information, opinion and views. There was no attempt to stimulate any kind of action among its audience, only present a well-argued case. So what went wrong? Ultimately the outcome of Suez was not the responsibility of the BBC or the entire British propaganda effort; since propaganda is only as effective as the policy it is defending, responsibility must lie with the way Britain handled the crisis politically.

In the post-Suez plethora of inquiries the BBC was wholly vindicated, both by its Board of Governors[214] and by the Hill Report.[215] The latter concluded that the BBC's autonomy 'should remain absolutely unimpaired and the government accepted this view'.[216] It affirmed that the 'impartiality and objectivity of the BBC is a national asset of great value, and the independence which the Corporation now enjoys should be maintained'. But the report also contained its fair share of failures; it certainly recognised and endorsed the importance of the external services but did not acknowledge that the BBC should be

involved in diplomatic efforts towards 'friendly' countries, thus implying that only their contribution to hostile propaganda was valued. In
this way the BBC had arrived full circle from the end of the Second
World War. While a doubling of the daily output in Arabic was recommended by the Hill inquiry, along with that of other services,[217]
this was to be at the expense of broadcasts to western Europe, while
services to Latin America were not restored.[218] But the envisaged expansion of Arabic was a case of closing the stable door after the horse
has bolted, and indicates a fundamental weakness in the connection
between external radio broadcasting and the shaping of foreign policy;
the latter must respond rapidly to events while the former must, because of the logistics involved, operate according to a long-term strategy. A spontaneous expansion of language services in times of crisis
is difficult, but not impossible. It was achieved by the Voice of America which successfully expanded its Arabic service between October
and November 1956, from just 1 hour 30 minutes to 14 hours 30 minutes per day.[219] The Hill Report's review of the Overseas Information
Services concluded that an improvement in this area was vital to the
effectiveness of the BBC: 'While stability and continuity of effort are
essential,' it said, 'our efforts must be able to react swiftly to a changing situation with a flexibility which permits, as the need may arise, a
switch from one area to another.'[220]

Set against the background of the Cold War the large-scale overhaul
of the BBC external services reflected the shifts in foreign policy that
characterised the end of the Suez crisis. It was inevitable that the BBC
would be subject to the prioritising of the Foreign Office concerning
the most important geographical areas and language services, but this
only hindered the diplomatic efforts of the BBC and, in turn, hampered Britain's overall conduct of its foreign policy.

Above all else, the Suez crisis confirmed that even the best propaganda cannot defend the most ill-judged and, to world opinion, most
questionable of foreign policies. In being seen as the injured party,
especially since the legal position was so vague, Egyptian radio had a
head start on the BBC. As it became increasingly clear that the military venture was vigorously opposed, particularly in the United States,
British propaganda weakened to an irrecoverable position. Actions do
indeed speak louder than words. As Thomas Sorenson has written, 'world
public opinion ... proved stronger than the combined military forces
of Britain, France and Israel. The invaders won a military victory ...
but they suffered a major political-propaganda defeat'.[221]

3 The Hungarian Uprising, 1956: Ambitious Aims, Limited Means

Listen to the tolling of Hungarian bells warning of disaster! Come! Save our souls! . . . We implore you in the name of justice, freedom and the binding moral principle of active solidarity to help us. . . . The shadows grow darker every hour over the Hungarian land. Listen to our cry . . . and act. SOS! SOS! May God be with us![1]

This is the hardest night Dubrovnik has ever known. SOS Croatia! SOS Europe![2]

INTRODUCTION

While Britain was struggling to manage the Suez crisis and come to terms with its weakened status in international affairs, Eastern Europe was in ferment. The 1956 Hungarian uprising in particular had enormous implications for western foreign policy and for international radio broadcasting. Miklos Molnar has written that 'never before had a medium of communication affected the course of events as profoundly as happened in this case'.[3] Moreover, Marshal Tito of Yugoslavia accused radio propaganda of having helped to generate the crises by interfering in the internal affairs of Hungary and Poland. Tito speculated that the Soviet government, watching this interference reach 'rather extensive proportions,' was nervous that 'unpleasant consequences could result if it [the Soviet government] left these countries completely and gave them a status such as that enjoyed by Yugoslavia; reactionary elements might then be victorious.'[4] Such Soviet anxiety was probably exacerbated by the other methods which the United States used to disseminate its propaganda in the satellite countries. The CIA, for example, flew balloons over the Iron Curtain which carried leaflets bearing such inscriptions as 'Hungarians for Freedom – All the Free World for the Hungarians.'[5] Quite possibly foreign broadcasts, combined with such CIA-inspired propaganda campaigns and coverage of the Polish crisis in the Communist media, did raise the level of both dissatisfaction and expectation within Hungary, and contributed to the revolution that occurred there.

The role played by Radio Free Europe (RFE) in the Hungarian uprising is the most notorious and well-documented.[6] The debate concerning just how much influence RFE actually had in stimulating and maintaining the uprising is fierce; whether broadcasts did incite the Hungarians and promise American military intervention has never been satisfactorily proven. The United Nations Special Committee which investigated the crisis in 1957 concluded that RFE had 'aroused an expectation of support'.[7] In terms of apportioning responsibility, however, this means very little. As this episode confirms the whole issue ultimately revolves around the question of *implication*; most writers categorically state that RFE 'implied' this, or that individual commentators 'implied' that. Determining both the intent and the interpretation of the broadcasts is therefore crucial. One must also consider the very real possibility that the Hungarian people heard exactly what they wanted to hear which, given the critical and stressful atmosphere of the time, is quite understandable. Another less generous theory speculates that perhaps they felt the need to find a foreign scapegoat for the failure of the revolution, and RFE fitted the role perfectly.

Less well known is how the BBC and Voice of America managed the crisis. Their broadcasts adopted a less hardline approach than RFE, but were therefore seen to be more effective and credible. In addition to being agents of propaganda and channels of diplomatic communication, they also relayed news and information to an audience which would otherwise have been denied a full picture of events. They were also responsible for assuring the suppressed Hungarians that they had been neither ignored nor forgotten by the west, and that their plight was the cause of considerable anxiety within the 'Free World'.

The coincidence of the Hungarian uprising with the Suez crisis was unfortunate. Anatol Goldberg, Head of the Russian Service (1953–7),[8] described Suez as a personal embarrassment since the Soviet media were now in a position to exploit the Middle East crisis and distract attention away from Hungary.[9] Inevitably perhaps, the Soviet media argued along similar lines themselves, and accused the BBC of using Hungary to divert attention from Suez![10]

Sooner or later most western international broadcasting stations were criticised for their treatment of the Hungarian uprising, albeit by differing individuals and organisations and largely coloured by their Cold War political perspectives. In stark contrast to the others, and RFE in particular,

the BBC emerged from its extensive coverage of the Hungarian uprising with its reputation intact, and with its beleaguered audience having placed an even greater trust and confidence in its services. This
was despite the ongoing Suez crisis, the enormous physical strain that
the coincidence of events imposed upon broadcasters, and their understandable urge to assist the Hungarian liberation efforts. Even the Foreign
Office praised the BBC for its treatment of the Hungarian problem,
recognising that Suez notwithstanding, 'considerations other than personal
feelings must prevail,' even if 'at times we have longed for blunter speech'.[11]

In January 1957 George Tarjan, Assistant Head of the Central European Service, visited the Council of Europe in Strasbourg to meet
Hungarians participating in the Congress of the Hungarian Revolutionary Council. There he conversed with General Béla Király, Commander of the Budapest Revolutionary Forces, who told him that 'if
there was one radio that enjoyed respect and authority during the revolution it was the BBC'.[12] RFE was by far the most popular station;[13]
broadcasting from Munich, it had the strongest signal, was the most
accessible, and it scheduled the most complete Hungarian programme.[14]
Yet officials at RFE themselves confessed that the BBC enjoyed a far
greater reputation among the better-educated, more informed and perhaps potentially more influential sector of the audience – in Sir Hugh
Greene's terminology, the 'disaffected'.[15] This was not coincidental.
As former head of BBC broadcasts to the Soviet Union and Eastern
Europe, and later Director General, Greene believed that this audience
had to be targeted since they 'tend to be receptive and attracted in
different ways by the freedom of the west. . . . A dictatorship,' he concluded, 'cannot ignore public opinion entirely and thus by a very gradual
process our propaganda may affect Soviet policy.'[16] Greene had made
an extensive contribution to the development of British propaganda
methods during the Second World War; as head of the BBC German
Service he collaborated with the Political Warfare Executive which
guided 'white' broadcasting to the enemy and occupied countries. Together they had believed it was necessary to encourage the German
opposition to Hitler and promote disunity whenever possible.[17] Undoubtedly these principles continued to guide Greene in his subsequent
Cold War propaganda activities, the success of which RFE ascribed to
the reputation the BBC had established during the Second World War.[18]
This prompted RFE to attest that 'among many more critical members
of the audience in Hungary, news is accepted as true only if confirmed
by the BBC'.[19] This was indeed a most commendable tribute to the
BBC's methods.

It is of minimal use and value to describe the BBC and VOA's handling of this or any crisis if nobody was actually listening to their broadcasts. It is therefore imperative to first establish that both stations did have an audience in Hungary and the Soviet Union. This is not an easy task; western broadcasters were bedevilled during the Cold War by a lack of reliable audience research methods, results and analyses. The usual technique – gauging audience size and reaction by the volume and content of mail received from target areas – was hampered in the Eastern bloc both by censorship and by fear of the consequences that letter writers often faced upon discovery. Evidence of an audience is therefore more often than not anecdotal, yet still encouraging and derives primarily from the valuable work carried out by RFE in its extensive interviews with travellers, defectors, refugees and the like. And of course the repeated and vociferous attacks launched by the media of the Eastern bloc upon western broadcasters at the height of the Cold War provide further proof that broadcasts were heard. If this was not so, how could they be criticised with such accurate references to specific broadcasts?

One USIA survey conducted amongst refugees in Austria discovered that approximately 80 per cent of Hungarians listened to VOA. This was later confirmed as accurate by an RFE enquiry,[20] although the fact that these were the results of American-sponsored interviews must throw some doubt on such exceptionally high audience figures for American broadcasts. The BBC has recorded no comparable statistics for their own ratings, yet there is still a large body of evidence to confirm the existence of an audience. It has been claimed that the BBC Hungarian service was widely listened to, but that jamming made reception virtually impossible. Nevertheless there was some listening to the BBC Home Service and the German and French language services. A correspondent with the *Observer* newspaper, for example, noted how during October and November 1956 a 'handful of Hungarian intellectuals' found refuge in his hotel 'to listen to the BBC news.' The fact that the news was mainly concerned with the Suez crisis led the Audience Research Department to conclude that they had been listening either to the French or English service.[21] The scope for penetrating Hungary's borders was therefore considerable, and the language abilities of the audience suggest that the level of their education was high; it was imperative that this audience be targeted. However, Hungarians who wished to hear the broadcasts still faced many difficulties. Although listening to western broadcasts was never officially prohibited, anyone caught spreading information derived from them was liable to be charged with anti-state activity, spreading 'warmongering rumours' and 'imperialist propaganda'. This would be followed by possible conviction and severe punishment.[22] This meant, as one USIA Research Report commented, that 'members of the foreign broadcast audience' lived in a 'systematically created environment of anxiety and intimidation'. Not surprisingly USIA found that with 'only a few exceptions, all foreign broadcast listening in Hungary is clandestine listening'.[23] Nevertheless, an awareness that the educated could listen to broadcasts in languages other than their own provided even more opportunities for the BBC to bypass the jammers and allow its audience to hear broadcasts not originally intended for them. This audience was sacrificed however by the Hill Committee which decided to contract or curtail altogether West European language services for reinvestment elsewhere within the BBC.

A letter from a leading workers' representative, published by the influential party newspaper *Szabad Nep* provides further evidence that the Hungarians listened to the foreign broadcasts, and that officialdom assigned considerable significance to their content. This letter requested that the Central Committee keep workers' committees informed 'in good time about the affairs of the country and the party, for we are in a very difficult position if the workers get to know something from the hostile radios sooner than we do'![24] There is perhaps no better confirmation than this of the potential power and influence of international radio broadcasting.

'GOOD NIGHT AND GOOD HOPE'[25]

P.F. Grey of the British Foreign Office emphasised that Britain must do nothing in its 'publicity'[26] to 'incite the peoples of Eastern Europe to uprisings which will be bound to fail'. Since Grey was such a vociferous critic during the Suez crisis it is most refreshing to find him offering praise for the BBC which, he said, 'has followed and is following a cautious policy in its broadcasts to the satellites'.[27] Indeed there is documentary evidence that the BBC deleted from its broadcasts anything that threatened such a discerning approach. On 27 October 1956, for example, the news bulletins contained a report of Hugh Gaitskell's speech at a Labour Party meeting in London. The original script read:

It was to be hoped . . . that the example of Poland and Hungary would be followed by other countries behind the Iron Curtain.[28]

These remarks were deleted from the bulletin that was broadcast, an editorial decision based on a fear that they might encourage further futile efforts at revolution. Thus despite what its critics assert about Suez the BBC was certainly sensitive of its power and often acted as its own censor where diplomacy may have been jeopardised. Some however were critical of such an approach. Barry Zorthian, in possession of the rather grand title of Assistant Programme Manager for Policy Application of the USIA,[29] believed that such self-censorship was the price to be paid for the reduction in Soviet jamming of BBC broadcasts which had first been observed in June 1956 (that is, prior to Khrushchev and Bulganin's visit to Britain). As evidence, Zorthian hurled at the BBC the words of a Soviet defector who is reported to have said that it was difficult to distinguish BBC Russian broadcasts from Radio Moscow.[30] As anyone who listened to Radio Moscow and the BBC regularly during the Cold War will testify, this is an unbelievably incredulous remark to make and is not substantiated by any evidence whatsoever. Nevertheless, the BBC must certainly be commended for not inciting the Hungarians,[31] and this was readily acknowledged by the Hungarians themselves. On 3 November 1956, Budapest Radio relayed a message of thanks to the BBC for its coverage of the crisis, and expressed appreciation for the objective information it had given the world about Hungary. 'We were particularly pleased,' it said, 'to note that there was no incitement to extremism and that the tone of the broadcasts expressed solidarity in our joy over victories and in our sorrow weeping over the dead.'[32] The BBC broadcast this on both its Hungarian and European services, and did the same with their own reply which it broadcast the next day, 4 November. This is worth quoting at length for it reveals what the BBC considered to be its purpose in such tempestuous times:

> The BBC in its transmissions to Hungary and the world during these historic days has tried to represent faithfully the admiration and sympathy of the whole British people for the sufferings, the victories and the courage of the Hungarian nation. In the knowledge that Hungarians have written a chapter in the history of Europe, we hope that the result will be for the Hungarian people based on justice and moderation . . .[33]

This is a most carefully worded statement; it is easy to see the delib-

eration that must have gone into its phrasing. It strives to retain traditional BBC balance by focusing primarily on the message from
Budapest, and by talking of 'the Hungarian nation' and the 'Hungarian
people' it avoids taking sides. Yet at the same time it expresses 'sympathy and admiration', and hopes for 'justice and moderation'. The
BBC was clearly telling the Hungarian people of where its sympathies
– and those of the people of Britain – lay, and thus reassured them
that they had not been forgotten. This was perhaps the most important
and probably most successful function which the BBC performed during
the crisis, and an examination of broadcasts throughout the whole period
reveals that this was indeed a priority.[34] The amounts of practical, medical
and financial aid donated to the people of Hungary by various organisations were documented day after day. The list of organisations and
individuals offering their support – financial as well as moral – seemed
to be endless. Among them were the British government, Hungarians .
living in Britain, the Red Cross, Save the Children, the TUC, the Lord
Mayor of London, and students of Oxford University.[35] Such sympathy was not limited to Britain; on 4 November, the day that the Soviet
troops re-entered Budapest and crushed the revolution, the BBC Hungarian news reported that 'horror and indignation . . . has been expressed
throughout the free world'.[36]

The Voice of America covered the crisis in a similar fashion, reporting events for the Hungarians themselves (local communication being
in a state of disarray) and informing them of world reaction to their
bid for freedom. The following for example is an extract from a VOA
Hungarian programme-lead broadcast of 24 October 1956:

> From every part of the free world voices express deep sympathy
> with the Hungarian people. The French Socialist Workers Federa-
> tion . . . discussed the Hungarian events and Robert Bathereau, Gen-
> eral Secretary of the Federation, said . . . 'I want to express my
> complete sympathy with all peoples who are struggling to be free of
> oppression.' The American press is discussing the Hungarian events
> under large headlines. The radio stations give the latest news in every
> half hour.[37]

During the crisis VOA assured its audience that the 'leaders of the
free world and the public follow the developments in Hungary tensely,
and important voices gave expression of their deep sympathies with
the Hungarian people'.[38] VOA christened the uprising a 'freedom revolt' and described the 'Soviet armed interference' as a 'violation of
the Hungarian peace treaty'.[39] Such overtly political language confirms

that the VOA was acting as the mouthpiece of American policy. Listeners were once again given a guarantee that they were not being ignored, especially at the highest levels; VOA reported how America, along with Britain and France, had 'requested the urgent convening of the UN Security Council' to discuss Hungary, while Spain had demanded the organisation initiate 'immediate steps'.[40]

The impact of such broadcasts was extensive; refugees and escapees were as encouraging in their praise of VOA as they were of the BBC: 'You were our hope,' said one. 'You kept the spirit up in us,' remarked another.[41] One BBC broadcast in particular stands out for the frank language and imagery it used not only to reassure the Hungarians, but in indicating to their Russian oppressors the scale of world opinion now ranged against them. In a talk entitled 'Hungary and the West' James Monahan, former Head of the West European service, related how a British reporter was asked by a Hungarian: 'Do they know in the west what these Russians are doing?' 'Well,' said Monahan, 'the meeting [of the Security Council concerning Hungary] now begun . . . is one immediate sign that the west does know.' In fact, he said, the west not only knew of the events themselves but judged them to represent the 'bankruptcy . . . of a system which has practised the enslavement of men's minds under a specious theory . . . Communism,' he declared rather prematurely, 'is a broken creed'. [42]

News and information were therefore the most valued services provided by the BBC and VOA at this time, especially if they focused on the struggles within the Soviet orbit and placed these in the wider context of Cold War superpower confrontation. One explanation for this was offered by a woman from Budapest answering questions in one of the many surveys conducted by USIA among refugees in Austria. She said that people ' are always expecting some great happenings, some significant event coming from the west, which has direct or indirect bearing on their future fate. They switch on their radios day by day with such hopes.'[43] According to these USIA surveys the BBC's news coverage was regarded as being the most reliable; on what was called 'timeliness', however, the BBC was said to have been 'definitely out of the running', while VOA was described as the most timely.[44] Such comments must of course be treated with a certain amount of scepticism; as Guillermo Santisteban, the head of Radio Havana's English language service in Cuba, remarked rather cynically but with considerable accuracy in 1986, 'whoever pays for the study always comes out on top'.[45]

The Monitoring Service

The Suez crisis confirmed that the monitoring service performed two invaluable functions: it acted as a channel of information so that states could relay their diplomatic intentions and messages to the foreign services of the British and American governments; and these governments were also provided with some indication of how their policies and objectives were received in the target country. But the versatility of the monitoring service was far from being limited. The Hungarian uprising added two further roles to its repertoire: the west was kept informed of events in a closed society, while the external services were provided with information which they could then broadcast back to Hungary.

Throughout the 1950s, access to Eastern Europe by western journalists was difficult and often impossible. Naturally the monitoring service was regarded as a vital source of information. British journalists did enter Hungary when the Iron Curtain was briefly lifted prior to the second Soviet invasion.[46] When it all too soon descended again at the beginning of November 1956, the BBC monitoring service became almost the only source of news available once more, and its reports served as a guideline for BBC Russian service programmes. This was a critical time however, and exercising caution in selecting material to be broadcast back to the Hungarians generated its own problems. Budapest Radio was the principal source for the BBC monitoring service throughout the crisis but it was, after all, a propaganda station, particularly once the Soviets assumed editorial control over its output. Western broadcasters therefore had to try and judge the intention and accuracy of broadcasts, and consider the possibility that transmissions from Budapest Radio to the west – which it certainly knew would be monitored, reported and perhaps re-broadcast – might serve specific strategic purposes.

The United States likewise benefited from monitoring reports. VOA disclosed to its Hungarian audience how it had managed to piece together 'fragmentary reports and appeals by Budapest Radio and despatches of foreign correspondents now in Hungary' which, said VOA, 'depict dramatic scenes, clashes between the rebels and the security police who have been aided by Soviet troops called to suppress the revolt. The free world received particularly shocking reports about planes firing into crowds, massed before the Parliament building in Budapest.'[47]

The value attached to monitoring reports by the media was therefore considerable, but the American government and State Department also profited from their services. On 23 October 1956, contact between the State Department in Washington and its embassy in Budapest was

lost. Until it was restored on 25 October the Department was compelled
to rely on Budapest Radio for news and information of the situation
inside Hungary.[48] In such circumstances both the British and the
Americans were forced to frame their reaction to events and base their
policy options according to the monitoring reports. Such top-level confidence in this channel of information is perhaps surprising but, when
placed in context, quite understandable; there was simply no other method
of obtaining news and information from Hungary. Considering the diplomatic implications of such dependence it was of course essential that
the reports first be accurate, and then be correctly interpreted by the
Foreign Office or State Department. This analysis then determined the
political response to their content and thus to the events themselves.

However, the British Foreign Office was not quite as dependent on
the monitoring service as the State Department. Unlike others, the British
embassy in Budapest did not rely on telephone and telex to maintain
contact with the outside world, using instead the Diplomatic Service
wireless system which could still be operated even in the most adverse
of circumstances. This, together with the BBC monitoring service, provided the basis for the dissemination of news to the non-communist
world. The Information Research Department approached the Reuters
news agency and offered them exclusive use of this information provided it was not attributed to either the Foreign office or the embassy.
Reuters eagerly accepted and decided to dateline it from correspondents in countries neighbouring Hungary.[49]

In a similar way the US Information Officer attached to the legation
in Vienna received information about the situation in Hungary from
returning correspondents and travellers, but primarily from refugees.
He then relayed this to the Munich Radio Centre news room which in
turn transmitted it to USIA in Washington.

Together these examples illustrate both the use of the embassies in
information work, and the importance of using the *authentic* media in
disseminating news and information for propaganda purposes; manu-
factured channels, such as 'The Voice of Britain' during the Suez crisis
and the clandestine 'Voice of the South Atlantic' during the 1982 Falk-
lands war, had their uses of course but enjoyed minimal success; they
were used, and were therefore regarded by their audiences, simply as
propaganda stations and as part of British psychological warfare operations. So unlike the authentic media, for example Reuters and the
BBC, they lacked credibility which is the vital ingredient necessary
for propaganda effectiveness.

A CAUTIOUS POLICY

It has already been demonstrated how Radio Free Europe was the target of criticism from a variety of sources. These alleged that its broadcasts had incited the Hungarians and made hollow promises of American intervention. But such accusations were not levelled at RFE alone. *The Times* newspaper for example reviewed how the west had, for years, told Hungarians that 'theirs is a bad inhuman system of government. Even the more moderate broadcasts from the west, such as those put out by the BBC, have held up western democracy as the best system of government. 'Even if such broadcasts did not call for the forcible overthrow of the Communist régime,' *The Times* thundered, 'they sowed in Hungarian minds the seeds of the present struggle.' The newspaper thus concluded that the Hungarians were justified in feeling 'utterly and completely' betrayed by the west.[50] This was however neither a fair nor accurate representation of BBC policy. It has already been suggested that when he was made Head of BBC broadcasts to the Soviet. Union and Eastern Europe in 1949, Hugh Greene relied on the methods which, as Head of the German Service during the war, he had perfected in collaboration with PWE, namely to ensure credibility through truthful reporting. He therefore defined the objectives of propaganda as being 'to get our audience to accept our view of events', and 'a subsidiary aim was to shake faith in Stalin'.[51] He remained cautious, however, as to how far such propaganda could and should go:

> ... no-one in his senses could believe that it should be any part of our objectives to contribute to the overthrow of the Soviet regime or to 'liberate' the Soviet peoples.... it was certainly part of our aim to keep alive their links with the west and the belief that somehow, someday ... things might be better and Russian rule might be shaken off. But in broadcasts directed from Britain to Eastern Europe we have always been careful to avoid any hint of encouragement to sabotage or revolt. ...
>
> ... Khrushchev has shaken faith in Stalin much more effectively than we ever could – and perhaps in doing so has helped to show our audience in Russia that we had been telling the truth about Stalin for many years.[52]

These were prophetic words indeed. Twenty-five years after they were recorded by Greene in his memoirs, Communism collapsed in Eastern Europe, and with it fell the various dictatorships which had clung to power under the tutelage of the Soviet Union. Of course it cannot be claimed that radio broadcasting alone was responsible for this remarkable turn of events in 1988-9; but by persistently eating away at the Communist régimes for 40 years, and maintaining the hope of liberation among the people, the western broadcasting stations certainly contributed to events. In this way then, Greene's observations bring us full circle back to the question of the intention of broadcasts. Radio was regarded as an invaluable weapon in helping the west to win the Cold War, but the BBC knew this would be best achieved by avoiding a hardline crusading approach. The events of the late 1980s certainly vindicate Greene's words. Barry Elliott, who at the time was the Head of the BBC Central European Services, echoed Greene's words when, in 1992, he explained the role of the BBC and his department in particular:

> In terms of keeping hope alive and spreading democratic ideas, of really putting it to the people that there were alternatives, yes, I think we did have a role. We were not propounding a change of régime – that wasn't part of our job – but we were stimulating the democratic process, and providing a whole range of views, by reporting strikes and demonstrations that people would not have heard about from their own media we encouraged them to come out and demonstrate.[53]

Following the violent suppression of uprisings first in East Germany, Hungary, and then again in Czechoslovakia in 1968, encouraging the people to 'come out and demonstrate' was a considerable risk, even if it did eventually pay off. It is uncertain that Greene would have agreed that this should have been an intention of broadcasts. But Greene and Elliott both confirm that broadcasts have something of a snowball effect on events. The policy of openness, or glasnost, pursued by Mikhail Gorbachev, together with the cessation of jamming, will have made their own contribution; the peoples of the Soviet Union and Eastern Europe, now able to hear broadcasts without interference or fear of being caught, were encouraged to listen to transmissions from the west. What is certain is that broadcasts latched on to these events and made the most of them, and it is further confirmation that international radio broadcasting plays a pivotal role in international politics, whichever process is adopted.

Returning to the events of 1956 we can see how such caution, championed by Hugh Greene, had possibly inspired the USIA. In 1952 the BBC told the USIA that they gave the satellites sympathy but not promises. Liberation is not mentioned as a political prospect. We do say that these crimes cannot continue indefinitely . . . We avoid the word 'liberation' almost completely, but we do try to give hope.

   . . . The BBC often says ' We don't want to write you off, but we are not preparing a war; there will never be a war unless the Soviet Union starts it.' We would not be so blunt as to say 'We won't start a war even to liberate you.'[54]

Yet initially the United States remained less appreciative of the limited power of propaganda than the BBC. The Formulation of Voice of America purposes, written in 1950, included the objective of helping to roll back Soviet influence short of war which would be achieved, it declared, primarily by propaganda.[55] In 1953 however, the Senate's Jackson Committee, established to review 'informational activities,' recognised the intrinsic relationship between word and deed, and warned of the dangers of subscribing to such objectives in propaganda when the Administration was unable to give any practical assistance in carrying them through. Its report said that the US

> will be judged not only by the things it is able to do, but also by the gap between these and its announced policies. A clear distinction must be made between policies and aspirations. Objectives with respect to which the United States commits itself to act must be clearly identified as distinct from those ends to which we, as a nation, aspire but regarding which the government is not committed to take action.[56]

'Had that distinction been clearer three years later,' observed Thomas Sorenson, 'the United States might have avoided acute embarrassment at the time of the Hungarian revolt.'[57]

Sorenson is credited with many propaganda successes in his time at USIA. His indictment is therefore surprising and in fact unfounded. VOA broadcasts remained excessively cautious not to foment trouble, despite the Cold War rhetoric of many American statesmen. Many became a little over-zealous in their caution so that at one stage 'the excellent and heavily praised commentaries' of Laszlo Boros, the Hungarian desk chief in Munich, were omitted from transmission. P. Nadyani, chief of the Hungarian desk in Washington, later described how his staff felt 'heartbroken' at his instructions not to report at length the statements made in the United Nations 'extolling the heroism of the Hungarians and how the free world must come to their aid, etc.'[58] Nadyani justified this by explaining that he 'didn't want the Hungarians to get a false sense of reality – what was said in New York may not mean the same in Hungary'. Moreover he recalled that VOA actually toned things down 'without falsifying anything. We paraphrased our delegate's words. They sounded promising by implication' – that word again – 'and when we heard them we felt it better to paraphrase rather than give exact words which might sound inflammatory'.[59] VOA neither encouraged nor discouraged the rebellion, striving instead to keep the Hungarian people informed of events as they happened, but at the same time supporting, as diplomats at the US embassy in Budapest said, 'the present spiritual restiveness of the Hungarian people'.[60] Thus broadcasts consisted almost exclusively of stilted heavy news and reports of world reaction, all carefully edited before being transmitted.

Still, no one could criticise VOA for not having the power of foresight, and briefing papers prepared at this early but critical stage described the ways propaganda would change in the event of renewed Soviet aggression. The emphasis in broadcasts would then be the struggle of the Hungarian people, illustrating how the 'Soviets stand exposed before the world and that bloody suppression of Hungarian freedom aspirations may well mark the beginning of the end of the Soviet empire.'[61] Grand words indeed, and a grand objective. Nevertheless VOA was criticised for being *over*-cautious in its attempt not to fan the flames.[62] It was often too defensive, being merely responsive, reactionary and negative. After all, as one USIA Research Report conceded, it was the Hungarian people themselves who were 'on the firing line'.[63] On 25 October 1956, for example, officials at the Munich Radio Centre wondered how a Hungarian VOA broadcast could tell its audience of the success of an Arctic expedition, elections in the Soviet Union and cancer research – all rather trivial news stories given that in Hungary 'people were dying in the streets,' and warned that 'such treatment could only cause dismay and resentment'.[64] The Radio Centre then judged that aggravation had been added by the fact that the BBC Hungarian service had broadcast two commentaries vociferously condemning the Soviet action and demanding the removal of whoever was responsible.[65] In other words the Munich Centre had claimed to witness a remarkable reversal; the BBC, usually calm and moderate, was broadcasting what were considered to be caustic commentaries, while the VOA, an instrument of the US's Cold War rhetoric, was criticised for its moderation. As this chapter will demonstrate however, neither the BBC nor the VOA operated in such clearly defined ways; both successfully combined criticism with restraint in their output during the Hungarian uprising.

Such emphasis on news coverage by VOA reflected the modification of station objectives that had occurred after the 1955 Geneva Summit. It also dated back to the Berlin uprising of 1953 when an intensive propaganda campaign, combined with a political policy of non-intervention, proved disappointing. Here was the first demonstration that the US would not be able to support its anti-Communist rhetoric by any practical means; Berlin was also a turning point for VOA and RFE which now carefully avoided calling for open rebellion in the satellite states. In such a climate it would have been easy for VOA to launch a vitriolic offensive against the Soviets, maintaining the idea of liberation behind the Iron Curtain, and reflecting the Administration's support of the right of sovereign people to choose their own governments. Representatives of VOA-Munich told a Conference of US broadcasters in 1956 that this was exactly what their station should have been doing:

> We ought [not] to have any illusions – if we are in the broadcasting business we are in it for a purpose, and that purpose after all is to put across points of view, concepts in which we have an interest . . . and that, of course, is the essence of propaganda. . . . You are not going to kid anybody on the other side of the Iron Curtain or anywhere when you have an official broadcast or a broadcast with a political objective that you are there simply by accident – you will be considered and identified at all times as a propaganda station and I don't necessarily think that that necessarily has a pejorative taste to it. . . . I don't want people looking down the necks of the broadcasters saying ' . . . are you indulging in propaganda?' because the answer should be, without any hesitation, 'Yes, we are, and we hope we are doing it successfully'.[66]

However such broadcasts would only have been denounced as not credible in a situation where word could not be supported by action; the US simply could not despatch western military aid to Hungary. President Eisenhower, all too aware himself of the use and abuse of propaganda, described Hungary as being 'as inaccessible as Tibet'.[67] So the emphasis was to be on news of interest to the Hungarian people, and presenting a picture of American life. Non-political Americana and human interest stories were considered important because the people of the Soviet orbit were said to be tired of the sober political news from their own media. Feeding their curiosity about life in America was a way of hooking listeners to other broadcasts while providing a more subtle form of propaganda.[68]

An equally important aspiration was fostering the idea of peaceful rather than forced change. A VOA policy guidance directive issued in June 1956 established the repudiation of Stalinism as an objective of programming in the hope that it might generate internal pressure within the satellite states. Encouraged by the de-Stalinization that began with the 20th Party Congress in Moscow, pressure from below was to be combined with pressure on the party itself. The output of VOA, together with the policies it pursued during the Hungarian crisis, must first be located within this framework before any attempt to make a credible evaluation of its role can begin.

REVOLUTION: PEACEFUL MEANS

The Voice of America and the BBC enabled listeners to learn of the mood of change and rebellion sweeping Poland and Hungary in 1956. Their own media deliberately played down their significance and often ignored them altogether, thus creating a large information vacuum which western stations could readily fill.

This combination of events during the first half of 1956 had compelled the Foreign Office and IRD to reappraise their propaganda policy towards the Communist orbit. The official record reveals just how necessary such a reappraisal was. Given the circumstances of the Cold War, and the importance which political circles attached to the Soviet bloc, it is rather surprising to find a minute by C.C.B. Stewart, Head of IPD, saying that '(a) this department is not organised to undertake such [information] work in Hungary or any other country behind the Iron Curtain, and (b) the information budget is drawn up on the assumption that no such work is to be carried out. . . . there is no expert in this Department on the satellites.'[69] This was hardly guaranteed to generate confidence at such a critical time!

What Stewart did not disclose of course, was that propaganda to the satellite states was the responsibility of the experts in the IRD, and in April 1956 they described the purpose of their activities in Hungary. The principal objective of their propaganda was to prise Hungary away from the Soviet Union. To this end IRD proposed directing propaganda towards the Hungarian people themselves in the hope of strengthening their resistance to Soviet Communism and reinforcing their opinions of Western values. In addition IRD suggested that Hungarians should be reassured of the west's willingness to help them towards the attainment of freedom. The means of achieving this centred on a debate which is integral to propaganda theory, namely that attitudes and opinions cannot be changed, only existing ones reinforced. On this basis the bureaucracy, intelligentsia and the privileged classes in particular were identified as targets of propaganda which would seek to intensify their latent doubts about Soviet policy, stimulate a revival of Hungarian nationalism, and counter Soviet accusations about the west. From a list of general themes, IRD suggested that:

1. The dogmatic and non-progressive nature of Communist doctrine should be highlighted.
2. Comparisons should be made between the 'free' world and the Communist bloc; the question 'What would Hungary be like if it was not Communist?' ought to be asked.
3. Propaganda should describe the international organisations Hungary would be eligible to join if it was not part of the Soviet bloc, together with the benefits of such membership.
4. Soviet exploitation and general neglect of the satellites should be exposed.
5. There should be extensive publicity about events in Poland and Hungary.
6. Propaganda should provide evidence of dissension inside Hungary.[70]

The IRD was pleased to note that the BBC Hungarian Service had already been pursuing corresponding themes in its broadcasts. These represented British policy, based as always on the necessity of 'peaceful methods' of change.[71] What was meant by the term 'peaceful change' is indeterminate and the official record offers no satisfactory clarification. Today such an expression may imply the achievement of reform and reorganisation through the ballot box rather than by violence; in Cold War Communist dictatorships however, there was of course no possibility of this, and it is this absence of democracy which makes the concept of 'peaceful methods of change' even more difficult to define.

'Peaceful methods', however they might be specified, were likewise at the core of American policy, compromising the more crusading approach of some propagandists. This comprised 'full objective news of all liberalizing developments elsewhere in the orbit; a wide range of materials inspiring nationalist sentiments of the Satellite people of all strata and indicating that continued use of Stalinist methods are inadmissible; reports of Opposition to Communism and Soviet policies; and sympathy of the west'.[72] In a Christmas message to Eastern Europe, broadcast by VOA and RFE and echoed in subsequent public statements, President Eisenhower announced 'peaceful liberation' to be a 'major goal of US foreign policy'.[73] The East Europeans however seem to have taken such pronouncements with the proverbial pinch of salt. The British embassy in Budapest reported that the messages had been branded by the Hungarian government as 'brutal interference' which aimed at the collapse of Communism and a return to the old, despised ways. Diplomats then noted how the people themselves wondered 'what Mr. Eisenhower could mean; they had heard such words before. By what peaceful methods did the President intend to reach his goal?'[74] No acceptable answer was recorded. Further evidence that Eisenhower's Christmas message was heard and was rejected as mere rhetoric is provided by Imre Nagy, former and future Premier of Hungary and unofficial leader of the Hungarian revolutionary movement. He wrote that no 'enemy propaganda, no Christmas or other "message", will destroy more completely the people's faith in Socialism and in a better, happier and more humane future than a forced return to the old, mistaken, anti-popular pre-June [1953 reformist] policy [initiated by Nagy as Premier]'.[75] This is one method of distinguishing British and American propaganda to Hungary specifically, but also during the Cold War as a whole. Both accepted the importance of radio broadcasting, and both acknowledged that one intention of broadcasts directed behind the Iron Curtain was to encourage change. The difference was that the BBC never explicitly described these intentions to its audiences in Eastern Europe, preferring instead to quietly get on with the job in its own particular way. On the other hand, USIA and VOA adopted something of a crusading spirit, and actually told the East Europeans the objectives of their propaganda. In this way false hopes that liberation would indeed occur were raised and American foreign policy was, by implication, indelibly tied to the fate of the Hungarian people. The Americans should therefore have not been surprised when they learnt that the Hungarians had expected military aid from the US.

In contrast J.G. Ward, Deputy Under Secretary of State at the Foreign Office, recognised the limitations of propaganda's ability to actually influence the course of events. He advocated that British propaganda should assert its wish to establish friendly relations with the people of Eastern Europe, and encourage national independence, together with the end of internal repression, again by 'peaceful means'. In addition the 'BBC Overseas Service should continue to broadcast to the satellites straight news and material showing that freedom is preferable to Communism,'[76] Ward remained unconvinced however of the value of distinguishing between the régime and the population in propaganda, despite its current effectiveness in Egypt and its tacit endorsement by Hugh Greene. Rather, Ward believed that British influence may be extended in the satellites by establishing closer political relations between the governments themselves.[77] This narrow-sighted recommendation, based more on a blind faith in the diplomatic process rather than the most fitting method of propaganda, was not put into effect; early in October 1956, immediately before the crisis erupted in Hungary, the Foreign Office registered how the satellite governments were now regarded as 'unrepresentative régimes imposed by force from outside,' enjoying 'neither the confidence nor the support of the vast majority of the peoples they govern'.[78] Accordingly the long-term objective pursued by the Foreign Office was the replacement of such governments 'by others freely chosen by the peoples of the satellites themselves and independent of the Soviet Union. The policy of [HMG] has been to do nothing which would encourage or strengthen the puppet governments of East Europe or which can be interpreted as approval of them.'[79] During the Hungarian crisis it was this set of principles, which included an explicit acknowledgement of the role of the BBC, rather than the recommendations by Ward, that governed propaganda policy towards the satellites. In this way the confidence of the people of Hungary was to be retained. These principles continued to guide BBC broadcasts through the next two decades and contributed to the overthrow of Communism in 1988–9.

VOA had yet another perception of how best to achieve 'peaceful change', and many programmes focused on the activities of the increasingly active Hungarian intellectuals. On 2 October 1956 for example, VOA reviewed the Hungarian press which included reports of how composers, writers and historians had demanded 'the truth'. 'Is it possible,' VOA asked, 'that if so many want the truth they should not obtain it?'[80] By broadcasting these demands VOA was not encouraging them, but simply articulating them to a wider audience, and particularly to the ordinary Hungarian people who may be sympathetic to their grievances. Then when composers and musicians published a manifesto demanding greater freedom of expression and knowledge of western music, the VOA Hungarian service immediately devoted a weekly broadcast to American music. Similarly back in December 1955, the US legation in Budapest had suggested that propaganda should take advantage of the Soviet Union's exploitative economic relationship with its satellites. This, it was hoped, would provide a context for further anti-Communist resistance by the Hungarian people; if it could be

demonstrated that 'the fruits of their labours are simply going to finance the Soviet economy and imperialistic adventures in the east,'
wrote diplomats at the legation, 'the media would have an excellent
argument with which to urge the maintenance of at least passive economic resistance'.[81] In addition, this would offer the Hungarians a pretext to participate in their own liberation efforts instead of relying on
the west, an anomaly that had been created by an acknowledged 'over
emphasis [of the] liberation theme over [the] years'. The American
legation considered that 'such an offensive should not be difficult to
mount or buttress with facts,' and recommended that the US offer sur-
plus agricultural commodities to the east 'whenever conditions appear
to so warrant'. This would demonstrate that the US was 'prepared and
willing to give concrete expression to its exercise of the golden rule,
thus alleviating in some measure [the] effects of captive peoples' sac-
rifices'.[82] This might be considered as merely an act of political re-
alism and traditional diplomatic practice, which it certainly was. But it
was moreover a significant admission that supporting propaganda with
concrete policy action is necessary if that propaganda is to be accepted
as credible. Again international radio broadcasting was used to directly
augment American foreign policy.

It was not entirely clear that the Hungarian students and intellectuals
were about to launch an anti-Communist, or indeed anti-Soviet revolution. It seems that their demands merely amounted to the wish for a
form of Communist organisation which was more acceptable to Hungarian conditions. On 23 October 1956, Budapest Radio quoted a leading
article in the Hungarian newspaper *Szabad Nep* which pledged its own
support for the students. This is noteworthy because *Szabad Nep* was
the official party newspaper and was thus required reading by all party
members. Since it was also regularly read out in radio broadcasts, the
paper therefore served to mould public opinion and so represented an
influential, if not official, endorsement for the uprising that could be
neither rejected nor ignored. 'We who have turned against the crimes
and mistakes committed in the immediate past,' it said, 'want to side
with the collective action of the youth . . . with all material and moral
support. . . . We welcome the position taken up by the University youth.'[83]
For western decision makers reading these monitoring reports it was
important that the paper agreed with the principle that 'friendship between the Hungarian and Soviet peoples must be intensified on the
basis of complete equality and in the spirit of Lenin, and emphasise
that both our Marxist–Leninist conviction and Hungarian patriotism
prompt us to do so'.[84] So rather than straining, and eventually break-

ing the relationship between the Soviet Union and Hungary, as western propagandists had hoped for, the insurgents were resolute that the relationship would remain intact. This implied a wasteful use of radio's contribution to the Cold War of words, with the objectives of propaganda remaining unfulfilled. But the west would not have long to wait for the situation to turn and lend credence to its aspirational propaganda.

The situation in Hungary began to deteriorate on 23 October when a mass of ordinary Hungarians, wishing to express their sympathy with Poland, marched through Budapest to the statue of General Bem, hero of the 1848–9 War of Liberation, idol of the poet Petofi, and a Pole; no anti-Russian or even anti-Communist slogans were voiced. Then all 50 000 demonstrators, later joined by a further 50 000, marched to Parliament Square, and it was then that events began to turn unpleasant. The Premier of Hungary, Ernest Gerö, misjudged the situation. and made a most offensive broadcast over Budapest Radio which merely angered the demonstrators and inflamed the situation.[85] In the ensuing chaos shots were fired, and what began as a peaceful demonstration quickly became a bloodbath. One historian of the revolution, Bill Lomax, has offered his own bitter opinion why the situation developed in this way:

> By evening Budapest was alive with rumours, whipped on [sic] by western radio broadcasts, that Soviet tanks had opened fire on a peaceful demonstration, murdering hundreds of unarmed civilians. In this world of distortion and propaganda, the British diplomatic service played no small part, announcing that more than twelve truckloads of corpses had been removed from the square, while the BBC reported the slaughter of over six hundred unarmed Hungarians.
>
> Up to this point popular feeling towards the Russians had been growing more and more friendly, but the spread of exaggerated tales of massacre was now to fill the Hungarian people with bitter hatred.[86]

Lomax seems to have confused the chronology here. As will be demonstrated below, Soviet troops did not actually enter Hungary until the next day, 24 October. More importantly Lomax's charge that BBC broadcasts were exaggerated cannot be satisfactorily proven. Lomax has actually implied in this quoted paragraph that such 'objective' and 'accurate' reporting as the BBC claimed to engage in may have had certain drawbacks. It is possible that by reporting the massacre simply as a news story the BBC may have contributed to generating a climate of suspicion and revenge among Hungarians listening to its broadcasts.

But if this hypothesis is accepted, then we are in fact guilty of under-estimating the intelligence and rationality of the Hungarians, even in such an inflamed situation. If the BBC was reporting the situation accurately, then the Hungarian people were only hearing from foreign broadcasts what they were able to experience for themselves; their actions were ultimately their own responsibility. By suggesting that Hungarians lacked the necessary perspective to correctly interpret broadcasts Lomax has presented a flawed, if not naive, argument.

At 2300 GMT the Hungarian external radio service, normally using three short-wave and one medium-wave transmitters, went off the air. Because all news now derived from Hungary's domestic services their propaganda value to the world-wide audience was minimal; domestic services are intended only for the native audience, and consist mainly of news and morale-boosting rhetoric. Any propaganda transmitted does not need to justify or explain events and actions to the outside world. Under such circumstances, monitored broadcasts from Hungary were useful as a means of gathering the latest information, but had little diplomatic value. The importance of this should not be overlooked. Because western journalists were not allowed into Hungary, and com-munication with embassies was virtually impossible during the revolu-tion – except as we have seen in the case of the British embassy – the monitoring service was the only source of news for western decision makers who were forced to shape their reaction to events according to what they read in the *Summaries of World Broadcasts*. President Eisenhower for instance, recalled in his memoirs that his Administra-tion had to rely on the monitoring of Hungarian radio reports during the crisis.[87]

At 0800 GMT the next day Kossuth Radio announced that the So-viet army had been invited into Hungary. The broadcast is worth quot-ing in some detail since it provides an account of the government's reasoning and justification for making this decision:

> The dastardly attack of counter-revolutionary gangs during the night has created an extremely serious situation. The bandits have pen-etrated into factories and public buildings and have murdered many civilians . . . The Government authorities did not reckon with these bloody and dastardly attacks. They have therefore applied for help to the Soviet formations stationed in Hungary under the terms of the Warsaw Treaty. In compliance with the Government's request, the Soviet formations are taking part in the restoration of order. The Government appeals to the inhabitants of the capital to keep calm,

to condemn the bloody havoc played by the counter-revolutionary gangs and to support everywhere the Hungarian and Soviet troops who are maintaining order. The liquidation of the counter-revolutionary gangs is the most sacred cause of every honest Hungarian worker, of the people and of the fatherland. At this moment we are concentrating all our strength on this task.[88]

It is unfortunate that there is no record of how western governments and their foreign services reacted to this spirited but convoluted defence of a most questionable action. We therefore have no way of ascertaining whether the west's response to the uprising was in some way shaped by such reasoning.

The first significant development after the massacre outside the Parliament building occurred when Kossuth Radio broadcast a communiqué issued by the Politburo of the Hungarians Workers' Party, announcing the replacement of Ernest Gerö by the recently rehabilitated János Kádár as First Secretary of its Central Committee. The broadcast claimed that 'the people of Budapest received this news with joy. In Angyalfoeld workers embraced and kissed one another and people hoisted the National Flag on their houses. Cheers echo everywhere!'[89] In his broadcast to the nation at 1109 GMT on 24 October Imre Nagy, the insurgent's preferred candidate and unofficial leader, presented his political agenda having been finally reinstalled as Premier of Hungary.[90] But not everybody was pleased with his appointment; L. Veress of the BBC, for example, denounced the new government as servants of the Communist dictators. He wondered why Nagy did not refute the claim that he had invited the Soviet troops into Hungary, and judged that as Prime Minister, he was 'therefore ... ultimately responsible'.[91] This is one of the risks of relying on monitoring reports. Veress had clearly gathered his information from the monitored broadcasts of Radio Budapest which had implied Nagy had invited in the Soviet troops. What Veress did not know however – and there was no way either he or the monitors could be aware of this fact at the time – was that Nagy's script had been prepared by others and that his broadcast was supervised by the AVO, the Hungarian Secret Police. A gun had been literally held to the Premier's head as he sat at the microphone and made his broadcast justifying the invasion.

In a later broadcast Nagy announced that his government would begin negotiations with the Soviet Union concerning the withdrawal of Soviet forces from Hungary.[92] In an effort to placate both Hungarians and Soviets, Nagy remained convinced that this would 'provide a firm

foundation for a sincere and true friendship between our peoples, for
our national progress and socialist future,' and he declared that 'the
ordering back of those Soviet troops whose intervention in the fighting was necessitated by the vital interests of our socialist order will
take place without delay after the restoration of peace and order'.[93]
This is yet another example of how radio was used as a channel of
diplomacy: in clear terms that nobody could misunderstand, Nagy stated
his government's intentions to the Soviet Union, reassuring Moscow
that friendly relations between their two countries would continue. This
was achieved by his repeated reference to 'socialism' and 'socialist order,'
together with such phrases as 'sincere and true friendship.' After all
Nagy was a committed Communist. In addition the wider world now
knew that the Hungarian–Soviet relationship would be sustained and
that its basis would continue to be socialism. All the American rhetoric
demanding 'roll-back' was therefore wasted; at this stage the new government had no intention of rolling back Soviet influence at all.

The BBC Hungarian service meanwhile assumed another function
of considerable importance; by reporting the curfew measures as broadcast
by Budapest Radio, the BBC performed as adviser to its Hungarian
audience. It announced that warnings had been transmitted 'to refuse
shelter to insurgents trying to escape; to bolt doors during the night
curfew which would continue until further notice; and to avoid going
out into the streets'.[94] In another broadcast on 25 October, the BBC
repeated Central Committee promises of amnesty for insurgents who
laid down their arms. Those who did not, it said, would be 'mercilessly
annihilated'. Such broadcasts continued through to 31 October 1956,
when the BBC directly relayed an appeal by the Hungarian Ministry
of Defence, requesting that the people avoid 'impeding the departure
of Soviet troops by any hostile action'.[95] At the same time VOA coun-
selled the Hungarian people to refrain from taking the law into their
own hands and to defer the fate of the AVO, now hunted out by vengeful
lynch-mobs, to the courts. In this way both the BBC and VOA provided a medium whereby rules for avoiding further bloodshed could
be transmitted. Was this an instance of radio being used as an instrument of international politics? Not really; but it did suggest that the
west, together with their radio stations, believed the change of government and the promised withdrawal of Soviet troops from Hungary to
be a start at least. The west had to take advantage of this if further
progress was to be made within Hungary specifically, and across Eastern
Europe generally. Any further disorder and chaos would only jeopardize
that tentative start, so it was necessary that the BBC and VOA not

only save lives of innocent Hungarians but also dampen the flames of revolution. Their broadcasts could then latch on to this change and hopefully encourage further change by 'peaceful methods'. In such difficult circumstances it is necessary to ensure that the Hungarians had an efficient news and information service they could rely on. So on 24 October 1956, the Voice of America decided to implement an emergency schedule. This ability to quickly change programming agendas as crisis situations demand is one of the finest attributes that sets VOA apart from other international broadcasters. Thus within an hour VOA was broadcasting live up-to-date reports (repeating broadcasts normally carried by relay) in no less that 14 languages, including those of the Eastern bloc, the main Soviet languages and, from 29 October, German. Moreover the new schedule expanded transmission times to the USSR and the whole of Europe. The events in Hungary were now to be a major news story carried to the Soviet orbit by all the relevant language services. VOA had responded admirably, and undertaken the task thrust upon it by events with considerable proficiency.

SERVICES TO RUSSIA

Radio Moscow remained noticeably quiet about Hungary's predicament, and this was a subject addressed by the BBC in its Hungarian news bulletins; these informed their audience that the ordinary people of the Soviet Union were quite unaware of the unfolding events.[96] George Tarjan of the BBC Hungarian Service sardonically attributed this virtual silence to the fact that after one year of de-Stalinisation under Khrushchev, 'it would be difficult to revive old slogans and to explain to the Soviet people that Russian tanks have been necessary in Budapest to kindle Soviet–Hungarian friendship'. Tarjan concluded his broadcast by warning that, 'tanks can defend the régime but they won't infuse any confidence, loyalty, zeal into the Hungarians'.[97]

One of the most prominent of BBC commentators was Maurice Latey who had established his reputation in the German service during the Second World War, and was later appointed Head of the East European services. His perception and talent for thoughtful analysis were demonstrated in a broadcast he gave on 24 October 1956 entitled 'Soviet Policy in Eastern Europe'. He asserted that there was now no possibility of either Hungary or Poland reverting to the status of mere satellites. 'Their people must either have better things,' he said, 'or else be held down by Soviet tanks. And the latter course would be both politically and economically disastrous for the Soviet Union.'[98] In other words, the Soviet Union could not hope to maintain a permanent presence in Hungary; not only would it be despised by the Hungarian people themselves and therefore lack political legitimacy, but world opinion would not tolerate such military occupation. In addition to these political considerations, Latey emphasised that the Soviet Union simply could not afford the finance required for such a venture. The importance of this broadcast was augmented by the fact that although Russian language broadcasts were jammed,[99] English language transmissions never were because Soviet statesmen themselves found them required listening.[100] So the above talk by Maurice Latey, and others broadcast in English, were almost certainly heard by Soviet decision makers and officials; their potential diplomatic value was therefore quite considerable.[101] For example, on 26 October 1956, Latey explained to the Hungarian people why the west could not intervene, but in broadcasting it in *English* on the European service (in addition to the Hungarian service), he also tacitly reassured Soviet listeners of western intentions in their foreign policy. 'We cannot intervene directly,' he said,

> ... because that would mean world war ... and even indirect invasion would make matters worse ... We are bound ... to applaud their [Hungarian insurgents] heroism, but we here on the sidelines cannot encourage one man to shed his blood since we ourselves can take no part.... If the Russians fear that the troubles in Eastern Europe are being exploited for western aims, the Red Army will stay. But if somehow they can be convinced that having free and independent countries on their borders will not threaten Soviet security, perhaps they will abandon a domination which has proved politically disastrous.[102]

It is most unfortunate that the impact of such broadcasts upon the English speaking Soviet population cannot be ascertained. We therefore have no way of knowing if the broadcast served to reassure the Russian people, or presented to them a successfully demonised portrait of Soviet policy.

In contrast to their seemingly preferential treatment of the BBC, the Soviets subjected VOA broadcasts in both Russian and English to constant jamming. Back in 1953 officials at USIA's International Broadcasting Service had written that 'Moscow should now be written off as far as VOA reception is concerned' because there was simply too much interference,[103] and nothing had changed by 1956. Yet there is still evidence that VOA had a sizeable audience within the Soviet Union, suggesting that the interference with broadcasts was not complete. It has been intimated by Irving R. Levine, an American correspondent with the NBC network, that by 26 November 1956, foreign broadcasts 'like the Voice of America' were compelling Soviet officialdom 'to acknowledge events to their own people that otherwise they would prefer to ignore'.[104] Hence Russian newspapers found themselves having to fill 'column after column' explaining to their readers 'why it was necessary for the Soviet army to intervene'.[105] The people knew that the Soviet version of events reached them several days later than foreign broadcasts. They were thus able to identify discrepancies between the two, and were then in a position to form their own conclusions. This was yet another instance of the BBC and VOA contributing their valuable services in order that their own propaganda efforts might be enhanced, but also for the benefit of the Soviet people themselves under the most difficult of circumstances. Consistent with 'peaceful methods' of change, the BBC and VOA provided news and information to an audience that would otherwise be denied the full picture of the unfolding situation. But this must of course be located within the Cold War framework; the full picture inevitably meant the western version of events. Nevertheless the Soviet people were at least presented with two versions which they could then interpret for themselves.

FROM MASSACRE TO NORMALITY

The period of 26 to 29 October was relatively quiet in the airwaves. Kossuth Radio documented the mopping-up operations, a task begun by the Soviet troops but gradually assumed by the Hungarian security forces. The restoration of order was similarly chronicled. The full scale of the tragedy was not known until after the Central Committee issued a statement on 26 October estimating that in Budapest alone, the number of injured ran 'into the thousands' and the dead 'into the hundreds'.[106] The BBC Hungarian Service was able to be more specific, placing the number killed at an estimated total of 8000 with 30 000 wounded.[107] These figures are a little high if we are to believe the official sources which provided statistics for a longer period, 23 October to 1 December. These established a figure of 19 971 wounded throughout Hungary, and 1945 dead in Budapest along.[108] Miklos Molnar cautions us to remember, however, that these figures do not include Soviet losses.

In order to end this 'fratricidal battle' the Central Committee advocated the election of a new government that would 'make good' the crimes and mistakes of the past, and fulfil the legitimate demands of the revolution. In addition, it called for negotiations with the Soviet Union 'on the basis of independence, complete equality and non-interference in internal affairs'.[109] This was a turning point, the repercussions of which seem to have completely by-passed the Hungarian government. Would the Soviet Union really permit free elections which the Communist party would undoubtedly lose? Could 'independence, complete equality and non-interference' really be achieved by a Soviet satellite state? Would the Soviets simply sit back and let these changes occur? These were questions that quite possibly raced through the minds of British and American foreign service personnel as they tried to interpret the meaning of these monitoring reports.

Kossuth Radio announced the new government the next day, 27 October, with Imre Nagy as Chairman of the Council of Ministers. In a series of 'biographical sketches' the station revealed that the majority of new ministers had been persecuted by previous régimes. Nagy, for example, was described as having taken a 'brave stand . . . against the Rakosi–Stalin tyranny'.[110] Following his dismissal in 1953 after he had tried to implement many of the reforms now demanded, 'he did not give up the fight. He became the rallying point of the country's patriotic forces, Communists and non-members of the party alike'.[111] Many at the BBC, however, were not convinced of the credentials of this new government and denounced it as 'not one for which thousands have died and many are losing their lives still'.[112] L. Veress, a passionately anti-Soviet and pro-Hungarian BBC commentator, judged the new government as having been 'formed quite arbitrarily by a small group of Communist party leaders . . . obedient servants' of the very Stalinists the revolution had opposed.[113] In the light of what followed, such admonitions were a little premature. The precise character of the revolution seems to have been overlooked: it was not anti-Communist; indeed thousands of Communists, who owed their allegiance to the Hungarian nation rather than the party, had participated in the uprising. Moreover Communist participation in the new government was essential if the Soviet Union was to be pacified.

PARTIAL WITHDRAWAL

On 28 October 1956, Nagy announced that he and the Soviet government had reached agreement, claiming that Soviet troops would immediately withdraw from Budapest, and that his government was opening negotiations with the Soviets.[114]

On the same day, 28 October, both VOA and the BBC reported a speech in which US Secretary of State Dulles had promised that all East European countries which achieved independence would receive American economic aid, regardless of the form of society they adopted.[115] This commitment was perhaps made in response to Nagy's earlier historic announcements, again suggesting the framing of foreign policy according to monitored radio broadcasts. On the whole however, the west greeted the news from Hungary with a degree of caution. The BBC said the Foreign Office would welcome the withdrawal of Soviet forces if it actually occurred; the right of the Soviet Union to station troops on the soil of signatories to the Warsaw Treaty was not disputed, but the Foreign Office did object to their deployment against civilians.[116] But Radio Moscow broadcast a government statement which suggested a willingness to comply with Hungarian demands, echoing Nagy's statement in declaring a withdrawal from Budapest and the start of Hungarian–Soviet negotiations.[117] Because of its political and strategic implications this broadcast was quoted at length by the BBC. Allen Dulles, Director of the CIA, reportedly described this broadcast as 'one of the most significant to come out of the Soviet Union since the end of World War Two'.[118] But did the CIA really have grounds to be that optimistic about Soviet intentions?[119]

TURNING POINT

Despite Soviet declarations of good intentions however, it was clear by 1 November 1956 that the Soviet troops were not completely leaving Budapest after all. Kossuth Radio reported that airfields belonging to the Hungarian airforce had been surrounded, but played down the implicit threat by quoting the Soviet embassy that this was 'to secure the air transport of members of the families of Soviet troops stationed in Hungary and the transport of the wounded'.[120] Then just after five o'clock in the evening, it was revealed that Nagy had a meeting with Yuri Andropov, the Soviet ambassador in Hungary and future leader of the USSR. Nagy told him that his government had received information that fresh contingents of Soviet troops were arriving in Hungary, and he demanded that they be immediately withdrawn. This was the first hint of the tragedy to come, and was also the first indication of the foreign policy that the Nagy government would pursue, which was anathema to Soviet interests. To illustrate how radio was used to project this foreign policy, broadcasts monitored at Caversham Park described Nagy's meeting with Andropov. Nagy reportedly told Andropov that 'the Hungarian government was giving immediate notice of termination of the Warsaw Treaty, and at the same time declared Hungary's neutrality. The Hungarian government,' continued Nagy, 'turned to the United Nations and sought the help of the four great powers in safeguarding the country's neutrality'.[121] This was the turning point; could the Soviet Union permit either Hungary's cessation from the Warsaw Pact or its neutrality?

The uprising was fast becoming a revolution and, for the Russians, going too far. The events that began on 1 November quickly gathered momentum over the next 24 hours. Kossuth Radio described how the Hungarian government had given three verbal notes to the Soviet embassy on 2 November. These denounced the Warsaw Treaty in light of the renewed troop movements and called for fresh negotiations with the Soviets again based on Hungarian neutrality, sovereignty, equality and non-interference. In the meantime, the station said, Hungary would demand the attention of the UN Security Council to 'call on the great powers to recognise Hungary's neutrality . . . and instruct the Soviet and Hungarian governments to begin negotiations immediately'.[122] Needless to say this chain of events was exhaustively reported by the BBC and VOA.

On 1 November 1956, the VOA Hungarian programme transmitted the full text of a speech made by President Eisenhower in which he reaffirmed that the US would continue to aim for the fulfilment of promises made at the UN's founding, namely that all occupied countries should regain their sovereignty and were entitled to self-government. Although this could not be implemented by force Eisenhower guaranteed that America would 'keep alive the love of freedom in these people'.[123] In other words, the President confirmed that American propaganda could not be supported by action, but nevertheless accepted the vitally important role that propaganda could still play. Eisenhower's words contained no suggestion that either the Voice of America or Radio Free Europe would actively encourage the revolution. Rather he offered a tacit endorsement of 'peaceful methods' of change. However the President could not establish the crucial fact of how such statements would be interpreted by the Hungarians. Once again American propagandists faced the perennial problem of balancing intention with possible interpretation.

Only two days later on 3 November, the British Foreign Secretary,

Selwyn Lloyd, informed the House of Commons that he had received notification that the Soviet military had indeed withdrawn from Budapest. However there appears to have been something of a breakdown in communication between broadcasters and the political machinery at this time; as Lloyd spoke, the BBC Hungarian service was earnestly broadcasting disturbing reports obtained by the west that all was not as it should have been. The BBC described how Soviet military units had surrounded three-quarters of Budapest and were in control of three airfields near the capital, in addition to several in the western provinces of the country.[124] The Voice of America warned that if there was any truth in these reports, 'this would be a dark day indeed,' but added that if on the other hand, 'the Soviets were to complete the withdrawal of their troops, then an era of justice and mutual trust would emerge'.[125] Unfortunately VOA's optimism proved groundless, and a 'dark day' did indeed envelop Hungary.

REVOLUTION CRUSHED

As they listened to what was to be a final broadcast by Imre Nagy in the early hours of 4 November 1956, BBC monitors became aware that something was critically wrong inside Hungary: 'In the early hours of this morning,' he said, 'Soviet troops launched an attack against our capital with the obvious ... intention of overthrowing the lawful democratic Hungarian government. Our troops are fighting. The government is in its place. I am informing the people of the country and the world public opinion of this.'[126] This was repeated in several languages – English, Russian, English again, French, Hungarian and German. Obviously Nagy hoped that this broadcast would be monitored in the west despite the fact that Hungary's own external services were no longer transmitting. Budapest Radio, quoting a report filed by Associated Press, confirmed that the UN Security Council had indeed received the text of Nagy's dramatic announcement. His diplomatic message had filtered through and found its intended audience, confirming yet again radio's contribution to international relations.

At 1100 GMT the BBC's Hungarian service proclaimed that Budapest Radio was 'now believed to be in Soviet hands'.[127] Reports described how communication with Budapest had been severed, and that the BBC was unable to contact its correspondents there. As the monitoring service had been dramatically deprived of its principal function of providing information, bulletins were now limited to reports filtering through via the Vienna channel. The news was therefore sparse, but the BBC was still able to report the most important development – the Soviet assault – and quote Nagy's final tragic broadcast.

In a later broadcast the BBC described how a Hungarian provincial station, controlled by the 'pro-Soviet Kádár government,' appealed at regular intervals to the population to support the new régime. The BBC also quoted from a broadcast by Kádár himself, justifying the renewed Soviet intervention in much the same language that had been used to defend the first Soviet intrusion of 24 October: 'We asked the Soviet troops to help us,' he said, 'in crushing the reactionary elements and to restore peace and order. As soon as this aim is reached, our government will suggest that talks be held . . . on the withdrawal of Soviet troops from Hungary.[128]

The Voice of America began its coverage of the events with straight factual reporting, but soon adopted a more strident tone. It now concentrated on assuring Hungarians that American, and indeed world, opinion were vehemently opposed to the Soviet actions, while also describing the west's diplomatic response. The news, it said,

> created great consternation and indignation, as only a few hours before . . . the Soviet delegate repeatedly stated that the Soviet Union is conducting peaceful negotiations with Hungary regarding the withdrawal of Soviet troops from the country. At the meeting of the UN Security Council, which ended only a few hours ago, Ambassador Lodge, Chief Delegate of the US, introduced a resolution calling on the Soviet Union to refrain from any kind of interference, but particularly armed interference. At the same time he called on all member states of the UN to co-operate in aiding Hungary.[129]

Again the Voice of America was able to reassure the Hungarians that their plight was not being ignored, but was the subject of much debate and consternation at the highest political levels. In addition the Hungarian experience was covered in broadcasts to all neutralist states.[130] This suggests that although the Americans recognised early on that their practical support of the revolution would be minimal, propaganda could continue to expose the Soviet atrocities to world opinion. In this way the VOA was actually used as a weapon of the Cold War.

The Response

The BBC adopted a surprisingly hardline approach and denounced Nagy's replacement as Premier, János Kádár, together with his government, as Russian puppets.[131] Indeed criticism was so vehement that in 1957 the Hungarian Foreign Minister sent a note of protest to the BBC about its Hungarian broadcasts, claiming they had used 'rude adjectives' in describing the Kádár government. Unfortunately no record of these adjectives seems to have survived![132] If such accusations were accurate, then they certainly reveal a great deal about the BBC, and may even force scholars to reappraise their opinions of what is often depicted as a rather staid institution!

From the outset Kádár was eager to use radio to project a favourable picture of his régime. Accordingly his broadcasts asserted that all open armed resistance had been overcome, but lamented that while law and order had been restored in Budapest, many parts of Hungary were still in turmoil.[133] In its account of such proclamations the BBC added that the restoration of order would precede negotiations for the withdrawal of Soviet troops, but decided to delete the scripted sentence, 'but the People's Democracy must be strong before such negotiations could take place'.[134] This was obviously judged to have specific political implications, namely that by restoring order in Hungary the Soviet troops would also renew its strength; in other words the Soviet intervention would have been portrayed as having been of benefit to Hungary. The BBC could not take the risk of such interpretation; such a message would not only have jeopardised the BBC's relationship with the Hungarian audience, but would also have reduced its effectiveness as an instrument of British diplomacy. Yet it is to the BBC's credit that despite the violence and the carnage, and inevitably heightened emotions, their broadcasts retained a modicum of balance. The Hungarian revolution and its violent ending did not precipitate the vociferous right wing response by broadcasters it could well have, but allowed instead for a moderate anti-Soviet and anti-Stalin criticism. Thus a *Review of the British Weekly Press* included reviews of such critical socialist publications as *Tribune* and *The New Statesman*, all of which incidentally cited Suez as having contributed to the outcome of the Hungarian uprising.[135] It was noted, moreover, that the Soviet action had generated an anti-Soviet backlash within the European Communist movement, compelling the BBC Diplomatic Correspondent to affirm that 'while the events in Hungary may well be a Russian victory, they are a defeat for Communism'.[136]

Nevertheless the BBC did allow a considerable amount of invective to be voiced in its commentaries. Commentaries were of course the opinion of the broadcaster himself, the 'independent expert', and did not necessarily reflect the views of either the government or the BBC.

Yet as the Suez crisis vividly demonstrated, they remained by and large consistent with the government line. One example of how commentaries could be quite forthright was revealed by the BBC's Martin Esslin.[137] In a broadcast of 13 November he described reports by correspondents which gave 'a vivid picture of the brief upsurge of political life, the resurgence of hope and freedom when the Russians launched their treacherous attack'.[138] Furthermore, he said, they depicted 'a people which may have been repressed by an unprecedented weight of armour – but whose spirit remains unbroken'.[139] Esslin then quoted the European correspondent of the *New York Herald Tribune*, who described the attack on the Kilrian barracks in vivid language and imagery. Its stirring language and powerful imagery are worth quoting in full:

> Two hours before the attack began, foreign embassies . . . began receiving frantic telephone calls saying that the Russians were shooting their way through the infants' hospital to get at the barracks. . . . Embassies began telephoning desperately in their turn. The lives of three hundred children were at stake. A truce permitting the evacuation of the children was demanded. Finally as callers telephoned in anguish again two hours later, a dismal message awaited them. The Soviet Embassy said it could not intervene; nothing could be done. Later further word spread; some of the children had been cremated.[140]

Combined with portraits of the devastation of Budapest, tales of heroism and martyrdom, and stories of the terror that accompanied the return to power of the AVO, such a broadcast is an indication of the type of picture the BBC was prepared to present its audience. The BBC did not mince its words when a graphical account of events was necessary and considered most effective.

The BBC was not, however, always quite this serious, but often used parody and satire to get its message across. The BBC archives contain a letter from Tangye Lean, Deputy Director of External Broadcasting,[141] which documents the content of Hungarian spoof notices and proclamations. One warned the population of Hungary – numbering ten million – that 'ten million counter-revolutionaries are at large.' Another, satirising the parasitic relationship between the Kádár régime and the Kremlin said:

> Wanted: Premier for Hungary. Qualifications: no sincere convictions, no backbone; ability to read and write not required, but must be able to sign documents drawn up by others. Applications should be addressed to Messrs Khrushchev and Bulganin.[142]

Obviously excited by these, Tangye Lean wondered whether it was possible to 'keep these in play throughout our output? . . . can we get more of them? They are the kind of thing that sticks deeply in the mind'. He believed that 'it would be a pity if their value got overlooked as long-term ammunition'.[143] From his days spent observing the work of the German service during the Second World War, Lean had obviously learnt that satire, humour and ridicule could be the most effective propaganda.[144] This had made a lasting impression and now, as deputy controller of the external services, he considered that such a strategy might again have its uses.

As Kádár assumed the mantle of power on 4 November 1956, a general strike was called throughout Hungary. The strike was immediately denounced as 'counter-revolutionary' and 'anti-socialist' by Hungarian radio, but was applauded by the BBC as an example of how the unity of a people could paralyse an entire country. Once again what was omitted from scripts is as significant as what was actually transmitted. While the BBC described the greater part of industry as being at a standstill, it cut out the scripted addition which quoted the Hungarian government as saying that 70 or 80 per cent of workers had returned to their jobs. *Szabad Nep*, it continued, 'says that workers will be given food at their factories if they return to work'.[145] Clearly the BBC believed that such reporting would only undermine the unity of the people and reduce the effectiveness of the strike weapon. Then following the tragic news that some strikers had been tortured, the BBC reported some workers were returning to work, but added that the majority were 'driven back by the threatening hunger rather than the ultimatum by the régime which expired today'.[146] Again this demonstrates how, by a careful selection of the facts and the calculated way in which bulletins were constructed, the BBC applied itself to a propaganda campaign against the Kádár régime which did not involve outright deceit.

In addition the unprecedented coincidence of events in 1956 also presented the BBC with the opportunity to bluntly accuse the Soviet Union of hypocrisy. A speech by Anthony Eden was broadcast in which he compared the 'brutal onslaught' on Hungary with the tripartite attack on Egypt when 'every conceivable precaution to avoid bloodshed' had been taken.[147] Describing how the French and British had 'welcomed UN observers who had not been allowed into Hungary' Eden concluded that for a 'country to enslave Hungary, and at the same time lecture us for our own action in Egypt, is nauseating hypocrisy'.[148] Eden of course overlooked the particulars of the Suez crisis, but this is not surprising; propaganda relies on truth and accuracy for its credibility, but these have more often than not been used in a selective manner. Propaganda thus did not deny Britain's mishandling of the Suez crisis, but just did not consider it relevant to the matter at hand!

P.F. Grey suggested that British propaganda to the Third World should, 'without playing down Moscow's imperialistic ambitions, draw attention to the sign of internal weakness within the Soviet orbit, and thus help to destroy the myth that history is on the Communist side'.[149] Throughout Africa and Asia in particular the Suez adventure had been vociferously condemned as 'constituting a greater danger to their own national interests than the Soviet action in Hungary'.[150] Both crises had been denounced as the result of colonialist acts directed against smaller powers, but evidence suggests that Suez was of more direct concern to world opinion than Hungary. 'In terms of coverage,' read one USIA Special Report written in November 1956, 'the non-Communist press of almost all the Asian countries has given greater attention to events in the Middle East. According more criticism is heaped upon Britain and France than upon the Soviet Union.'[151] To counter such adverse opinion BBC broadcasts throughout the world presented a contrast between 'imperialist Russia clamping new fetters on subject peoples after an experiment in elementary freedom,' with Britain granting independence to former colonies and inviting them to participate in a 'voluntary' Commonwealth.[152]

The BBC and VOA therefore successfully forced the Kremlin to acknowledge events they had desperately tried to quietly brush aside. In turn the Soviet people were able to recognise the discrepancies between the two versions of events. In this way both stations were instrumental in exposing the fact that Soviet public opinion was far from united. Reports reached the United Kingdom from Moscow describing how University students, expressing sympathy with Poland and Hungary, had been openly critical of the Soviet regime and demanded an end to one-party government.[153] According to the *Daily Telegraph* this culminated with the closure of Moscow University after students, refusing to accept their government's version of events, posted up copies of the BBC bulletins concerning Hungary. The University rector angrily tore them down, confident that Moscow Radio was reliable.[154] One objective of British propaganda had been to encourage 'the growth of critical faculties, especially among the Soviet youth.' and such episodes are indicative of its success.[155]

AFTERMATH

On 6 January 1957, the BBC monitored a broadcast which contained an explicit diplomatic message from Kádár to the American government, announcing that Hungary would accept an offer of financial assistance, 'even one from a capitalist state,' provided it was unconditional. The broadcast recalled the 'hollow promises' of the US following 'liberation' when Hungary received no money at all, and concluded that the 'western dollar imperialists were willing to finance counter-revolutionaries but they are not showing any eagerness to give economic support to the worker–peasant state'.[156] One prevailing theme of this book is that there must be a consistency between propaganda and deed. However such lapses can be forgiven given the circumstances that prevailed in Hungary in 1956. Dulles and Eisenhower had certainly offered economic support to Hungary on 31 October 1956, but after Soviet. troops and tanks had so mercilessly suppressed the revolution, it was surely a little too much to expect the US to now keep its word.

British treatment of Hungarian refugees became the subject of vociferous criticism in January. For example Britain was accused of recruiting Hungarian miners to 'depress the standard of living of British miners'.[157] Allegedly, the flood of refugees had caused British public opinion much concern, even to the point where stories were circulating concerning Communist infiltration of the refugees.[158] Such broadcasts were designed to perform two principal tasks; they represented propaganda for the Hungarian domestic audience, designed to heighten their awareness of the supposed treatment of their brethren in Britain and thus further alienate them from the west. But more generally they were an attempt to create a momentum of support for their plight to the advantage of the Hungarian state. The refugees themselves, and perhaps their family and friends back home, no doubt sensed that such propaganda was complete nonsense. Throughout December 1956 the BBC operated a refugee message service which, for security reasons, ensured that both sender and intended recipient remained anonymous. Between 10 December 1956 and 4 January 1957 when the service was suspended, over 1000 messages had been broadcast at a rate of around 60 per day. This must rank as one of the most popular, if not most successful, functions provided by the BBC at this critical time.[159] By engaging in such public diplomacy, the BBC subtly affirmed their commitment to support the Hungarians in the admittedly small way they could. But small or not it was certainly appreciated by both the refugees and their families in Hungary. The west's link with the Hungarian people themselves was therefore strengthened, providing firm foundations on which radio broadcasts could build once the situation stabilised.

REFLECTIONS

> The crisis in Hungary [wrote Miklos Molnar] was not a crisis on an international plane, not a crisis of European or world significance. It shook world opinion, with repercussions which went far beyond the framework of a Soviet–Hungarian quarrel; but the matter was finally arranged between the two parties involved, even if the outcome was unequal. Strictly from the point of view of international relations, this crisis, a tragedy for one of the actors, may be written down in international history as a crisis with a happy ending. The conflict was limited; it had no far-reaching effects; peace was saved and equilibrium restored.[160]

Miklos Molnar was right; the Hungarian uprising had no far-reaching implications for international politics, nor even for Soviet–American relations. Just three years later, Krushchev visited the United States where he was received with warmth and successfully carried off a public relations coup. It would seem that both superpowers had put the events of 1956 firmly behind them. Britain too had to accept Hungary as a matter of fact rather than an obstacle to furthering its foreign policy, although the situation that prevailed in Hungary by the end of 1956 was certainly not viewed with any overwhelming sense of optimism; the British embassy in Budapest, for example, merely described it as 'about the best that we can hope for'.[161] There was very little that could be done except for sustaining the propaganda effort and continuing the provision of relief and welfare assistance. In short the British response to the crisis, like the American, had been minimalist based more on a realistic appraisal of the delicate situation rather than a crusading idealism. There was a confirmed commitment to non-incitement in propaganda and support for resolutions passed by the UN. Equally there was a considerable amount of political vacillation concerning the closure of diplomatic missions and recognition of the Kádár government. The Foreign Office even advised Selwyn Lloyd to accept the situation in Eastern Europe as a *fait accompli*, suggesting that Britain use it advantageously to reach a compromise with the Soviet Union over Germany.[162] There were indications that the Soviet Union was prepared to reciprocate; on 17 November 1956, the Foreign Office received a Soviet note which contained very detailed proposals for disarmament and the reduction of forces in Germany. Lloyd acknowledged that these proposals were probably intended primarily as propaganda, but said that did not warrant their outright rejection. Indeed, he announced to the House of Commons, they had been 'studied to see whether they contain any new constructive ideas which might be followed up'. Hungary might be used as a bargaining chip after all; Lloyd would insist first on compliance with UN resolutions, and would convey a willingness to negotiate the future of Germany if the Soviet Union withdrew its troops from Hungary.[163] Whether it was propaganda or not, the Soviet note certainly contributed to the shaping of British foreign policy at this time.

Meanwhile, the BBC itself continued to be employed as an instrument of Britain's diplomatic efforts when, throughout 1957, its broadcasts inferred that Britain did not favour either János Kádár or his régime. Accordingly although interest was expressed in developing a relationship with Hungarian radio based on an exchange of cultural material, political considerations remained paramount and the Head of the Central European Service refused to comply with such requests.[164] Not everybody, however, shared this view. Cyril Connor, Head of External Services Liaison, stated that BBC policy was to 'differentiate in satellite countries between the broadcasting organisations and their governments; and to promote exchanges pretty freely'.[165] Nevertheless, Connor later admitted that intensified jamming had compelled the BBC to be 'less favourably inclined towards Hungarian radio at the moment than to some of the other satellite countries'. He decided that, under present circumstances, exchanges would not take place, but pointed out that this could change in time as the situation improved. The situation must have improved remarkably quickly, for by December 1957 an exchange of music and sports material was established. Connor declared his unease at dealing with the Kádár regime but, true to the spirit of Hugh Greene, suggested that 'there is a difference between supplying a limited number of British programmes for the benefit of the Hungarian audience whom we like, and approving the Kádár régime which we detest'.[166] We cannot know of course whether the Hungarian people themselves saw this development in such rational terms. It is possible that they viewed them as the latest in a long line of sell-outs by the west. Nevertheless, this was a risk that had to be taken. It is after all far better that the ordinary Hungarians receive some British propaganda than none at all.

In the aftermath of Hungary, with the importance of radio propaganda recognised and acknowledged by the government, the BBC Eastern European services benefited from the reorganisation of broadcasting that was recommended by the Hill Committee. The expansion of services to Russia and Poland were deemed Priority I proposals; the Czech and Hungarian language services were accorded Priority II, but were still allocated the same budgetary share of £10 000.[167] The *extra* cost of this expansion, one apparently not appreciated by the government, was the contraction or curtailment of West European services to finance it. This is a particularly salient issue given, it will be recalled, that many educated Hungarians were keen listeners to the BBC's French and German language services. Proposals to reduce these services merely deprived this audience of yet another source of objective and accurate news and information. Perhaps a government does know the cost of everything and the value of nothing after all! Moreover, the government failed to appreciate that the credibility of the BBC, and therefore its propaganda effort as a whole, hinged on its broadcasting to both east and west; anything less would encourage speculation that the BBC was merely an instrument of anti-Communism. In a situation when governments are unable to offer any practical assistance, maintaining the credibility of broadcasting stations should be a priority.

For their part the United States Information Agency, and the Voice of America in particular, continued to concentrate their programming on the Hungarian revolution and its suppression. When the UN produced its Special Report on Hungary in 1957, 'the Agency blanketed the world with the text and commentary'.[168] But its style had considerably altered. Gone was VOA's strident and crusading anti-Communist invective, reflecting both the failure of the US to intervene in the crisis and the relaxation in East–West tension that ensued. Thomas Sorenson has described Hungary as a 'hard but useful lesson' for the USIA, but especially for VOA. Thereafter, he said, the station 'put greater emphasis on the credibility of its output and less on the "hard sell"'.[169] A report to Congress seven months later concluded that heavy propaganda of the type that characterised VOA output before Hungary 'is not only inappropriate to the official voice of the United States Government; it also simply does not work'.[170] The report went on to describe how 'tighter controls were established and language broadcasts were submitted to even more rigorous review before they went on the air.[171]

Thus it seems that the Hungarian uprising would prove as useful to the Voice of America as the Suez crisis was to the BBC. Yet as the following chapter on the Cuban missile crisis will demonstrate, the Americans seem to have forgotten the lessons of Hungary fairly quickly; American propaganda targeted Fidel Castro and actively encouraged the people of Cuba to rise up and overthrow their leader to no avail.

Both the BBC and the VOA seem to have been relatively well prepared for the Hungarian uprising, but this is not surprising given that the propaganda agencies of their governments focused their attention on the theme of combating Communism. The cardinal opportunity presented by the uprising lay in the ability to test these propaganda instruments in Cold War crisis circumstances. On reflection things appear to have gone well. Perhaps it was the coincidence of Hungary with Suez, and the subsequent scathing attacks on the BBC from within government circles that has provided the pretext for cynicism regarding BBC–government relations at this time. Yet if they prove anything, the different outcomes of both the Suez crisis and the Hungarian uprising suggest that where the interests of the government coincide with the principles of the BBC, there can be harmony; in concerns peripheral to the Cold War, like Suez, opportunities to achieve harmony were often set aside.

Radio's use as an instrument of international politics was actually quite limited during the Hungarian uprising, but this was not through want of trying by the western broadcasters. There were few diplomatic machinations simply because there was nothing to negotiate. The west was presented by the Soviet Union with a *fait accompli*, and broadcasts could only describe to the Soviets how their actions in Hungary would adversely affect their conduct of international relations, especially important when it is recalled that the Soviets did not jam English language transmissions by the BBC because officials listened to them. Hungarian radio used the medium as a channel of diplomatic communication much more than western stations. In the early days of the uprising, for example, the newly-installed Nagy government broadcast messages of reassurance to the Soviet Union that its Communist credentials would not be replaced.

Radio did, however, perform a series of other vital functions during the Hungarian uprising of 1956. Western broadcasts provided a news and information service, first to the Hungarians themselves, and also to the Soviet people who were unaware of their government's actions until they heard about them from the BBC or VOA. At the same time the BBC monitoring service provided a channel of information for western governments which were more or less completely denied information from other sources; these reports then contributed to the shaping of policy towards the crisis. Radio broadcasts assured the Hungarians that their plight was not ignored, but was actually the cause of considerable concern at the highest levels, and coverage of the UN proceedings by the BBC and VOA confirmed this. Broadcasts meanwhile continued to express hope for change by 'peaceful methods' which, together with the careful selection and presentation of the facts that characterised BBC and VOA broadcasts at this time, contributed to the eventual downfall of Communism some 30 years later.

4 The Cuban Missile Crisis, 1962: Two Colossi, A Trembling World

INTRODUCTION

Throughout 1957, the repercussions stemming from the coincidence of the Suez crisis and the Hungarian uprising continued to make western statesmen nervous. Thus the launch of the first man-made satellite by the Russians on 4 October 1957 was an added concern, although American propaganda desperately played down its significance. *Sputnik*, as the satellite was christened, was dismissed as 'a nice technical trick', while the space-race which ensued was flippantly described as 'an outer-space basketball game'. President Eisenhower himself recorded that Sputnik had not raised his apprehensions by 'one iota'.[1] Given the strategic implications of Sputnik this is astounding. As Martin Walker has observed in his history of the Cold War, the US 'was now in pawn to superior Soviet technology'.[2] Disregard of Sputnik did not therefore reflect genuine indifference, but rather the elaborate efforts of American propaganda to save face. Sputnik transformed the international system, just as the Soviet manufacture of the hydrogen bomb had back in August 1953. Consequently the history of the Cold War during the 1950s and early 1960s was stained by a succession of crises which threatened to spiral out of control into nuclear confrontration – Lebanon, Quemoy and Matsu, Berlin, and even the Suez crisis had its nuclear dimensions.

In October 1962 the United States and the Soviet Union clashed over the siting of nuclear missiles on the island of Cuba, situated just 90 miles off the coast of Florida. President Kennedy's management of the crisis has since entered diplomatic legend, but equally remains the subject of heated debate, especially as the relevant archives continue to be opened on both sides of the former Iron Curtain.

Whatever doubts there may be, there can be no denying the fact that the Cuban missile crisis represents a crucial turning point in the history of international broadcasting. The episode was certainly characterised by the familiar propaganda, rhetoric and continuous sparring of claims, counter-claims and threats that had been a feature of all crises in the age of mass communication. However for the first time the leaders of the two powers had talked directly to each other over the radio and conducted their diplomacy in the knowledge that the speed of the electronic media would facilitate settlement. Khrushchev, aware that speed was of the essence, broadcast his messages proposing and agreeing to resolution knowing that they would be received and reported long before the official diplomatic communiqués could reach their intended destination.

Thomas Sorenson, a Deputy Director of the USIA during the Kennedy Administration and author of *The World War*, described the Cuban missile crisis as 'a unique challenge' for the USIA which was presented with a 'unique opportunity to play an unprecedented role'.[3] In contrast its former Director, George Allen, accused USIA efforts of having done 'more harm than good' because Castro was left in a position to 'pose with convincing evidence as the target of the largest concentration of propaganda effort unleashed against an individual since Stalin tried to purge Tito by radio in 1948'. Since USIA was used as a 'propaganda agency', Allen believed that 'nothing has served to label the USIA more indelibly than the anti-Castro campaign and nothing could have helped Castro more'.[4]

Before USIA, and with it the Voice of America could rise to the 'unique challenge' posed by the Cuban missile crisis, it had to endure the test of America's own Suez, namely the Bay of Pigs invasion in 1961. This proved to be as much a watershed for VOA as Suez was for the BBC.

BACKGROUND

In 1953, VOA was subjected to a wide range of sweeping economy measures which clearly reflected the political priorities of broadcasting. Portuguese and Spanish to Latin America were among seven languages cut, while direct broadcasting to that area was curtailed altogether so that resources could be poured into fighting the Cold War in Europe and the Far East. Latin America was served by private North American short-wave broadcasters, in particular station WRUL in which VOA invested the princely sum of $200 000.[5] VOA's activities in Latin America were now confined to supplying local stations with material – discs, tapes and scripts – for re-broadcasting.[6]

However rapidly changing circumstances in foreign policy soon indicated the error of applying such heavy-handedness; the Cuban revolution of 1959 determined that the VOA resume its Spanish-language broadcasts to Latin America in 1960. By the end of 1961 the region was receiving 8 hours 45 minutes' worth of original programming in Spanish per week, while on 6 August VOA began transmitting in Portuguese on short-wave to Latin America, a service that had been suspended in 1953. In addition to 185 hours 30 minutes of original programming in English world-wide, by 1962 VOA broadcast to Latin America in Spanish (61 hours 15 minutes), in Portuguese (21 hours) and Russian to Europe (42 hours), while the total English language output directed to Latin America amounted to 31 hours 30 minutes.[7] A 1961 USIA survey found that VOA ranked below the BBC amongst audiences in Latin America, but could derive some comfort from the fact that both were 'decisively above WRUL, Radio Moscow and Radio Peiping'.[8] VOA-Spanish was the most popular, a discovery of particular interest to USIA given the brief period it had resumed broadcasting prior to the survey, not to mention the short duration of its programme.

Meanwhile competition from Communist broacasters was intense, consisting of 120 hours from the Soviet Union and its satellites, 38 hours from China, and 109 hours from Cuba itself.[9]

After the revolution American propaganda predicated that Americans were largely sympathetic towards the changes in Cuba (even at the height of the missile crisis VOA was directed to assure Cubans that America was not intent on turning the clock back[10]), thus countering Castro's own propaganda which invariably portrayed the US as the greatest threat facing the Cuban people. Meanwhile the continuing danger of Communist encroachment was of course a prominent theme. In this way radio broadcasts were actively involved in America's public diplomacy with the Cuban people themselves.

At the same time radio's more aggressive power was not neglected; overthrowing the Castro régime, with propaganda playing a prominent role, remained a policy pursued by both the Eisenhower Administration in its final days and the new Kennedy Administration. So in February 1961 VOA began transmitting a series of anti-Castro broadcasts targeted at Cuba, the Caribbean and South America.

In April 1960 USIA executives mooted the possibility of establishing a medium-wave station broadcasting in Spanish to Cuba from the United States. This was based on the judgement that there was 'little confidence that VOA short-wave broadcasting has any real impact or listenership'.[11] The case for such a station was forcefully reiterated in

December 1960 when the American embassy in Cuba vividly described how ordinary Cubans were denied access to news and information about developments in their own country, the wider world and about American policy. 'Short-wave radio,' it said, 'reaches a limited and unrepresentative audience in Cuba'. The embassy therefore advocated that VOA broadcast on long-wave which 'reaches into over a million Cuban homes' from transmitters on surrounding land and sea. Since the VOA would broadcast 'the facts' which would have 'sufficient propaganda impact – without need for embellishment or exaggeration,' the embassy affirmed that the VOA would be listened to and believed.[12] However, the embassy failed to explain exactly why VOA – an agent of the American government – would be so trusted by the Cubans. The size of an audience, actual or potential, is not a sufficient criterion by which the effectiveness of propaganda can be judged; simply because broadcasts were heard does not mean that the messages they contained were absorbed and acted upon which is, after all, the true test of propaganda.

THE BAY OF PIGS: A LESSON LEARNT?

The Bay of Pigs invasion is crucial to our understanding of how VOA was used as a channel for diplomatic communication during the missile crisis. This is explained by the very failure of the invasion which, it can be argued, derived in part from USIA being denied any involvement in the decision-making process. This is not surprising given that the operation was shrouded in secrecy and was known only to a select few. However, it *is* surprising given the wealth of talent and expertise within USIA which could have been deployed against the possibility of failure.

Ed Murrow, Kennedy's appointment to head USIA and a full member of the National Security Council, had no opportunity to convince his colleagues of the invasion's psychological aspects. Its success ultimately depended upon a spontaneous rising of the Cuban people in support of the invasion, but the prospect of this actually happening was questionable; reports prepared by the Office of Naval Intelligence challenged assumptions that such popular support would be forthcoming, and the USIA itself was reserved as to how such an action would be received by Cuban and world opinion. Many of the techniques used to reach such conclusions were quite elaborate and reveal an American sophistication in research that had been perfected during the Cold

War and during the Hungarian uprising in particular. In 1960 for example, one USIA official had gone 'undercover' at a Latin America Youth Congress to determine the level of support for Castro and the Communists, and to identify weak spots that could be exploited by propaganda.[13] Another survey conducted in Cuba reinforced such doubts since it discovered Castro was popular among the people.[14] What happened to these findings is not, however, consistent with the sophistication with which they were sought; they were made available to USIA who had sponsored the surveys, but the exclusion of Murrow from the planning stages of the invasion meant that the White House remained in ignorance of them. Indeed Murrow only learnt of the invasion from a *New York Times* reporter![15] Cuban and foreign opinion were essential in securing the success of the scheme for, as Sorenson has written, the invasion 'violated the cherished Latin American doctrine of non-intervention, appeared to pit a great power against a weak one . . . involved [the US] in the kind of sudden aggression we had so often criticised and, worst of all, was unsuccessful'. Like Suez, he concluded, 'it was wretchedly conceived and clumsily executed, and could not and did not succeed before world opinion was aroused against it'.[16] Apparently Arthur Schlesinger Jr., a senior Kennedy adviser and future historian of his Presidency, later found the survey prepared by Naval Intelligence and wished he had seen it earlier so he could have advised the President that a Cuban uprising was most improbable.[17] But the enterprise had been hijacked by the CIA whose senior operatives had become emotionally involved with the downfall of Castro to the detriment of both the plan itself and the work of other government agencies such as USIA who could perhaps have foreseen the consequences of launching a premature invasion.[18]

Consequently the embarrassment of the Bay of Pigs alienated world opinion against the US for many years. There was also the justifiable worry that the diplomatic repercussions would generate problems for all of those involved, including the VOA and USIA, in competing with the Soviet Union for trust, affection and loyalty, especially in the developing world. As one Kenyan newspaper, the *Daily Nation*, so wryly but accurately asserted, 'Khrushchev sits back and chuckles over a crushing propaganda victory which has cost him not an ounce of effort.'[19]

It was a hard but nevertheless valuable lesson: the failure of the Bay of Pigs invasion highlighted the consequences of excluding USIA from the planning stages of foreign policy. In its immediate aftermath Ed Murrow was made a member of a special group whose activities were confidential given that its objective was to unseat Castro.[20] Then in 1962, Donald M. Wilson, Murrow's deputy, was officially designated a member of the Executive Committee, or Ex. Comm. as it became known, a special Presidential committee established to manage the missile crisis.

STOP DOING WHAT YOU HAVE NO INTENTION OF DOING

Despite the fiasco of the Bay of Pigs invasion, the CIA was not prepared to accept the longevity of Castro's power in Cuba. In what almost became a personal vendetta against the Cuban leader, further plans were made to achieve his overthrow. Thus Operation Mongoose, the largest of CIA covert operations, was launched headed by Kennedy's favourite psychological warrior, General Edward Lansdale. Described as 'a prototype destabilization or "bleeding" campaign',[21] Mongoose was an orchestrated attempt to unseat Castro from power. To achieve this Lansdale is reported to have said: 'We want boom and bang on the island.'[22]

The Administration's attitude towards Cuba was adopted by VOA, whose 'underlying policy' in the period immediately prior to the missile crisis was 'to expose, weaken and isolate the present government there with a view to its eventual elimination and replacement by one friendly to the US'.[23] In other words VOA was not only directly involved in American foreign policy towards Cuba, but was considered central to the unseating of a leader of another sovereign state. Even if VOA's responsibility to the United States government is accepted, this application of the station's resources was most questionable, and required elaborate justification. So it was alleged that Castro had 'betrayed a legitimate national revolution' and had attempted to 'subvert existing governments'. The revolution had promised to remain 'as native as [Cuban] palms' but had become 'as native as Russian missiles and troops'.[24] This overlooked the fact, of course, that the relentless American subversion against Castro, the economic embargo of Cuba, and the Bay of Pigs invasion had together forced Castro to rely on the Soviet Union to a greater extent than he would otherwise have liked.

VOA reflected policy decisions in other ways, largely due to the appointment of Ed Murrow as director of USIA. Apparently 'Kennedy gave Murrow his full confidence; no government information chief had been so close to a President.'[25] His predecessor, George Allen was determined that VOA be less propagandistic and hard-line, and thus enhance its own credibility. Under Murrow this movement gathered momentum since he was himself a reputable journalist and a former director of CBS News, and under his guidance both USIA and VOA received a much needed boost of professionalism. His first decisions responded to initiatives from the new President and were to have much bearing on the crisis that followed. In an attempt to both publicise and counter increasing Communist expansion into developing areas, Murrow strengthened VOA's signal to Africa and Latin America. According to Schlesinger Murrow in this way 'revitalized USIA, imbued it with his own bravery and honesty and directed its efforts especially to the developing nations where, instead of expounding free enterprise ideology, it tried to explain the American role in a diverse and evolving world'. USIA therefore became 'one of the most effective instruments of Kennedy's Third World policy. . . . Under Ed Murrow the Voice of America became the voice, not of self-righteousness, but of American democracy.'[26] This was no exaggeration. Murrow was certainly one of, if not the, most popular of USIA directors, held in great esteem by friends, colleagues and audiences alike, and his personal vision continues to shape many USIA activities today.

The Soviet media vociferously criticised such an ordering of foreign policy priorities. In particular, radio broadcasts repeatedly attacked American policies towards Cuba and denounced what they considered to be US-sponsored aggression against the island in preparation of a further invasion attempt in the near future.[27] In both its Spanish broadcasts to the Caribbean and English broadcasts to North America, Radio Moscow described how Washington was directly arming and financing Cuban insurgents, in addition to recruiting more than 500 of them for the American armed forces.[28] Upon reading Michael McClintock's enlightening study of American unconventional warfare methods, together with the evidence provided by the Bay of Pigs invasion, such conspiracy cannot be lightly dismissed.[29]

Such aggression allowed an unscheduled Moscow home service transmission on 2 September 1962 to explain that Soviet ships were carrying cargoes of weapons to Cuba merely for the island's defence, an argument which Soviet propaganda maintained throughout the missile crisis.[30] Moscow said that the increasing paranoia against Cuba had been encouraged by the American press which, it alleged, was intent on 'deliberately playing up reports of Soviet military and technical assistance to Cuba'.[31]

Whether it was deliberate or not remains unclear. The American media certainly added to America's anxiety about Cuba, and the combined pressure of press speculation, public opinion and the upcoming mid-term elections plainly forced Kennedy to respond. The media were spurred on by a report prepared in August 1962 by the Director of the CIA, John McCone, which accurately predicted that Soviet military assistance to Cuba would dramatically increase over the coming months and would eventually have offensive capabilities. Senator Kenneth Keating's startling revelations that Surface-to-Air Missiles (SAMs) were actually located on the island likewise contributed to the hysteria. Lack of concrete evidence, however, and repeated Soviet assurances that the missiles were intended only to defend Cuba, compelled the Adminisration to publicly dismiss such conclusions.

Perhaps the reports were merely the product of an over-eager press establishment, but whether they were or not is largely irrelevant; the significant factor is that the Soviet leadership monitored and interpreted American press reports and concluded that the US was preparing to take some action over Cuba. This is indicated by a statement reportedly authorised by the Soviet government and transmitted by Tass on 11 September 1962 which directly warned the US that its 'provocations' might 'plunge the world into thermonuclear war'. The American government was advised to exercise restraint and to calculate the risks it was taking. The statement then intimated that since Soviet missiles were so powerful, it was unnecessary to locate them surreptitiously outside the Soviet Union.[32] This last sentence had clear diplomatic motivations in that it sought to reaffirm the Soviet commitment that missiles in Cuba only had defensive capabilities, an assertion which was also central to the succession of personal bilateral communication which occurred between the US and the Soviet Union at this time. The statement warned that an American-inspired 'aggression' against Cuba would therefore be met with a 'crushing retaliatory blow', but maintained that the Soviet Union would nevertheless continue to seek a 'lasting peace'.[33] Over the next 24 hours this statement was repeated in Moscow's home service no less than four times, and was summarised in all the foreign language services, including English for North America. It was therefore intended as an important communication, and is thus worthy of serious consideration.

Such a diplomatic communication was undoubtedly the subject of intense scrutiny by analysts in Washington. There was as yet no valid reason why its intention should have been questioned since, it must be reiterated, there was still no firm evidence that potentially offensive weapons were being installed in Cuba and private diplomacy had reassured the Americans of Soviet intent. However the chronology of events as presented by Martin Walker, a serious journalist and scholar who has made a commendable start to analysing the recently-opened Soviet archives, suggests that the statement must now be dismissed as part of a sophisticated Soviet campaign designed to misinform and deceive the US.[34] He has described how the political situation was dramatically transformed on 8 September when Medium-Range Ballistic Missiles were unloaded in Havana. A week later another shipment arrived carrying weapons which could easily have reached Washington, DC and have knocked out most of America's Strategic Air Command bases.[35]

If we accept the traditional interpretations of events, reinforced by the discrepancies between Walker's chronology of 8 September and the Soviet communication just three days later, then we can observe the clear success of the Kremlin's efforts to cover up its actions in Cuba by means of an elaborate disinformation strategy.

So by this stage several key themes were starting to emerge as part of the Soviet Union's propaganda offensive, the most forceful being that Cuba was seeking to defend itself against proven American aggression. Another focused on America's relationship with its allies, especially Britain, who were consistently warned of the commercial risks of participating in America's embargo of Cuba. Britain was repeatedly denounced as a weak nation, vulnerable to America's arm twisting techniques' and was evolving into 'one of the states of America, so that all orders from Washington have to be carried out without a word'.[36]

In a similar way, Moscow criticised the stand taken by Cuba's Latin American neighbours. Support offered by the Organisation of American States for the blockade of Cuba was described as the consequence of its members' dependence on the US who had engaged in feverish 'diplomatic pressuring'.[37] This was in fact quite an accurate observation. The unanimity of the OAS for this move was secured, according to the historian Barton J. Bernstein, by 'some deft coercion';[38] and the fact that the OAS agenda placed discussion of Cuba before the question of economic aid suggests that US aid would be dependent on support for the quarantine. Thus Radio Moscow seized the opportunity to deliberately play up the American influence over the conference.

Next, Radio Moscow turned to address the people of the US themselves, warning them of the consequences of their government's actions. Using the supposed evidence of a Gallup poll which discovered that Americans were not in favour of an invasion of Cuba, the commentator Alexsandre Yevstafyev directly addressed 'those . . . who have apparently been so taken in by the anti-Cuban hysteria that they are ready to give Washington the green light for an armed attack on Cuba. Do you realise the significance and possible consequences stemming from a US attack on this small Caribbean island?' he asked. 'It will bring neither America nor its leaders laurels or success. . . . Playing with dynamite today may lead to real trouble tomorrow.'[39] In sharp contrast to ealier efforts, these attempts to achieve an intimacy with its audience made this propaganda and its accompanying threats all the more effective and credible. It was hoped that by personalising the issues each individual listener would be compelled to consider and evaluate the possible consequences of their government's actions; each then had a personal stake in the diplomatic procedure which would determine their future.

Another approach used primarily in Soviet broadcasts to the US was to appeal to America's sense of its own colonial history. Speeches by George Washington, which embraced his aspirations for national sovereignty, non-interference and the opposition to oppression, were echoed to expose the hypocrisy of the Kennedy Administration.[40] Of course such radio propaganda overlooked the fact that the Kremlin had violated such cherished principles in its own backyard, most recently in Hungary.

Significantly Radio Moscow appealed to history in other ways. For example in a Spanish-language broadcast to South America the expression 'Yankee' was used instead of 'American'. Soviet propagandists had chosen their words with great care, and this indicates the level of their sophistication; for the people who live South of the United States, the term 'Yankee' has a unique meaning which conjures up images of a past relationship based on exploitation and dependence.[41]

All of these broadcasts are examples of how the Soviet government channelled its diplomatic effort towards the people themselves, often blurring the fine distinction between public diplomacy and propaganda.

AN EXCHANGE OF STATEMENTS

On 13 September, President Kennedy held a press conference in which he suggested to the world how America would react to any aggression originating from Cuba. 'If at any time,' he said

the Communist build-up in Cuba were to endanger or interfere with our security in any way . . . or if Cuba should ever attempt to export its aggressive purposes by force or the threat of force against any nation in this hemisphere, or become an offensive military base of significant capacity for the Soviet Union, then this country will do whatever must be done to protect its own security and that of its allies.[42]

According to Michael Beschloss, Khrushchev reacted angrily to Kennedy's speech and, knowing his words would be reported to the American President, expressed his determination to resist any blockade of Cuba. As expected the message was then offered to President Kennedy, filed under the heading 'More rude noises from Khrushchev.'[43]

But it was the series of developments which unfolded on the 22 October which most clearly illustrate the growing role of radio communications in the mounting crisis. Ten American radio networks were requisitioned by the federal government so that an address by President Kennedy could be relayed to Cuba at precisely the same time as it was watched by American TV viewers.[44] In addition the speech was carried live by VOA and followed by Spanish and Portuguese translations to Latin America, while the European services relayed the speech in Russian, French and Spanish. The speech has been variously described as the 'best weapon in the [USIA's] arsenal'[45] and 'perhaps the most important address of the Cold War'. Given its obvious diplomatic nature and that in part it was addressed to Khrushchev himself, it can be reasonably assumed that it was monitored in the Soviet Union. In addition Soviet Ambassadors in the target countries could summarise the speech for Moscow, and Dean Rusk provided the Soviet Ambassador to the United States, Anatoly Dobrynin, with a copy of the text. Such a combined information effort was directed towards guaranteeing that the Kremlin would learn of the speech's content. It was therefore vital that the media handle the speech with extreme sensitivity as to its diplomatic importance. Thus Thomas Sorenson, Deputy Director of Policy and Planning at USIA, drafted a directive on the speech for 'all media elements'. Its objectives were described as (i) to obtain the understanding and the support of the Cuban people for the blockade and 'any subsequent action which may be required', and (ii) to 'encourage Cuban opposition to and non-cooperation with the Castro r‹gime and the Communists, *stopping short of premature or ineffective uprisings*' [emphasis added]. The directive continued by instructing the media that they should not use 'any comment, regardless of source, which is not wholly consistent with the lines set forth in the President's speech and this instruction'.[46]

Such caution indicates that at long last the harsh lessons of Hungary and the Bay of Pigs had been learnt. Moreover the very existence of the directive reveals that the Americans had finally accepted consistent international propaganda to be pivotal in the successful projection of a specific diplomatic line or policy.

Extra vigilance also had to be taken in the actual text of the address. This task fell to Theodore Sorensen, a Kennedy aide and speech writer, who spent long hours drafting the address apparently after studying speeches made by Wilson and Roosevelt at comparatively critical junctures in their Presidencies. To illustrate the consistency of the projected government line, almost the exact same words are to be found in Thomas Sorenson's directive as were included in Kennedy's speech.

The speech did not mince words; it described the build-up of missiles in Cuba as 'secret, swift and extraordinary,' a 'sudden clandestine' move which was 'deliberately provocative and unjustified' and in clear violation of 'Soviet assurances and in defiance of American and hemispheric policy'.[47] Kennedy then outlined the response he intended to take: Cuba would be quarantined on 24 October,[48] and any ships found to be carrying weapons would be turned back. By imposing a quarantine the President had ingeniously shifted the onus of responsibility on the Soviet Union to prevent escalation of the crisis. Surveillance of Cuba would be stepped up, while American troops would be stationed at Guantanamo; and perhaps most ominously of all, Kennedy guaranteed that a nuclear missile attack from Cuba on any nation in the western hemisphere would be regarded as a Soviet-inspired attack on the US 'requiring a full retaliatory response upon the Soviet Union.' He continued: 'I call upon . . . Khrushchev to halt and eliminate this . . . reckless and provocative threat to world peace, and to stable relations between our two nations. I call upon him further to abandon this course of world domination and to join in an historic effort to end the perilous arms race and to transform the history of man.'

To conclude his broadcast Kennedy turned to directly address the 'captive people of Cuba'. First he assured them of his friendship, sharing both their 'aspirations for liberty and justice for all', and their sorrow as the 'nationalist revolution was betrayed' and the 'fatherland fell under foreign domination'. Then Kennedy steered towards isolating the Cuban government from the people:

Now your leaders are no longer Cuban inspired by Cuban ideals. They are puppets and agents of an international conspiracy which has turned Cuba against your friends and neighbors in the Americas

– and turned it into the first Latin American country to become a target for nuclear war. . . .

... [The US] has no wish to cause you to suffer or to impose any system upon you. We know that your lives and land are being used as pawns by those who deny your freedom.

By addressing this last passage to the Cuban people themselves, Kennedy had deliberately bypassed Castro altogether. In this way the Soviet Union alone was made responsible for the possible consequences of violating the blockade, while the issue itself was no longer a localised incident involving the US and Cuba but was now a crisis in Superpower relations. Yet the Cuban press and radio service completely ignored Kennedy's message to the people of the island, while the VOA Spanish-language broadcast on medium-wave from Key West was apparently audible but other frequencies were subject to jamming.[49] Kennedy's appeal was therefore lost on all ordinary Cubans except those who happened to be listening to the Key West frequencies.

Sorenson's directive to USIA continued where Kennedy's speech left off, being much more forceful in its denunciation of the Soviet Union, more descriptive of 'the sordid history of Castro's sell-out of the revolution to Communism', and more vigorous in its warnings of the risks which now faced Cuba.[50]

According to Raymond Garthoff, a Soviet Affairs Assistant in the Department of State, the Russians interpreted Kennedy's speech as implying that the missiles would be used as an excuse for invading Cuba. However, he has written, the Soviets 'had no way of knowing that Kennedy had rejected even stiffer language hinting at the removal of Castro . . . what they did hear seemed ominous enough'.[51]

And it is VOA's broadcast of Kennedy's speech in the Russian language which provides yet further evidence of the important diplomatic role assumed by radio during the crisis. A full 14 hours drifted by before Moscow's newspapers finally reported it, omitting its more conciliatory passages and even failing to mention the missile bases themselves. Neither did they report the President's guarantee that the Soviet Union would be held responsible for any attack on the US launched from Cuba, inviting in response a full retaliation. In fact the British Cabinet learnt on 23 October that the blockade had received no publicity whatsoever within the Soviet Union. The Cabinet judged this to mean that 'Mr Khrushchev had left himself room for manoeuvre' without feeling the pressure of public opinion which might have been aggravated by Kennedy's words.[52]

Listeners to Radio Havana were also unaware that the OAS had endorsed the blockade of Cuba, while the British embassy in Warsaw reported that the speech had not been published in Poland.[53] An enormous information vacuum had been created throughout the world and, intense jamming notwithstanding, it was important that VOA at least attempt to let Cubans, Russians, Poles and no doubt countless others behind the Iron Curtain, know what was being deliberately kept from them by their own governments. However the success of these efforts appears to have been minimal: by the end of the crisis on 28 October, the British Foreign Office noted that the Russian media had presented a 'confused picture' of the events. Confused is actually something of an understatement; taken in its entirety the list of items neglected by the Soviet media is a remarkable read, and one is left wondering just what facts the Soviet media *did* report! For one thing American evidence of a military build-up in Cuba was denounced as fake; at the same time important aspects of the crisis were withheld from the public altogether, including American charges of Soviet deceit and the actual stationing of rocket bases on Cuba. In addition, Russians were deliberately kept ignorant of the fact that a Soviet tanker, the *Bucharest*, had been intercepted but allowed to proceed and that Khrushchev had issued instructions to Soviet shipping to stay well away from the interception area.[54] What is certain is that the 'confused picture' of the crisis meant that the Russian people were oblivious of its impact and implications. Sir Frank Roberts, British Ambassador to Moscow, reported that the 'Moscow public have been less excited and apprehensive about the Cuban crisis than they were at the height of the Berlin crisis'.[55] Roberts explained that one reason for this was that 'news was released to the Soviet public in such a way that the crisis was never fully evident to them until the high point of danger was past'.[56]

Not surprisingly VOA focused on the extensive support that the blockade received world-wide. This required programmes to broadcast the American version of the 'truth', and to this end a massive media operation was launched on 25 October 1962. To overcome Communist jamming, the accumulated power of no less than 52 VOA transmitters was harnessed to broadcast eight-and-a-half hours of saturation broadcasting on 80 frequencies.

While VOA was engaged in such frantic propaganda activity, American radio and television were subject to strict news management. Directors were asked to 'exercise caution and discretion' in the publication of information 'considered vital' to national security.[57] This included discussion of plans for weapon employment and the types of weapons themselves, their capabilities, and possible targets, as well as intelligence estimates of enemy plans or capabilities. In short the media were told to refrain from providing any information which might 'reveal the success of United States intelligence efforts or operations', plans for emergency mobilisation and procedures, and supply capabilities. The White House judged the publication of such information to be 'contrary to the public interest' in such a 'tense international situation'.[58] Was this censorship or was it news management? Identifying the one from the other is problematic. It would of course be too simplistic and too easy to portray the Soviets as engaging in censorship, while the west practised news management. There is a world of difference between war and peace, and such practices as were demanded of the media by the American government during the missile crisis are understandable and perhaps more justified in wartime. A crisis, however, is not a war as Britain found to its dismay during Suez. In crisis circumstances such 'news management' could well be construed as the prelude to censorship and raises many doubts about the free flow of information in the democracies.

The Soviet Response

In reply to Kennedy's speech the Soviet government issued, 'with what for the Russians is unusual speed',[59] its own statement, broadcast by Moscow's home service and transmitted by Tass, and touching upon many of the themes that had already been addressed by the Soviet media. Sir Frank Roberts, the British Ambassador in Moscow, believed this statement would inevitably be 'only the first shot in a heavy barrage of propaganda'.[60] Yet USIA still blindly described the Soviet media as 'defensive', deliberately avoiding the 'real issues' to rely instead on 'anti-American vituperation'.[61]

The Soviet statement dismissed Kennedy's speech as an example of American aggression against a sovereign state and of their willingness to provoke war.[62] Once again, the statement threatened that Kennedy himself must assume responsibility for 'recklessly playing with fire' and pushing the world towards the brink of thermonuclear war by flouting international law and the Charter of the United Nations, which included piracy on the high seas. This was followed by the repeated diplomatic assurances that the missiles in Cuba were designed only for the island's defence. Moreover the 'Soviet Union has already repeatedly declared that not a single nuclear bomb would fall on the

United States or any other country, unless an aggression is committed. The nuclear weapons which have been created by the Soviet people and are in the hands of the people never will be used for the purpose of aggression.'[63]

This was a theme that Khrushchev returned to in his historic 'letter to Kennedy' broadcast on 27 October, reiterating that 'the weapons . . . are in the hands of Soviet officers. Therefore any accidental use of them whatsoever to the detriment of the United States is excluded.'[64] Together these statements reflected a genuine concern within the Soviet leadership that the US feared the possibility of Castro gaining possession of the missiles, thus providing an excuse for a quick first strike against Cuba. The Soviets, anxious that this be prevented at all costs, insisted that such a move by the Americans was unnecessary. The initial promising tone of the statement was compromised, however, by the threat that 'if the aggressors touch off a war, the Soviet Union would strike a most powerful retaliatory blow.'[65]

The statement then echoed the now familiar theme of hypocrisy in America's aggressive policy towards Cuba, and how it was

> well known that American statesmen are fond of speaking about their devotion to the principles of international law and harangue about the necessity of law and order in the world. But in point of fact they apparently believe that laws are meant not for the United States but for other countries. The establishment of the actual blockade . . . is a provocative move, an unheard of violation of international law, a challenge to all peace-loving nations.
>
> . . . The arrogant actions of American imperialism could lead to disastrous consequences to all mankind, unwanted by a single people including the United States.[66]

In contrast the Soviet Union was said to have offered Cuba a means of defence, thus carefully avoiding any suggestion that this was a dispute between America and the Soviet Union. It was also possible that the Soviet presentation of the dispute, 'Great power America bullying small power Cuba'[67] would be appealing to audiences in the developing world. The statement intimated that the Soviet Union aspired to the withdrawal of all foreign troops 'from alien territories to within their national boundaries. If the United States shows real concern,' it continued, 'for consolidation of friendly relations with other states and tries to secure durable world peace, as President Kennedy declared in his speech on 22 October, it should accept the Soviet proposals and withdraw its troops and military equipment and close down military bases on foreign territories. . . . However the United States . . . stubbornly refuses to accept this proposal.' Listeners were informed that the Soviet delegate at the UN had been instructed to call for an immediate meeting of the Security Council to discuss 'the violation of the United Nations Charter and threat to peace on the part of the United States of America'.[68]

In his expert study of the statement, R.H. Mason of the Foreign Office noted how its political content was minimal; in fact it revealed very little about Soviet intentions. There was, for example, no reference to Berlin, despite the constant worry that this would prove a vulnerable spot in the event of US–Soviet hostilities.[69] This may have been designed to reassure the west that, for the time being at least, Berlin was safe and so the Superpowers together could resolve the immediate crisis as necessary. Mason judged the statement as having given 'the impression that the Russians were caught off balance by President Kennedy's statement, that they were surprised at its vigour, and that their first instinct is to be cautious. It is particularly note-worthy,' said Mason, 'that they have avoided engaging their prestige beyond the very minimum that was essential,'[70]

Sir Frank Roberts, in a most accurate projection of Soviet propaganda themes, largely agreed with Mason's assessment and doubted that the Russians would 'take any action beyond propaganda until they see how things are going [at the UN]; and I would not expect Khrushchev,' he wrote, 'to make a direct challenge to President Kennedy in the present charged pre-election atmosphere when he fully recognises the impossibility of an American back-down.'[71]

COMMENTS

Together the American and Soviet statements of 22 and 23 October made very little constructive contribution towards finding a resolution to the crisis. Kennedy's announcement of the blockade signalled to the Soviets that he intended to escalate his response as the crisis proceeded and accorded to them full responsibility for disregarding the consequences. McGeorge Bundy, Kennedy's National Security Adviser, said he knew of 'no public document in the nuclear age that more faithfully reports a major course of action by a President and the reasons for his choice'.[72] There was no avoiding the fact that Kennedy had addressed the Soviets and Cubans directly and had presented the American case in plain terms and in clear language – the essence of public diplomacy.

It might credibly be argued that Kennedy should have first allowed private bilateral diplomacy to resolve the crisis when he met with the Soviet Foreign Minister, Andrei Gromyko, on 18 October, before publicly announcing that the missiles in Cuba had the capacity to be used offensively against the US.[73] Had this effort failed, Kennedy's broadcast statement of 22 October would certainly have carried greater force since world opinion would perceive the Soviets had been responsible for the breakdown in diplomacy. Kennedy however had chosen to issue a public ultimatum to the Soviets without negotiation, making a quiet withdrawal by the Soviets now impossible.[74] If this really represented a suspension of diplomacy, then its implications for the role of international radio broadcasting in the foreign policy process were considerable; VOA was actually used as a means by which Khrushchev could be publicly humiliated, a weapon of Kennedy's Cold War crusade. It also suggests that Kennedy overlooked the contribution which the VOA could make in shaping public opinion, as well as in assisting American diplomatic efforts, for short-term political gain.

This is a plausible theory, but is inconsistent with both the demands of the diplomatic process and the urgency of this specific crisis. It is a theory which overlooks the vital fact that any diplomatic manoeuvring threatened to create a situation where the missiles would have been operational and the Americans would have been presented with a near *fait accompli*. Kennedy could not afford to let the Soviets stall for time during what would probably have been a series of protracted negotiations. Kennedy also felt justifiably aggrieved by the way the Soviet leadership had lied to him about their commitment to Cuba all along, forcing him to conclude that there was simply nothing to negotiate. In the event Kennedy's response was the right one to make at such a critical hour.

In contrast the Soviet statement was a general reply full of rhetorical imagery and implied threats but made no attempt to directly answer American charges of deceit. In fact by focusing on US–Cuban relations the statement avoided the crisis's Superpower dimension. Even the American Jupiter missiles in Turkey which were to play a pivotal role both in the propaganda war and in the resolution of the crisis, were not yet regarded as crucial and were mentioned only in passing by broadcasts. For example, in a programme to North America on 17 September, Radio Moscow's Vladislav Kozykov had talked of American military bases 'thousands of miles from US shores and right next to the frontier of the socialist countries.[75] Broadcasts, however, avoided discussing the Jupiters by name until 27 October as part of Khrushchev's publicly demanded terms for the resolution of the crisis.

As late as 1962 the Soviets were hesitant to use the media for anything else except propaganda, this being the main role assumed by Radio Moscow since its inception in the early 1920s as an instrument of Communist agitation and as a means by which the objectives and progress of the Bolshevik revolution could be projected. That this was to change was to mark a most significant turning point in both the history of Soviet broadcasting and in the crisis itself.

FURTHER SABRES ARE RATTLED

In the days following the exchange of statements Radio Moscow relied heavily on familiar themes, but the rather staid and repetitive nature of broadcasts was enlivened on 24 October by Radio Moscow's resort to one curious form of propaganda, a technique that had been developed and used to capital effect by both the Allies and the Axis powers during the Second World War. In a feature entitled *Stop and Think, America!* Moscow's North American listeners were treated to a conversation between two voices, one which restated the American case, the other which criticised it, beginning each condemnation with 'That's a lie'. This was an attempt to engage ordinary Americans in a rhetorical dialogue on the premise that they were the ones who would suffer for the reckless policies pursued by their government. Hence the more formal diplomatic-media contact with American leaders themselves was by-passed. The broadcast itself began by humanising the issue and building an intimate relationship with its listeners by calling on various named cities in the US, and to

> the Pittsburgh steel smelter, the New Orleans longshoreman, the Californian farmer, Oklahoma rancher and Harvard student. Your leaders are prepared to plunge you into a reckless attack on tiny Cuba. Tomorrow you may be drafted and sent to the slaughter. . . . You must stop and think today – what is America headed for?[76]

The broadcast reassured its listeners that the Soviet Union had merely offered Cuba assistance to consolidate its defences, and did not have any bases on the island. Meanwhile 'the whole world' was said to be aware of the 'spies, wreckers and paid agents of the Pentagon and CIA who do subversive work against the Cuban Republic' who 'fired the sugar cane plantations . . . blew up factories and dropped bombs on women and children and the aged'. (Moscow neglected to mention that such spies who were engaged in subversive work could not have enjoyed much success if indeed the 'whole world' knew about them!) Washington, it said, had 'turned a deaf ear on all proposals' to find a peaceful resolution.

After this fierce tirade, the first Soviet voice then proceeded to chart the remarkable progress of the Cuban revolution to date and described its many social and economic achievements. These were accomplished, concluded the broadcast, because Cuba had 'freed itself from foreign domination of all kinds'.

The second voice then used the tried and tested propaganda method of appealing to history, a theme guaranteed to pull the heart-strings of every decent and patriotic American! 'The forefathers of present day Americans laid down their lives in the war against the British colonisers, for the sake of freedom and independence. Then why do America's leaders of today refuse the Cuban people the right to be free and independent,' it asked. 'Why should the Cubans be deprived of a right that every nation enjoys?' The words of America's founding fathers on national sovereignty and independence were then quoted. Americans were told that their leaders had 'spat on the finest revolutionary traditions of their nation. They have buried the legacy of George Washington and Thomas Jefferson.' Returning to the present crisis the broadcast evoked various acts of international law to prove the illegality of the blockade, while the second voice warned that an attack by the US on any other nation would spark a thermonuclear war – with 'disastrous consequences for all humanity. The American nation,' he said, 'would suffer as much, perhaps more, than other nations,' while his colleague assured listeners that the 'Soviet government makes no threats.' He continued:

> It reiterates . . . that if no aggression is committed, no Soviet nuclear bombs will drop on the USA or any other country. . . . But if aggressive elements precipitate a war, the Soviet Union will retaliate with all its power. The Soviet government feels it its duty to warn the US government most seriously that it will be assuming a grave responsibility for the fate of peace and will be playing recklessly with fire if it carries out the measures announced by President Kennedy. The Soviet government urges America's leaders to consider the situation realistically and display reason and common sense. [77]

This passage, combining reassurance with threats and hopes, clearly illustrates how the Soviets' diplomacy was augmented by radio broadcasting.

Such vehemence was not reserved for the US alone; one Radio Moscow commentator, Vladimir Alexsandrov, was most critical of the British response to Kennedy's announcements. In an English-language transmission intended for the United Kingdom he asked, 'what contribution have the leaders of British policy made to preserving the cause of peace, or what do they intend doing?'. Alexsandrov then claimed that he had been 'eagerly awaiting Mr. Macmillan's statement in the House of Commons, for Britain,' he conceded, ' is a great power and one can expect from her more than anyone else decisive action to save peace.'[78] Alexsandrov was here merely raising the reputation of Britain in preparation for its subsequent deflation. He was 'deeply disappointed' that Macmillan did not condemn Kennedy's actions, nor did he declare any foresight as to how the crisis could be eased. 'So one has to say,' concluded Alexsandrov, 'that official London has not taken a stand worthy of the government of a great power, a country perfectly capable of calling to order its NATO partner.' In the political climate of the early 1960s, such abiding faith in the power of Great Britain to exert an influence over the United States was quite incredible, even more so given that the Suez crisis had demonstrated only too clearly how the United States could pressure its Atlantic partner into reversing its policies.[79]

Such sharp criticism of the British government continued even after the immediate crisis had abated. With the same misplaced confidence he had earlier displayed, Alexsandrov told his British listeners that the government could have restrained Washington and prevent the US from taking 'rash and dangerous steps'. Lord Home, now derided as another 'advocate of American aggression', was attacked for his enthusiastic defence of the US, while his accusations against the Soviet Union, Cuba and Communism in general for 'all the sins he could think of' were considered monstrous. Above all the crisis had suggested to Alexsandrov that Great Britain continued to be dependent on its Atlantic partner.[80] Radio Moscow was here simply responding to the British government's public declarations of support for the American position; in private, however, the legality of the blockade was vigorously challenged. On 26 October 1962, the Secretary of State for the Colonies went further and instructed the Acting Administrator of St Lucia to 'deal with any requests for facilities from bloc or Cuban ships or aircraft exactly as you would deal with similar requests from any other ship or aircraft. In other words,' he wrote, 'it is NOT (repeat NOT) our intention to offer the Americans any special help in enforcing the blockade.'[81] Had the Soviets been aware of this contradiction between

British announcements and privately-expressed sentiments, their propaganda would have been considerably more forceful.

U Thant, the Secretary-General of the United Nations, was becoming increasingly active in searching for a settlement to the crisis. Combined with feverish behind-the-scenes diplomatic activity, a resolution appeared to be possible but still not probable. However a move initiated by Khrushchev which seemed to take everybody by surprise brought the end of the crisis so much closer.

MOSCOW CALLING!

By 26 October, Russian intelligence was under the impression that an American invasion of Cuba was imminent. At 3 a.m. the next day, 27 October, Castro visited the Soviet embassy in Havana and said that he was expecting either an American airstrike or invasion within 24 hours. Cuba's *Revolución* newspaper accused Kennedy of 'sabotaging prospects of peace with plans of invasion and bombardment', while emphasising the determination of ordinary Cubans to resist 'aggressive Yankee imperialism'.[82] The crisis was gathering momentum and such indicators suggested that it was nearing its climax, though its outcome was still very uncertain.

Following Kennedy's positive response to U Thant's efforts, Moscow Radio on 27 October broadcast a message direct from Krushchev. Its timeliness is suggested by Martin Walker who has described how as it was being transmitted, events at the quarantine line were becoming more urgent, with one vessel directed towards it.[83] The implications of any message transmitted at this moment were therefore considerable. Fully aware of this Khrushchev had spent a long time perfecting his message, dictating it, typing it, correcting it, and re-typing it several times.

'Esteemed Mr. President,' began the message, 'this reasonable step on your part [Kennedy's positive response to U Thant's appeal] strengthens my belief that you are showing concern for the safeguarding of peace, and I note this with satisfaction.'[84] Khrushchev sympathised with Kennedy's 'concern for the security of the USA, Mr. President, because this is the first duty of a President,' but wondered what he should make of American actions 'which express themselves in the fact that you have surrounded the Soviet Union with military bases, surrounded our allies with military bases. . . . Your rockets are situated in Britain,' he said, 'situated in Italy and aimed against us. Your rockets are situated in Turkey too. And you are worried by Cuba?... You have placed destructive rocket weapons, which you call offensive in Turkey, virtually on our doorstep.'[85]

Hoping to find a resolution soon which still might avert war, Khrushchev offered Kennedy the following proposal:

> We agree to remove from Cuba those means which you regard as offensive means; we agree to carry this out and to declare in the United Nations this pledge. Your representatives will make a declaration to the effect that the USA... will remove their analogous means from Turkey. Let us reach agreement as to the span of time needed for you and us to bring this about, and after that persons enjoying the confidence of the UN Security Council could check on the spot the fulfilment on the promises given.

This would be followed by a 'solemn promise' made by the Soviet Union under the auspices of the Security Council, to 'respect the inviolability of the frontiers and the sovereignty of Turkey, not to interfere in its internal affairs, not to invade Turkey and not to make its territory available as a bridgehead for... an invasion of Turkey'. In return Khrushchev demanded that the US make a similar pledge in respect of Cuba, that is, declare its respect for the 'inviolability' of Cuba's frontiers, its sovereignty, 'and that it undertakes not to invade itself and not to make its territory available for such an invasion of Cuba'. Linking the resolution of the missile crisis with other international problems, Khrushchev believed that such an agreement could serve as 'a good beginning' on a number of unsolved issues, and used the occasion to announce the Soviets' willingness to discuss the possibility of a mutual nuclear test ban. Khrushchev warned, however, that these matters must 'await a solution to clear up the international atmosphere. We are ready for this.' Illustrating the diplomatic content of this radio communication, the message included an explicit assurance that the weapons were not controlled by Castro. In other words Khrushchev was signalling to Kennedy that there was no need to attack Cuba before the missiles were operational to prevent a possible irrational first-strike by Castro. The statement concluded amicably: 'These, then, are my proposals, Mr. President. Respectfully yours, Khrushchev.'

This was broadcast at 1400 GMT in the home service and, given the urgency of the moment, was immediately repeated before being broadcast again at 1500 GMT. A commentator in Moscow's home service remarked that the fate of mankind depended on whether the American government agreed to Khrushchev's offer.[86]

But this was not the first diplomatic communication offering terms of settlement: on 26 October Khrushchev had sent a letter to Kennedy, acknowledging the existence of the missiles for the first time, and guaranteeing their removal in exchange for a pledge that no invasion of Cuba would take place. Susan Strange has suggested that this letter shows Khrushchev still saw a need at such a critical moment for quick, personal and confidential communication.[87] It is difficult to understand how Professor Strange could thus describe a message which took 12 hours to finally arrive in four out-of-order sections in this way. From the fact that two messages were sent, one private and conciliatory, the other pubic and hard-line, Kremlinologists reasonably assumed that the Soviet leadership was experiencing its own internal problems. According to Dean Rusk, Russian experts within the State Department believed that 'the comrades in the Kremlin had probably been pulling guns on each other during the last 48 hours'.[88] British analysts disagreed. R.H. Mason at the Foreign Office wrote to Sir Frank Roberts in Moscow that there was 'no sound evidence . . . of disputes and dissensions in the Soviet leadership. But so far as I am aware we have never had such evidence of divisions in the Soviet leadership until after the event. After all,' he continued, 'it is only quite recently that we have been discovering the extent and ramifications of the anti-party group.'[89]

This may seem like a peripheral issue, but deducing the motives for Russian actions over the weekend of 26–7 October can reveal a great deal about the Soviet conception of propaganda and media diplomacy. It also suggests that a nation's priority during crises is the state of its internal political structure, rather than the image it project outwards.

Three possible explanations can be advanced for the contradictory character of Khrushchev's messages: (i) He had acted without full authority in sending the first message and had been overruled by hardliners.[90] This continues to be the interpretation of events most favoured by historians, but as yet there is a lack of satisfactory evidence to affirm its accuracy. (ii) The Soviet government had decided it could get more than the first message was asking for, that is, some sort of Cuba–Turkey deal. Again this remains a possible explanation but cannot be substantiated beyond reasonable doubt. (iii) The proposal to remove missiles from Cuba in exchange for the withdrawal of Jupiters from Turkey may well have been a deliberate gamble aimed at exerting pressure on the US to accept the first message. Robert McNamara, US Defense Secretary, rejected this last idea, asking: 'How can we negotiate with somebody who changes his deal before we even get a chance to reply and announces publicly the deal before we receive it?'[91] According to Arnold Horelick, an analyst for the RAND Corporation, Khrushchev's wish for a deal involving the Jupiters was an 'improvised fall-back'. In 1963 he wrote that if it had been a prepared fall-back, Soviet propagandists were left mysteriously unprepared for it. On 28 October *Izvestiya* described proposals of a settlement involving a reciprocal exchange between the US and Soviet Union as the product of the 'unclear conscience' of their American authors.[92] This suggests either that the second message was hurriedly prepared given the pressing urgency of the matter and was indeed improvised, or the Soviets did not yet appreciate the need to maintain a consistency in propaganda. However, given the tight control exercised by the Soviet political establishment over propaganda this is most unlikely. Indeed the issue is made farcical by the fact that Khrushchev's son-in-law was the editor of *Izvestiya*. It is quite possible, therefore, that there was a breakdown in family communications, in addition to a breakdown in the more traditional chain of command within the Communist party!

Unfortunately for the time being at least, we can continue to only speculate as to why two messages were sent. But at least we know much more than most of the Soviet Communist party and the Russian public at that time. In a speech to the Supreme Soviet in December 1962 Khrushchev maintained that the missiles had been located in Cuba for defensive purposes, but more importantly he neglected to mention the fact that he had sent two entirely different messages to Kennedy. Obviously by controlling the flow of information in this way Khrushchev hoped to retain his authority and temper some of the criticism that was being hurled at him from all sides which accused him of being a reckless adventurer and a coward for capitulating.[93]

Knowing that the terms of Khrushchev's second message would appear reasonable to world opinion, Kennedy drafted a reply and showed it to David Ormsby-Gore, the British Ambassador to Washington and Kennedy's close personal friend. The second message had demanded the removal of Jupiter missiles from Turkey, a 'reciprocal concession'. Although he felt that this had been a last minute addition the Ambassador nevertheless believed that the terms of settlement 'had considerable merit,' especially since Kennedy accepted the Jupiters had very little significant military value.[94]

According to Ormsby-Gore, the Soviet offer made American unilateral action difficult, since any such move would appear to world opinion as if America was not prepared to make concessions for peace. This was an accurate assessment; the second Soviet statement had certainly

backed Kennedy into a tight corner and limited his freedom of manoeuvre, prompting him to delay his response and step up aerial re-
connaissance of Cuba. 'The trial of wills is now approaching a climax,'
wrote Macmillan to Kennedy; 'Khrushchev's first message, unhappily
not published to the world, seemed to go a long way to meet you. His
second message, widely broadcast and artfully contrived, adding the
Turkey proposal, was a recovery on his part. It has made a considerable impact.'[95]

Following considerable and often heated debate within the Ex.Comm.
about how to respond to the apparently contradictory messages transmitted from Moscow, Kennedy decided to ignore the second Soviet
message altogether, and replied instead to Khrushchev's first privately-
sent letter. Robert Kennedy later venerated this as an example of his
brother's acumen as a skilled diplomat.[96] There have, however, been a
number of notable dissenters who have expressed their disagreement
with this description of the President. The veteran statesman, Dean
Acheson, criticised the decision to ignore the first letter as 'another
postponement of action while Soviet work on the missiles drove on'.
Describing this as 'a gamble to the point of recklessness,' Acheson
did concede it was nevertheless 'skilfully executed': 'If there were
divided counsels in the Kremlin – as there were in Washington – the
new message proposed to exploit them.'[97]

Before any message was sent it was important to anticipate the possible Soviet propaganda which might be disseminated in reply, especially
if it continued to equate Soviet missiles in Cuba with NATO missiles
in Turkey and Italy. The USIA directive which resulted from this is a
remarkable example of the foresight which American propagandists
displayed at such a critical time, as well as a recognition of the crucial
link between politics and propaganda. The directive thus followed the
Administration's line that the missiles in Cuba were fundamentally
'different is conception and purpose' from those in Europe. A 15 Heads-
of-Government NATO meeting held in 1957 had been motivated by
'Soviet sabre-rattling' to locate the Jupiters in Turkey. Khrushchev had
been informed of this decision, whereas in contrast, deception and
disinformation had marked the Soviet attempt to cover up the existence of missiles in Cuba.[98]

It is interesting that similar themes were considered useful in British propaganda overseas, and this can be illustrated with reference to
Yugoslavia. Of course this should not be judged as typical of propaganda to the satellite states on this matter since Yugoslavia's status in
the Communist world was unique. As staff at the British embassy in

Belgrade suggested, Yugoslavia's turbulent relationship with the Soviet Union was a valuable theme which propaganda should exploit. Inevitably Yugoslavia was hostile towards America's Cuban policy, and labelled the US as hypocritical in its response to foreign bases while highlighting how the sovereign Cubans had eagerly welcomed Soviet aid and protection. The British embassy warned that criticism of foreign bases was 'likely to be directed here at all major members of NATO. . . . In countering such criticism in BBC broadcasts etc., intended for Yugoslavia,' advised the embassy, 'it would be desirable to stress the point that Stalin's aggressive foreign policy led to the creation of NATO and that the continuing necessity for defence bases on foreign territory results from the continuance of such Stalinist tendencies in Soviet foreign policy today'. In this way British propaganda was to take advantage of the historical animosity between Yugoslavia and the Soviet Union, noting that the 'term Stalinist still connotes aggression in Yugoslavian official vocabulary'.[99]

Now prepared for any propaganda eventuality the US issued a statement on 27 October 1962 welcoming Khrushchev's public initiative, but affirmed that before any 'sensible negotiation' could occur, 'the first imperative must be to deal with the immediate threat' posed by the Soviet offensive missiles in Cuba. It was therefore important to outline the American position in the clearest possible terms:

> [As] an urgent preliminary to consideration of any proposals work on the Cuban bases must stop; offensive weapons must be rendered inoperable; and further shipments of offensive weapons to Cuba must cease – all under effective international verification.[100]

The official Soviet response on 28 October was preceded by an announcement by Radio Moscow at 1405 GMT (9 a.m. Washington time) that an important government statement would be transmitted, the broadcast apparently beginning even before its textual editing had been completed. No clearer warning could be issued to the BBC's monitors at Caversham Park that they should prepare to receive and report what followed.

Once again Khrushchev addressed Kennedy personally as 'esteemed Mr. President', informing him that 'the Soviet government, in addition to orders previously issued for the cessation of further work on the [Cuban] building sites for the weapons,' had 'issued a new order; for the weapons which you describe as "offensive" to be dismantled, packed up and returned to the Soviet Union'. Yet although he was announcing his intention to climb down, Khrushchev was obviously not prepared to let the occasion slip by without first rattling a few more sabres. After reviewing the record of Soviet assistance to Cuba's defence and America's piracy, he once again described how Cuba was under a consistent threat of 'aggressive forces which did not conceal their intentions to invade Cuba's territory'. Nevertheless he accepted Kennedy's assurances that Cuba would not be invaded, and thus conceded that 'the motives which prompted us to give aid of this nature to Cuba are no longer applicable. Thus '[A]ll necessary conditions for the termination of the conflict which has arisen' were in place.[101] Moreover Khrushchev added that he was prepared to engage in constructive dialogue concerning NATO–Warsaw Pact relations. 'I also wish,' he announced, 'to continue an exchange of opinions on the prohibition of atomic thermonuclear weapons, on general disarmament and on other questions concerning the easing of international tension.'[102]

The significance of this broadcast, and the importance attached to it by the Soviet leaderships's insistence that it be monitored and reported, can be adduced by the fact that it was repeated four times in the home service and no less than 13 times in the North American service between 2200 GMT on 28 October and 0330 GMT on the 29th, in addition to several repeats in Spanish for Cuba. Dean Rusk told Ormsby-Gore that although the American government's 'public comment will be reserved in tone until such time as they have worked out some sort of immediate detailed problems arising from Khrushchev's latest message,' the Administration was 'in fact immensely satisfied with it'.[103] This was a gross understatement. In fact Washington was positively jubilant as it heard the message. Bundy said he 'felt that the world had changed for the better,' while Don Wilson, acting as USIA director after Murrow had fallen ill, 'felt like laughing or yelling or dancing'. The President himself said he felt 'like a new man. Do you realize,' he asked his friend, Dave Powers, 'that we had an air-strike [against Cuba] all arranged for Tuesday [just two days later]? Thank God it's all over.'[104]

Kennedy decided to accept the terms of the message in the same way that he had received it – over the radio. James A. Nathan has described this as a 'considerable departure from diplomacy'.[105] But there was nothing diplomatic about this particular communication; it was not an act of negotiation or the basis for further discussion, but was rather a public announcement of intention which, by its very nature, lacked flexibility and the propensity for compromise. If either side did try to bargain they would appear to be retreating in the face of public opinion, and as a result their reputation would be tarnished.

This has both its advantages and disadvantages; one benefit of using the media to engage in diplomacy makes retreat over an issue, or once a decision has been reached, difficult.

At the same time, however, there is a considerable risk involved. Traditional diplomatic negotiation, conducted in private, allows for compromise, flexibility and any necessary face-saving actions. These have all been jeopardised by the growing tendency to use the electronic media in foreign policy. It has already been suggested for example, that Kennedy recognised this and dubiously used it to his advantage at the onset of the crisis by publicly announcing his knowledge of the missiles in Cuba. This made quiet retreat by the Soviet leader impossible, and only exacerbated the crisis. One central argument of this book is that the use of the media in the foreign policy process is not a substitute for traditional diplomacy, and this is clearly demonstrated by the Cuban missile crisis. A recognition of this is suggested not only by the many private communications which passed between various representatives of the belligerents, but also by the fact that a 'hot-line' was established soon after the Cuban missile crisis to allow quick but private communication between the leaders of the Superpowers. This can be considered as an important compromise between relying on traditional diplomatic channels and full dependence on public diplomacy, while retaining the all-essential private element that many diplomatic situations still demand.

Kennedy's welcome of Khrushchev's decision was duly reported by Tass and in Moscow Radio's home service on 28 October and his reply was given textually in an unscheduled bulletin early the next day, though it was not published in Russian newspapers until 30 October. The Soviet media still presented a very one-sided picture of events, and their treatment of the resolution was designed to strengthen Khrushchev's image as a hero who had taken a firm stand to avert war. North America was told by Radio Moscow that the Soviet government's decision to end the crisis should not be regarded as a sign of weakness. On the contrary, it had 'displayed forbearance ... in an effort to keep world peace. It did a service to all of humanity with a courageous restraint and refusal to be provoked, for it saved the world from thermonuclear disaster. This was a display of might and statesmanship, not weakness. Only a country confident of its strength could take the stand the USSR has taken.[106] That the town of Khrushchev quickly changed its name to Kremeges was purely coincidental, and should not be taken to indicate any prevailing displeasure with the ageing Soviet leader!

Thus the Cuban missile crisis was resolved. Both the Soviets and the Americans has used the radio to communicate directly with each other, complementing the traditional channels of diplomacy and negotiation. Khrushchev used this method knowing the situation demanded that his words be monitored and reported long before the official communiqués reached the Oval Office, and in the circumstances time was certainly of the essence. Khrushchev's first letter of the 26 October had been subject to a long delay in its transmission to Washington from the embassy. This was a gamble the Soviet leaders were no longer prepared to take. The time saved by using the radio was actually a full two hours, a lifetime between peace and nuclear holocaust. The value of the BBC monitoring service was therefore recognised by both sides, and its contribution to the diplomatic process was confirmed. It admirably overcame the inevitable time problems caused by recording, translating, verifying and then sending the material to the recipient. Khrushchev's message was instantly translated, and its content immediately teletyped to the appropriate quarters.

In contrast to both Superpowers, the British government was slow to recognise the diplomatic power of radio. In his memoirs, the British Prime Minister, Harold Macmillan, lamented his decision to send his government's message to Khrushchev, which affirmed British support for America's demands, using conventional channels. He recalled that the message was 'sent off at 12 noon [on 28 October]. As we were all finishing luncheon together, the news came (by radio) that the Russians had given in.' Macmillan noted that the British message was not published until after the Russians had made their public climb-down: 'It almost seemed as if we had sent the telegram backing the horse *after* the race.'[107] Just how much this was of concern to the Cabinet is revealed in documents not opened until the early 1990s. The record shows how the Prime Minister expressed his disappointment that his message

> had been delivered in Moscow at about the time that Mr. Khrushchev despatched and gave publicity to his final decision to withdraw the missiles under United Nations supervision. This sharpened the political dilemma in which the government found themselves. In fact we had played an active and helpful part in bringing matters to their present conclusion, but in public little had been said and the impression had been created that we have been playing a purely passive role.[108]

INCIDENT CLOSED

In a display of statesman-like caution Kennedy was adamant that there should be no overt victory celebration marking the end of the crisis for fear of provoking a hard-line coup against Khrushchev, and in the long-term such prudence paid off. Michael Beschloss has commented: 'Testifying to the difference between the journalism of 1962 and that of a later age, most of the reporters obeyed the request.'[109] According to Sorenson, however, the Voice of America was not as responsive, choosing to report American 'jubilation' despite official directives calling for refrain from such celebration.[110] In addition to the tentative diplomatic progress that was made, the Soviets ended all jamming of western broadcasts; in return the US abandoned its use of the 173 kc wavelength, which had been assigned to Moscow Radio by the 1948 Copenhagen Convention but hijacked by VOA in 1953.

In the end Khrushchev did have to pay a high price for the resolution of the crisis, one aspect of which was a striking downturn in Soviet–Cuban relations. Khrushchev had decided to withdraw the missiles without consulting Castro who first heard of the settlement from the radio.[111] He tried to temper Castro's indignation at having been slighted in this way but told the Cuban leader he would not reveal the reply to Kennedy's message since he would hear it on the radio. It did little good: 'We felt great indignation,' Castro has since recalled. 'It was deeply humiliating.'[112] Indeed, Castro's humiliation was succinctly described by Alfred Sherman in a 1963 BBC General News Talk. '1962 has been a poor year for Castro,' he said. 'Exposed at home and in the eyes of Latin America as a pawn to be bargained over by Kennedy and Khrushchev, unable to dislodge his Latin American rivals and unable to fulfil his promises to his own people.'[113] Western propagandists made an intensive effort to exploit this clearly defined rift within the Communist bloc. The British Ambassador in Havana, Sir Herbert Marchant, believed that it was now the 'most opportune moment for maximum information efforts by the United States with their radio programmes'. One reason was the possibility (though not probability) of a 'sudden and dramatic turn against the Government'.[114] The main reason however, was an avowed concern among European Ambassadors to Cuba that 'neither Castro nor Communism has yet been discredited in the minds of most government supporters. [The] Onward crusade of Khrushchev,' wrote Marchant, 'defiance of Castro against the inhuman Yankee, food blockade, brotherly support of Communist countries, have all been played up to the exclusion of the facts. From the version of events at present available to the Cuban public it would appear that the United States and not Russia have climbed down, and that Castro and Khrushchev (in that order) have succeeded in frustrating imperialist aggression.' Marchant advocated that radio programmes (whether he was referring to the BBC is not made clear) should 'emphasise the satellite status of Cuba', and demonstrate how Castro had been completely excluded from the present dialogue between the Superpowers. Marchant then suggested that the main effort of such propaganda should be in Spanish language broadcasts on medium-wave, while short-wave broadcasts were no longer subjected to jamming, the target of propaganda – the ordinary public – did not own short-wave receivers.[115]

Then again on 1 November 1962, Marchant told of how most Cubans who relied on their own media for information were still unaware that offensive Soviet weapons had been at the heart of the crisis, preferring instead to blame 'Yankee aggression'. He then described how: 'Disruption of normal life of business and industry, extra staff and militia duties must lower morale of doubters and unbelievers. I believe,' he said, 'the Voice of America factual programmes are just right at this moment for this news-hungry public. Result of wide enquiries during the last three days fully supports my belief that medium-wave is most important channel.'[116] Why Marchant should be praising VOA to the Foreign Office in this way remains unexplained. It nevertheless indicates that the power of radio communication was recognised by the British foreign policy elite, and such an admission is most significant.[117]

Relations between the Soviet Union and China, already very tenuous and set on their own collision course, also suffered from the outcome of the missile crisis. The Chinese now labelled Khrushchev a reckless 'adventurer' and 'appeaser', while the *People's Daily* lamented the fact that in 'no circumstances can the people of the world trust the empty promises of the American aggressor'.[118] The *People's Daily* published the exchanges between Kennedy and Khrushchev without comment. According to staff of the British embassy in Peking, this left the Chinese reader 'free to put two and two together and conclude that Khrushchev has sold out Castro for no good reason'.[119]

As late as 6 November the Chinese press still concentrated on Cuba, despite China's ongoing border dispute with India being of more immediate concern. Officials at the British embassy reported how Peking was 'plastered with Castro's portraits, pro-Cuban slogans and Cuban flags; . . . So far from showing any tendency to cut losses,' they said, 'Chinese have done everything to magnify crisis and to evoke crescendo of pro-Cuban fervour. [The] Crisis is represented as direct confrontation between Cuban revolution and aggressive American imperialism.'[120]

Such criticism seemed all the more justified when problems arose over the speed of the dismantling and the question of on-site verification. Again the airwaves were filled with claims and counter-claims as both sides accused the other of reneging on the agreements. The US believed that the blockade should remain until all the missiles were dismantled and shipped away; in turn Tass accused the US of 'trying to evade its ... commitments to ... respect [Cuba's] sovereignty and not attack Cuba' despite the fact that the Soviet Union was engaged in 'honestly fulfilling its commitments and had already dismantled launching pads and rockets'. Radio Tirana, broadcasting from Albania, had already warned the Cuban people to look to their own experience to see that 'Kennedy and the imperialist monopolies represented by Kennedy cannot be trusted',[121] while Havana Radio said that Cubans 'do not believe in the words of Kennedy, but moreover, Kennedy has not given any word. And if he gave it he has already retracted it.'

The BBC joined the debate when its commentator, S. Mayers, reflected on the fact that had the Soviet Union not 'rashly intruded into the western hemisphere with powerful offensive weapons, the crisis would never have arisen in the first place.' In spite of Khrushchev's guarantees of withdrawal, he said, the UN had been unable to verify it was proceeding. 'Because of this,' concluded Mayers, 'and because there has been no agreement either on international arrangements to prevent any re-introduction of Soviet offensive weapons in to Cuba – again promised by Mr. Khrushchev – President Kennedy has not felt able or obliged to give a formal pledge that Cuba will not be invaded.'[122] Such comments are consistent with a report prepared by John Drinkall of the Information Research Department which outlined probable Soviet propaganda themes and possible responses following the resolution of the immediate crisis. As has already been suggested, the Soviet media was vociferous in its attempts to portray Khrushchev as a peacemaker. Drinkall advocated a response designed to illustrate how Khrushchev's actions had been provocative (the 'worst example of "brinkmanship" the world has yet seen'), deceitful to the west as well as the Cuban and Russian people, and 'without regard for the interests of the Cuban people'.[123] In his judgement Soviet propaganda would focus on the success of the Cuban venture and try to show how Cuba's independence had been secured, while the US were forced to give an assurance that there would be no invasion, all of which was achieved by the deployment of defensive missiles. Soviet propaganda had also

compared Turkey and Cuba; hence Drinkall reiterated that US bases
in Turkey were designed to counter Soviet aggression and expansion
as part of a regional defence permitted under the UN Charter, and that
their installation had been far from clandestine. He believed that the
Soviets would then try to portray themselves as a government working
through the auspices of the UN, in contrast to the United States which
used that organisation merely as a 'rubber stamp for aggression'. Drinkall
countered this by writing that the 'Soviet government is only supporting the United Nations because it is embarrassed at having been caught
out. Soviet actions in Cuba were entirely contrary to the spirit of the
UN.' Should the question of Berlin be raised, Drinkall advised its ac-
knowledgment as a legitimate subject for negotiation, but improve-
ments would be created *only* via negotiation, not by provocation. In
conclusion, Drinkall recorded that the missile crisis had 'shown the
extent to which the Soviet Government is prepared to involve small
nations in power politics. It should serve as a warning to nonaligned
countries considering close links with the Soviet Union'.[124]

Now while it is impossible to say that the BBC followed this and
similar reports to the letter, it is clear that many of the themes addressed
in BBC broadcasts did at least correspond to such advice as was offered; and given the close IRD–BBC link which has been described in
previous chapters, it is not impossible that this report *was* seen by the
BBC and used in its output. Until the relevant IRD documents are
declassified, however, this must remain the subject of speculation.

In the context of the Cold War, the defusing of the Cuban missile
crisis represented a step of progress in the conduct of international
relations: it had been the first real crisis of nuclear proportions; it
provided the pretext for further negotiation between the Superpowers
that paved the way towards an eventual, but short-lived, détente; and
it facilitated their relationship in that the need for a direct line of communication between the White House and the Kremlin – the so-called
'Hot Line' – was recognised and accepted. More importantly for the
purposes of this study, while Kennedy and Khrushchev conversed with
each other through traditional channels, radio had been explicitly used
as an integral part of the diplomatic procedure, marking a watershed
in global broadcasting on a series of levels. The Soviet Union was
forced by circumstance to recognise that the value of radio was no
longer rooted merely in propaganda, the importance of the monitoring
service was acknowledged, and public opinion was accorded a position as a contributory factor in the formulation of political foreign
policy. At the start of the crisis the British Ambassador in Havana, Sir

Herbert Marchant, had advocated the launch of a 'really serious propaganda exercise' by the US. 'I mean really serious and probably expensive, but still cheaper than a war.'[125] Such an observation implies recognition that propaganda can often be a substitute for military conflict, as the missile crisis vividly illustrated.

Together the Bay of Pigs invasion and the Cuban missile crisis had confirmed the importance of harmonising government action with propaganda and broadcasting policy. It had not been easy; the gravity of the crisis had forced the USIA into supervising VOA broadcasts to a degree that had so far been avoided. The crisis also opened up deep wounds between VOA and its parent agency. Director of VOA, Henry Loomis, told Ed Murrow that the station 'failed to sound convincing because of our monolithic tone. . . . During the . . . crisis,' he said, 'we were required to distort and concentrate our programme at the expense of credibility and relevance to our audience.' Loomis believed that by broadcasting Presidential and State Department pronouncements, the Voice suffered from a markedly dull output and at the same time revealed itself to be a propaganda station.[126] However, given the scope and nature of the crisis, this comment is unjustified. At a time when the political risks were incredibly high, when the future of the whole world was at stake, audiences to foreign radio broadcasts (which inevitably increase at times of major crises) were more interested in government pronouncements of intentions rather than often wild speculation. As America's involvement in Vietnam continued to escalate this dichotomy posed by VOA's dual purpose was exacerbated, and the relationship which the government enjoyed with its propaganda agencies was to prove crucial.

5 The Commitment to Vietnam: Hearts and Minds

Listening to the Voice of America is like letting a thief into your house who will steal your soul.

Viet Cong poster[1]

INTRODUCTION

The showdown over Cuba, together with the construction of the Berlin Wall in 1961, produced a refreshing new element of stability within the international system; the Cold War in Europe had reached an impasse, and each side was now more certain than ever of its relations with the other.

Wishing to capitalise on this new order, President Kennedy publicly suggested on 9 June 1963 that the superpowers explore the possibility of arms control, beginning with a nuclear test-ban. The President took this opportunity to announce a unilateral US moratorium on aboveground nuclear tests to prove his sincerity. The Voice of America carried the speech in Russian, and only one paragraph which talked of 'baseless' Soviet claims about American purposes was jammed. However, such interference in western radio broadcasts stopped almost immediately, suggesting a new era of détente was emerging in both politics and international radio broadcasting.

In return for the American moratorium the Soviets agreed to allow their nuclear power stations to be inspected, and within six weeks of Kennedy's speech they signed a Limited Test Ban Treaty with the Americans.

So the United States had discovered a renewed confidence in foreign policy after the disasters of the previous two years, and it is possible that this may account for the intensified American effort in Vietnam. But as the record would show, America's involvement in South East Asia belied such optimism.

The protracted and complex nature of the wars in Indo-China render any attempt to trace the whole of the American propaganda and information efforts impossible. This chapter will therefore assume a narrower focus than previous chapters and examine two specific events from the long American commitment to Vietnam, both of which clearly demonstrate the involvement of radio broadcasting in diplomacy. First, the events of 1963 are analysed, when Buddhist demonstrations and the continuing corruption of the South Vietnamese regime provoked an American-backed coup. This had enormous implications for the Voice of America and forced the station to reappraise its role in American foreign policy.

Next there will follow a discussion of how the VOA explained the escalation of American involvement which occurred in the immediate aftermath of the so-called Gulf of Tonkin incident. This suggests that the station still suffered from an acute identity crisis which made its work at best difficult, at worst inefficient.

MEANS AND ENDS

In 1961 Ngo Dinh Nhu, the powerful brother of the President of South Vietnam, flippantly remarked that western propaganda simply did not exist.[2] But it seems that Nhu overlooked the long history of USIA's involvement in the region; USIA had established posts throughout Indo-China – in Cambodia, Laos, and of course in Vietnam itself – as early as the 1954 Geneva Conferences on South-East Asia. This was regarded as necessary since these were areas 'expected to be ideological battlegrounds with Communist infiltration and subversion literally at the Paddy level'.[3] A year later VOA was broadcasting to the Far East in English (1 hour), Mandarin (1 hour 30 minutes), Cantonese (1 hour), Vietnamese (1 hour) and Russian (3 hours). A 30 minute service in Cambodian was then added, only to be dropped again in 1957.

The pattern of this schedule was a reflection of the way American interests in the Far East dictated which of its global involvements were of more importance and required a greater information/propaganda effort. The cost of this expansion of broadcasting was the termination of all short-wave transmissions to western Europe in French, German, Spanish and Italian. Allied audiences were therefore sacrificed yet again to the crusade against Communism, this time in the Far East. However, by the end of 1961 the growing tension in South East Asia and America's expanding commitment necessitated the inauguration of Thai and Lao language services, in addition to the resumption of Cambodian.

So western propaganda against Communism in South East Asia did indeed exist. Whether it accurately reflected reality in that part of the world, or was ultimately successful, are entirely different questions.

The VOA also faced the added challenge of balancing its commitment to objective programming with its obligations to the foreign policy interests of the government. Ed Murrow's successor as Director of USIA, Carl Rowan, had no doubts as to where the responsibility of his agency should lie. VOA commentaries, he said, 'express ... the official opinion of the US government ... When there is a crisis, or when we are militarily engaged as we are now in Vietnam ... we simply cannot afford to have the intentions and objectives of the US government misunderstood by other governments'.[4] However, on assuming directorship of VOA in 1967, John Daly pondered on the identity crisis suffered by the station throughout its relatively brief life, and expressed his determination to have VOA report the division in the United States over Vietnam 'fully and fairly'. After all the Vietnam war was exciting news, and the priority of VOA was to report it. The drama then provided the pegs on which to hang the propaganda objectives.[5] But at the same time its political obligations as a government agency could not simply be ignored. As the Americans evacuated Saigon in 1975 the impact of this identity crisis proved overwhelming. Fearing that VOA broadcasts might only aggravate the panic among Saigon's civilian population the American Ambassador, Graham Martin, demanded that the station desist from reporting the situation. The politicians cared little for the argument that this would undoubtedly injure VOA's already fragile credibility, especially since all the major international stations would be covering the events anyway.

In contrast to VOA, the BBC's coverage of the Vietnam war was never attacked as being either too 'left' or too 'right'; instead Julian Hale has expressed his personal disappointment that the BBC was too balanced, that it presented the events from a 'centrist bias' rather than adopting a judgemental position on issues which could be considered morally and politically just. According to Hale, President Johnson was 'centerist' and such a position was therefore most preferable to the BBC.[6] But such criticism has no foundation whatsoever. BBC broadcasts were, as always, based on the premise that the 'objective truth, in so far as can be established – however unpalatable – is ultimately the most effective form of propaganda'.[7] The BBC's Vietnamese Programme Organiser, L.P. Breen, has testified that one reason for the BBC's popularity among the Vietnamese people during the war was their perception of its objectivity and impartiality.[8] Such a reputation was beyond the Voice of America because it was quite clearly the mouthpiece of the American government itself, and was heavily involved in its propaganda strategy.

Breen's testimony that the BBC's Vietnamese service had a large audience is based on his observations of the war taken in its entirety. In the early days of 1960, however, the Foreign Office could only describe the audience as 'faithful but probably small'. Little listening was reported in Saigon itself, but there was believed to be a 'respectable amount' elsewhere.[9] This small audience evidently included a number of influential figures. In 1959 the American Consul reported that Ngo Dinh Can, brother of the President and the unofficial leader of central Vietnam, was apparently a frequent listener to the BBC (as well as VOA) on a most impressive-sounding 'Zenith transoceanic portable radio'.[10] In addition, local stations often re-broadcast BBC material, but the Foreign Office was concerned that 'neutralist politics are making this increasingly irregular'.[11] By 1961 the Foreign Office had realised that the BBC could no longer compete with the combined Communist broadcasting force of North Vietnam, China and Russia, nor indeed with American or Australian efforts, while the extreme range made the audibility of BBC broadcasts 'relatively poor'.[12] Moreover, in what can now be viewed as a remarkable admission of guilt, the Foreign Office accepted that the BBC Asian services had been 'starved of funds'.[13]

Until such problems could be overcome, the United States remained the driving force behind propaganda to and within Vietnam, and there was sufficient evidence to suggest that its message was getting across. In September 1963, for example, the National Security Council learnt how the rural hamlets of South Vietnam were 'hanging on every word and living off VOA'[14]; in addition Murrow told the President that hamlet dwellers preferred 'uncensored VOA reports' to Vietnamese radio.[15] VOA therefore had an obligation to be accurate and trustworthy as a source of news and information. At the same time, however, it had an undeniable responsibility to American foreign policy. Murrow's words had implied that whatever VOA said, the South Vietnamese people listened – a promising position indeed for propaganda to find itself in – and so the government had to ensure that the people heard exactly what it wanted them to hear.

One of the most important tasks of American propaganda was to foster democracy in South Vietnam. To achieve such aspirations propaganda targeted three distinct groups:

1. Communists and their supporters in the South who were urged to abandon the fight;
2. the masses and élites of North Vietnam who were encouraged to

challenge the growing threat of Chinese imperialism and believe
that the ruling Communist party had betrayed the people; and
3. non-Communists in the South who were urged to support and
co-operate with their government and appreciate the merits of
living according to democratic values.

Such a strategy had actually been developed by none other than the
BBC's Hugh Greene when head of the British Emergency Information
Services in Malaya. The success of this campaign guaranteed that the
Americans would apply it as their model in Vietnam,[16] but with a number
of destructive modifications. In particular USIA sought to encourage
Vietnamese interest in the capitalist system by stressing the riches and
high standards of living it could bring. As a means of combating Communist dogma, however, such a strategy proved counter-productive in
the long term; the very poor merely felt aggravated and more disil-
lusioned with 'exploitative' capitalism. In turn the attraction of Communism, which invariably portrayed itself as a friend of the poor,
preaching social, political and economic revolution to create equality,
would grow. This inevitably assumed an added anti-American dimension, with Communist propaganda describing the war as a 'national
salvation struggle' against a 'foreign invader' and 'colonial oppres-
sor'. 'Every day', read a Viet Cong directive, 'a cadre of the party in
charge of propagandizing the masses must unveil the barbarous and
cruel face of the enemy to the population so they can be aware of the
pitiless plot and plundering activities, warfare and eager preparation to
turn South Vietnam into a US colony.'[17] Such themes were effective
because they played upon a natural Vietnamese hatred of anything which
remotely resembled colonialism.

   This tendency of Communist propaganda consistently to present the
government in Saigon as a puppet of the west meant that American
and South Vietnamese propaganda were constantly on the defensive
and was merely reactive. As Robert Chandler has written, the main
reason for the failure of American propaganda was its inability to 'cope
with the "foreign invader" stigma' and, more importantly, 'make up
for the weaknesses of the Saigon government'.[18]

CRISIS AND COUP

The repressive nature of Ngo Dinh Diem's régime had been an acute
embarrassment to the Americans since the late 1950s and contributed

to their hesitation to commit larger numbers of American combat troops to Vietnam. Loyalty to Diem was based far less on his democratic credentials (few and far between anyway) than on the fact that he was quite simply anti-Communist. President Kennedy himself defended American support of Diem in the flowery but largely meaningless rhetoric at which he excelled: 'We must work with some countries lacking in freedom in order to strengthen the cause of freedom,' he said in 1961.[19] Perhaps *Pravda* was not wrong when it later accused Kennedy of 'incomprehensible upside-down logic!'[20]

In December 1959, the American Ambassador to Saigon, Elbridge Durbrow, believed that the United States could not avoid being identified with Diem, though he considered this neither here nor there as long as 'the image the Government of South Vietnam presents is one which is, on balance, in conformity with our interests'. Besides, it was hoped that America's efforts to democratise South Vietnam would off-set the more negative aspects of the relationship.[21] Only four months earlier, however, Durbrow had been very concerned by Diem's denial of basic democratic rights when he blatantly manipulated what were supposed to be free elections.

This turn of events gave Hanoi's propaganda machine the ammunition it sought: Saigon's ability to present the elections as the very epitome of democracy was vastly outweighed by Communist exposure of their illegality and their violation of the Geneva Agreements.[22]

This parody of democracy was not the only problem; another was Diem's attitude – and that of Washington itself – to reunification. America's psychological warriors were required to counter the penetration among the civilian population and the military of VC propaganda which denounced the Diem régime and portrayed it as being 'opposed to . . . unification'. This, however, was American disinformation since an anonymous hand-written note on the text of this 1961 Basic Counter-Insurgency Plan read: 'easy on this [reunification]; he does oppose'.[23] The Americans had fashioned their Vietnam policy in the belief that the Geneva Agreements had effectively partitioned the country, and that the two halves were independent and sovereign states. The Agreements had not in fact made this provision, but the Americans knew that if they accepted the idea of Vietnam being one country, the pretext for the war and especially their growing involvement quickly vanished.

By 1963 the US could no longer bury its head in the sand and hope that Diem would just go quietly away. The war was slowly escalating beyond initial expectations, and American policy-makers gradually accepted that a stable régime in the South – specifically one that would not seek a compromise with the Communists in the North to hold on to some semblance of power – was crucial. Central to this was the removal of Diem, but planners would have been satisfied with the demise of his powerful but dangerous and hated brother, Ngo Dinh Nhu. The latter was seen to be the real power behind the throne and the main reason for the lack of popular support for the war effort. This was clearly recognised in 1962 by J.I. McGhie, Director of British Information Services in Saigon, who observed that while Nhu and his domineering wife preserved their 'position of unrivalled power' they would 'remain unrepentant opponents of any political reform. The picture', he concluded, 'is indeed a black one'.[24] But Nhu had also made himself personally unpopular; in the course of one discussion with an American diplomat he had made a series of brazen anti-American comments. He then 'capped all this with the reckless (and psychotic?) remark that the US should now mount an atomic attack on Peking'.[25]

It is not surprising then that staff at the American embassy should support Nhu's removal – the new Ambassador, Henry Cabot Lodge, was a vociferous advocate of such a scheme – and believed that VOA could play a fundamental role in exerting pressure on Diem to this end.[26] This was to be achieved by broadcasting a series of 'utterances' in Vietnamese on 'basic American ideals such as free speech, free press, habeas corpus, due process ... all men created equal, government is the servant of the people etc. At present,' said Lodge, 'virtually all these principles are being flagrantly violated in Vietnam.' Confident that ideas carried greater force than commercial or political sanctions, Lodge wanted VOA to 'arouse' Vietnamese opinion so much that the people would complain to him about the denial of democracy; this would then 'provide leverage to US foreign policy objectives' since Diem was greatly troubled by the power of ideas and the public opinion they fed.[27] But the Secretary of State for Defense, Robert McNamara, was not convinced, fearing that such a course of action would only 'inspire Diem to eject the USIS, which would be disastrous'.[28] More importantly, President Kennedy believed that Washington could make more propaganda capital out of the damage which Diem's repression had caused to the fight against the Viet Cong.[29]

Some of the embassy's recommendations were nevertheless adopted. In October 1963 VOA began to broadcast a series entitled 'Roots of Freedom' twice a day in Vietnamese and three times a day in English. Of only five minutes' duration, programmes addressed such grandiose themes as Thomas Jefferson and the Declaration of Independence, Tom

Paine and the Prince of Liberty, Abraham Lincoln and Government of the People, and Woodrow Wilson and the Rights of Small Nations. Whether they were effective is questionable; many of the abstract philosophical themes which these programmes discussed must surely have gone over the heads of ordinary peasants struggling to survive in Vietnam. Yet ever blinkered to reality, the State Department, provided with three sample scripts to give a flavour of the series, endorsed the idea.[30] Perhaps no other single act demonstrates so clearly the close relationship between VOA and foreign policy élites at this time.

To the problems posed by the repressive nature of Diem's régime were added the brutal suppression of Buddhist demonstrations in South Vietnam and the coup d'état that followed. The American political establishment continued to present itself as loyal to the régime but correspondents, living and working among the South Vietnamese, were fully aware of its almost complete lack of popular support. They did not lose sight of this contradiction; the head of USIS-Vietnam and former *Time* correspondent, John Mecklin, described how he 'found it hard to accept the embassy's sanguine views of ... Diem and even harder to accept [the American embassy's] policy of inadequately informing, if not misleading, the press'.[31] Nevertheless, a number of reporters refused to believe that the Administration could be misled by its own officials, and berated the VOA for carrying disquieting reports. Marguerite Higgins, a prolific and vehement pro-war reporter for the *New York Herald Tribune*, was said to have been 'distressed' by VOA's apparent reliance on dispatches by, among others, David Halberstam and Peter Arnett. She described such correspondents as 'a cabal of young men dedicated to pulling down Diem and whose reporting was synchronized distortion'.[32] VOA assured Higgins that many sources were used and urged her to examine the transcripts for confirmation. 'Maybe so,' said Higgins, 'but the fact was that the Voice, by feeding anti-Diem copy back to Saigon, was exacerbating an already difficult situation; they should depend more on State and CIA reporting'.[33] Marguerite Higgins was unaware that such 'anti-Diem copy' which fuelled popular sentiment against the régime was exactly what the State Department and the CIA wanted. This episode therefore illustrated how the VOA was directly involved in American policy towards Vietnam. Higgins also neglected to mention that Diem was already engineering his own downfall quite efficiently! His fate was finally sealed as trouble flared between his government and the Buddhists.

The Whole Place is Going Sky High![34]

On 8 May 1963, Buddhists gathered in Hue to celebrate the birthday of Buddha and protest against the government ban on the display of religious flags. The day began peacefully, but for some unexplained reason government troops opened fire into the crowds killing nine people. As 10 000 Buddhists marched to protest the killings two days later, Diem jailed the leading monks and their supporters. The government, increasingly isolated from the people, required a scapegoat for this latest setback in public relations, and therefore described the deaths at Hue as the responsibility of a Viet Cong terrorist attack.[35] However, the Buddhist movement was undeterred and, gathering momentum, spread rapidly throughout South Vietnam, taking root in the schools and universities. The western journalists in Saigon at first simply reproduced the official account of events, but they soon discovered contradictions once dramatic eyewitness stories began to pour in. According to Peter Arnett, the Buddhists realised that the correspondents were the 'crucial link to world opinion', and he has described how the protests grew after the people heard reports of the situation in foreign radio broadcasts.[36] The government feared that such demonstrations might provoke a new wave of social dissension, exposing an already vulnerable South to yet further Communist infiltration. This was certainly suggested by the monitoring reports of 'enemy' propaganda broadcasts. On 16 May 1963 the 'Liberation Broadcasting Station', controlled by the National Front for the Liberation of South Vietnam (NLFSV), condemned what it described as the 'bloody repression' of the Buddhists in which 12 had reportedly been killed and a further 100 arrested. Another commentary asserted that such demonstrations would continue until the United States had left Vietnam and the Diem government was destroyed.[37] But neither Diem nor Washington appreciated that the NLFSV was not a Communist organisation (although Communists were undoubtedly among its ranks); rather the Front was an umbrella organisation which included many non-Communists, united only by their common objective of overthrowing Diem, expelling the Americans, and reunifying Vietnam under the terms of the 1954 Geneva Agreements. In fact it is virtually impossible to identify a strong and close relationship between the Communists in Hanoi and the NLFSV. Had the differences between the two – often the cause of heated debate – been recognised, they might have been favourably exploited in propaganda. But by contextualising the war in the black and white language of being either Communist or non-Communist, the United

States failed to understand the real character of its enemy, and therefore lost an opportunity to isolate and fight it on its own terms with credible propaganda.[38] Even the British made this mistake. For example F.H. Johnson at the British embassy in Saigon denied that the broadcasting station of the NLFSV was genuine at all, let alone broadcasting from within Vietnam.[39] This impression persisted until April 1962 when the embassy received indication that Hanoi would begin to supply the NLFSV with aid and men, thus suggesting the North's direct intervention in the war since they would 'clearly have not authorized such a statement unless they were prepared to meet any demand for "men and materials"'.[40] J.I. McGhie perceptively noted that this pledge would not go any further unless the United States escalated their own commitment to the South.[41]

The Americans overlooked such reasoning, and USIA officials continued to describe the NLFSV as 'phoney' and the Viet Cong as 'a force with faceless leaders, puppets who take orders from Hanoi', while the claim made by Communists that this was 'an indigenous, patriotic rebellion' was itself denounced as 'absurd'.[42]

'Communist' was therefore merely a convenient catch-all term which was applied by Diem's régime to anyone who opposed it and, of course, was used in similar fashion by the Americans to justify their presence in Vietnam. Hence it came as no surprise when the Women's Solidarity Movement, spearheaded by the 'Dragon Lady' Madam Nhu, implied that the Buddhists had been infiltrated by the Communists. When one monk, Thich Quang Duc, set himself alight in the streets of Saigon as a protest on 11 June 1963, Madam Nhu casually remarked that all that the Buddhists had done was 'barbecue a bonze'.[43] But this act of self-immolation was of a deeper significance; once photographed, the world had a greater sense of the passion with which Diem was opposed.[44]

The Americans, now anxious that the matter be settled quickly but peacefully, and already implicated by Communist propaganda in the Buddhist suppression, threatened to dissociate US policy from Diem and demanded that Madame Nhu remain silent instead of merely aggravating an already delicate situation. But the Americans were not counting on Ngo Dinh Nhu's own brutality; on 21 August 1963, with his special forces disguised as airborne troops, he launched a raid against Buddhist pagodas. President Diem immediately declared a state of martial law in the hope of sustaining the illusion that his brother's actions had been fully supported by the army and the political establishment.[45]

Unaware of what had actually occurred, VOA, the embassy in Saigon, and even the CIA assumed that the pagoda raids had been carried out by the South Vietnamese Army (ARVN). Its generals, already plotting to overthrow the government, feared that this indictment would seriously weaken the army's morale and undermine its popular support. It was therefore important, they believed, that VOA vigorously refute the idea that the ARVN had been responsible for the raids.[46] Lodge agreed, and so on 26 August 1963 VOA confirmed that it had been 'Vietnam's secret police – not the army – which made the raids against Buddhist pagodas'. It continued:

> American officials said that based on latest reports from Vietnam the army agreed to the plan to put the nation under military law – but it did not know about the police plans to attack the Buddhists. These Washington officials say the raids were made by the police under the control of President Diem's brother, Ngo Dinh Nhu.[47]

In this way the ARVN were absolved from any guilt and Nhu was held entirely responsible. Yet the broadcast, cleared it might be added by the State Department, included an explicit warning that the United States might reduce its aid to Vietnam by $1.5 million per day if Diem did not dismiss those who had carried out the pagoda raids – namely Ngo Dinh Nhu. Hence VOA was again directly involved in American foreign policy. The United States was already sending signals to Diem that he was disliked in Washington – stories had 'leaked' out that Lodge personally objected to his style of rule, and President Kennedy had publicly criticised him. Nevertheless Lodge was furious with VOA and he cabled Washington from Saigon that the broadcast had 'just destroyed the chance of achieving surprise with a Generals coup'.[48] Nhu complained that American statements about Vietnam were 'accepted at face value by many other governments and [the] US was therefore injuring Vietnam's standing with foreign governments'. He then denied the allegations contained in the report 'in as much as it was the generals themselves who had specifically demanded the actions [against Buddhists]'.[49] Roger Hilsman, Assistant Secretary of State for Far Eastern Affairs, told the President that VOA had broadcast this threat 'contrary to explicit instructions that [it] should not become involved in speculation'.[50] Weldon Brown disagrees: 'Speculations about consequences were permissible', he has written, 'as long as labelled speculation', but admits that in this case 'a mix-up occurred, and the full story of our demands and threatened punishments got reported as our official view in Vietnam and the US'.[51] As Michael V. Forrestal of the NSC staff observed, VOA had 'goofed badly', and he told the

President that the attempt to 'correct the VOA broadcast itself is producing bad speculation in the wire services'. He added that Roger Hilsman was 'taking steps to get control of all US government output'.[52] VOA later announced that the State Department denied that aid to Vietnam was in jeopardy, but it was too late; the damage had already been done. Not only had irreparable harm been done to relations between the US and Diem, but the government's Vietnamese opposition had been led to believe that his downfall was imminent. VOA's involvement in American foreign policy had gone too far.

Coup

The strange thing is, however that VOA's involvement continued, based on a recognition that information and propaganda were vital to American policy towards South Vietnam. Attention now focused on how to overthrow Diem, an extremely sensitive political issue which required very delicate handling by the USIA. It is therefore not surprising that several USIA representatives – Ed Murrow and John Mecklin in particular – participated in high-level policy meetings at which the possibility of a coup was discussed, and that they even suggested methods by which the coup might be achieved. Murrow for example described how USIA would continue to 'give ample coverage in news output of expression of US displeasure with aspects of Diem régime', and would 'watch out for, and pick up, third country, Congressional and US nongovernmental comment critical of the repressive aspects of the Vietnamese government'.[53] In other words USIA and VOA could feed resentment of Diem, and in this way information would not only play a crucial role in American foreign policy, but would also become involved in shaping the internal affairs of Vietnam itself – not for the first time and certainly not for the last. South Vietnam's own media had already detected such an approach within USIA output. For example USIS press round-ups were criticised for being completely opposed to the South Vietnamese government, while VOA was said to have been 'consistently hostile . . . and launched a call for [indistinct word] rebellion last month'.[54]

So propaganda and diplomacy worked side by side with American foreign policy objectives until the Ngo family was finally removed from power in November 1963 by its own army. The change in government and speculations about American involvement (encouraged by such VOA broadcasts as those detailed above) now made propaganda difficult. However USIA projected an image of 'business as usual' in

Vietnam and throughout the world; USIA declared that the basic issues at stake in Vietnam remained constant, that the fight against Communism in South East Asia would continue. But life would not be that
easy; USIA, together with the government it represented, faced fresh
challenges as successor régimes could not sustain power and as the
war escalated beyond expectation. In addition USIA also had to de-
cide when to announce that aid would continue to be provided to the
new government. Accurate timing was essential if the US was not to
be viewed as having collaborated with the generals who had over-
thrown Diem. In the event USIA decided to be deliberately vague and
instead declare that America would 'continue to support the Vietnamese people in their efforts to defeat the Communist enemy and
build a better future', which measures up to much the same thing in
guarded diplomatic jargon.[55] Nevertheless support for the new régime
was unequivocal: 'This is the best chance of a successful coup we are
ever likely to have', noted one briefing paper, suggesting that USIA
should deny any foreknowledge about the coup.[56] The agency could
be economical with the truth when it suited it, and when it served
American policy.

The crisis generated by the Buddhist demonstrations, their suppression and the coup d'état had an enormous impact on VOA and USIA.
At long last USIA was a participant in high-level policy meetings at
which major political decisions were discussed and made. As we have
seen, Mecklin and Murrow were strident advocates of a coup against
Diem. Nevertheless USIA and VOA vigorously defended their own
independence, and there were moments when their interests conflicted
with those of the government. The unfortunate incident when VOA
broadcast threats made by the State Department to reduce American
aid in the aftermath of the pagoda raids is one example of this, and
was symptomatic of a deeper malaise. In situations where VOA had to
weigh its role as a source of news and information against its obligations to government, the station protected its responsibility as a news
organisation first and foremost. But the State Department would continue to do everything in its power to ensure that VOA remained a
malleable instrument of its policy. It was in fact quite an unsuccessful
partnership from a presentational point of view, but this was perhaps
due as much to the policy itself as the propaganda; the propaganda
could not hope to survive intact as long as questionable policies were
pursued on the ground in Vietnam.

The coup had resolved very little. Indeed in March 1964 Robert
McNamara told President Johnson that since Diem's murder, the situation

had 'unquestionably been growing worse'.[57] While VC control and influence held steady, and actually increased in some parts of South Vietnam, the new régime's power was weakening. Casualties from among the ranks of the South Vietnamese army steadily mounted, while attacks against American personnel were also rising. The stage was set for an unplanned escalation of a war that nobody, not even the new President of the United States, Lyndon Johnson, sufficiently understood.[58]

ESCALATION

As the war escalated following the so-called Gulf of Tonkin incident, American propaganda assumed a new and vital role, yet propagandists (and especially John Mecklin) became increasingly speculative, optimistic even, about its methods and possible influence. Such faith is worth considering in some detail because we will then have a greater sense of how a 'credibility gap' in the propaganda was created, and furthermore it will suggest some reasons why media diplomacy in this particular case failed. It must be pointed out that the secondary literature on propaganda and the VOA is rather unclear on this period of the Vietnam war, and so we must rely increasingly on the words of the participants themselves, many of whom expressed an unfounded confidence in America's renewed efforts.

For example propaganda became part of a strategy of gradual escalation which was prepared by McGeorge Bundy, a Presidential aide on National Security, and was designed to exert 'maximum psychological effect on the North's willingness to stop the insurgency'.[59] This involved, among things, exploiting the North's 'considerable internal difficulties', encouraging 'the fears and grievances of the population', and weakening Hanoi's 'capability for supporting the Viet Cong. If conditions have not required such an effort in the past,' wrote John Mecklin in March 1964, 'the struggle has now reached a degree of crisis where the US should not overlook any opportunity, however marginal, to hurt the enemy'.[60]

VOA's output was expanded so that it could reach North Vietnam much more successfully than in the past. This would become more urgent should military action against the North begin in earnest. According to Mecklin such development would make a 'maximum, crash effort' by VOA essential to 'spell out US intentions to [North Vietnam], as well as the rest of the Communist bloc. Since the object of such action would be to hurt the North Vietnamese and alarm the rest of the bloc,' he wrote, 'its effect would be the greater as the fact of our action and its motivation is the more widely known'. Preparations should then be made for 'massive, sustained VOA support' of such actions.[61] On the other hand if the US decided against any such course of action, Mecklin considered it 'equally essential' that 'VOA avoid empty threats – except as unavoidable in reporting news of the debate inside the US'. In this way any accusation of 'hotairmanship' might be avoided.[62]

Next, VOA's method had to be considered. American propaganda had so far made no attempt to take advantage of the failures of the Communist government to meet its promises to the people of North Vietnam, even after a decade in power. Mecklin therefore believed that by comparing the lifestyles within the two halves of Vietnam, broadcasts to the North might encourage popular discontent. Mecklin conceded that this was a 'difficult theme', but maintained that it might work with 'extensive research' and careful targeting.

So Mecklin identified which audiences should be targeted by the expanded broadcasts, the most significant of which were those 'most likely to have access to radio receivers'. Government officials and the officer corps of the military who were torn apart by factional disputes were therefore targeted. The intellectuals, students and remnants of the middle class were particularly important since intelligence reports had suggested that Hanoi was now having to respond to their demands and grievances. Propaganda could therefore serve to aggravate discontent by publicising their demands to a wider audience. Because such audiences had been 'instrumental in forcing liberalization of Communist régimes elsewhere,' Mecklin believed that they 'conceivably could play a similar role in North Vietnam'.

Finally Mecklin identified the peasants as a target of this renewed propaganda effort. Although most village radios were controlled by the party cadres for communal listening at fixed hours, it was assumed that whatever VOA had to say would reach them eventually, even if by word of mouth. 'The régime could not ignore widespread unrest among the peasants', wrote Mecklin, ' . . . and they should be considered a major target'. But Mecklin was careful to draw the line at incitement, stressing the VOA should not 'stimulate specific actions either by the North Vietnamese people or government'.[63] Obviously the lessons of Hungary and the Bay of Pigs had been well and truly learnt!

But was there any evidence that such an audience existed in North

Vietnam, or was Mecklin simply being overconfident of VOA's strength? In 1961 USIA had estimated that VOA had an audience of just 4 per cent in the North due to tight surveillance and a rather small ownership of radio sets.[64] As late as 1964 VOA still had 'very little evidence of any substantial listenership in the North or among the Viet Cong'.[65] However, lack of hard evidence is no guarantee of a complete absence of listeners; it must be remembered that audience research in North Vietnam was nonexistent, and instead USIA had to rely on the anecdotal and questionable testimonies of defectors, or 'ralliers' to the South; and given the importance of propaganda to that region, VOA and USIA *had* to assume that there was some listening, even if it was as small as four per cent of the population.

Yet John Mecklin protested that VOA was 'delivering only a marginal service into an area of immense importance to the US', and he advocated beginning at least a one-hour programme for the North, thereby increasing the total Vietnamese airtime by 50 per cent to three hours per day.[66] Considering the importance which the United States attached to Vietnam and its growing military involvement, this was wholly insufficient. To be effective the propaganda output should have kept pace with the political and military commitment to Vietnam. Instead propaganda and policy were out of synchronisation. However, the prevailing political climate was not favourable for anything more; the North was assumed to have become 'a stable police state whose people exert relatively little influence on the government and that the limited airtime available for Vietnamese language broadcasts would be more usefully directed to the region where the issue was in doubt.'[67] In North Vietnam the distribution of short-wave radios was limited to officials – a valid and quite necessary target for purposes of diplomatic communication, but it was vital that the masses themselves also be reached – and listening was controlled in 'standard police-state fashion'. In addition jamming was widespread, but this was merely one more fragment of evidence that a 'valuable and potential audience' existed.[68] Nevertheless, Mecklin was confident that if VOA said something that the North Vietnamese wanted to know, a surprising number would always find ways to listen and then pass on information by word of mouth. 'This was spectacularly the case in the South during the Buddhist crisis,' he testified, 'and it has happened repeatedly in other parts of the world. It is axiomatic in international radio broadcasting that jamming can almost always be circumvented by a determined listener'. Mecklin therefore suggested that any expansion of broadcasting operations to the North should be via medium-wave to reach the largest audience. Moreover broadcasts should be scheduled for a time of day considered to be safe, namely the evening when, under the cover of darkness, clandestine listening carried fewer risks of reprisal by the Communist authorities.[69]

Meanwhile the South was not to be ignored since 'that is where the present trouble largely lies'.[70] Propaganda now targeted North and South Vietnam simultaneously because, Mecklin acknowledged, 'any message that is really worthwhile in the South is bound to be at least as worthwhile north of the parallel. It increases credibility and effectiveness to let people feel they are listening in on each other's VOA broadcasts'. Mecklin concluded that 'a radio signal is indivisible and so should be the Voice of America'.[71]

There is a crucial reason for describing Mecklin's reorganisation of propaganda at such length: for all of his optimism and painstaking effort, broadcasts had absolutely no effect whatsoever on Hanoi's determination to continue supporting the VC. In this instance the influence of media diplomacy to alter Hanoi's political frame of reference was clearly limited. The weakness of the propaganda was itself one of the reasons for the failure of the diplomacy, since the latter was designed to persuade Hanoi to end support for the VC and negotiate a settlement; the main reason was the insufficiency of American power which neither the best propaganda nor diplomacy could work with.

Sending an indivisible radio signal and message is relatively easy if propaganda is consistent not only with policy, but with the acceptance of that policy at home, and if that propaganda does not deviate on either the domestic or international fronts. At the start of the 1960s the strength of the Cold War consensus was sufficient to approve of American involvement in Vietnam, subjecting this justification to neither scrutiny nor debate. Questionable acts can be accepted much more readily if the policy behind them is also accepted.

But the war escalated, the consensus began to crumble. More and more American bodies were returning home in bags, television began to show pictures of the devastating nature of the conflict, the anti-war lobby began to assert itself, and a fierce debate opened within America's political circles.

Both USIA and VOA were now forced to confront a unique challenge: the war had to continue to be projected as justified to world opinion, but also had to retain the support of both the South Vietnamese government and the people themselves – the first to sustain the fight against 'Communism,' the second to ensure its success. To succeed in these multiple objectives on multiple fronts, VOA had to guarantee credibility, which meant that defeats as well as victories had to be reported at a time when defeats were becoming much more numerous.

This need to preserve credibility often collided with VOA's obligation to act as the mouthpiece of the American government, which required it to explain and justify American policy, and project it in a most favourable way. Thus the Vietnam war precipitated an acute identity crisis, and this conflict of interests habitually had serious and harmful effects – for VOA itself, for VOA–government relations, and ultimately for American diplomacy, as the events of 1963 clearly demonstrate.

Meanwhile VOA virtually ignored the developing debate on Vietnam and thus suffered from a loss of credibility as the Communists began to use the widespread American dissent as ammunition for its own propaganda. VOA could not lie; it could not contradict such reports for the simple reason that they were true. But neither could VOA grant the debate the coverage it demanded, for then it would surely have been accused of undermining South Vietnamese confidence in the US, and weakening the morale of American combat troops and the whole justification for being there in the first place. Such issues as Civil Rights and the events at Little Rock could certainly be covered; but these were *domestic* issues, not part of the sacred area of foreign policy, despite the fact that they had just as much if not more negative propaganda value for the Communists.

The Vietnam war scarred the VOA almost as severely as the United States itself. Only after a number of re-examinations of its operations, involving an extraordinarily quick turnover in staff and directors, could VOA fully recover.

CONCLUSIONS

The Vietnam experience offers two key lessons for radio propaganda. The first is that there can be no substitute for indigenous propaganda. This requires more elaboration. Just as professional diplomats must learn to adapt to any new environment and work within it, so propagandists must bridge the culture gap, thoroughly understand the traditions, family life, social practices and value systems of the country they are targeting. In Vietnam the success of this was constrained by the failures of Saigon's propaganda itself. At first broadcasting policy closely followed the political choice of non-escalation which confined American involvement to advising and assisting the government of South Vietnam to fight its own war. Thus between 1958 and 1963 the joint efforts of the US government and the USIA were directed towards establishing a strictly Vietnamese press and broadcasting system. As General Edward Lansdale noted, the South required a 'vastly improved radio broadcasting means',[72] since its own was poorly organised, too negative and heavy, long-winded and boring, and was designed more to spread government information than counter enemy propaganda.

But it was not to be: American impatience with Vietnamese efforts persuaded USIA that it had to assume a more dominant role in order to do the job which the Vietnamese were so obviously incapable of doing themselves. Barry Zorthian mourned this decision: because indigenous propaganda understood the ethics, values and customs of its audience and could adapt them for its own requirements, the expanded American effort was 'doomed to failure before it started'.[73]

However, it is quite extraordinary that in fact the USIA is well suited for such a task. For example USIA certainly did carry out extensive surveys into existing conditions and audience requirements throughout Indo-China. In July 1961 for example, John Anspacher of USIS-Saigon reported that 'under way is a two part study of Vietnamese society, embracing its demographic composition, general economic and educational levels, influence patterns . . . social relations etc'.[74] To account for the propaganda defeat in Vietnam one can only assume that either the results of these surveys were not made available to the relevant propagandists and foreign policy élites, that they were not used adequately, or that they were simply ignored. Since national policy must be consistent with propaganda, and since such research would be of enormous benefit to American foreign policy overall, this was a momentous oversight.

The expanded propaganda effort into North Vietnam had several serious diplomatic implications. In its broadcasts to North Vietnam, VOA decided to use the serious economic difficulties the regime was suffering as a prominent theme. John Mecklin, however, warned that this should be done 'with utmost caution':[75]

There is less reliable evidence about North Vietnam than perhaps any other Communist country. Since propaganda about, say, rice rationing with inaccurate information is instantly ridiculed, making the rest of the message suspect too, it is essential to avoid specifics in the absence of solid intelligence. This is particularly the case in material directed to [North Vietnam] since the [South] for years has been broadcasting to the North with reckless indifference to credibility.[76]

In Vietnam messages were often received by eavesdropping audiences for whom they were not originally intended, but eventually had to accommodate. This is clearly illustrated with reference to the role of China and coverage of its involvement.

In March 1958 USIS-Saigon used the story of refugees from China and Hainan arriving in South Vietnam. USIS and the Vietnam Press news agency supplied a number of media outlets, including VOA, with details of their interviews with the refugees. This was regarded as a 'substantial' opportunity to report a story which would 'damage the opposition, enhance the prestige of western-oriented free nations, and echo the thesis that although Communism has swallowed large territories, frequent rumblings of indigestion cannot be stilled'. The report concluded that USIS would continue to 'assure that these embarrassing sounds are amplified'.[77]

By 1964, USIA's use of the so-called 'China-card' assumed new dimensions, as it decided to play upon the traditional enmity between Vietnam and China, and portray the war in South Vietnam as an example of Chinese imperialism. Vietnam was thus warned of the 'angry slippage toward total, helpless colonial captivity'.[78] In addition American propaganda adopted a surprisingly racist tone: the Chinese, described as a naturally greedy race, would loot and exploit Vietnam if they were allowed a foothold in the country, which was guaranteed if the VC were victorious.[79] But the dangers of this were also recognised. Murrow described how USIA could only reach North Vietnam by radio, and warned that 'we must constantly keep in mind that anything which VOA broadcasts in the Vietnamese language can be heard by listeners in both North and South Vietnam'.[80]

There were various diplomatic problems associated with using China as a propaganda theme. For example, by placing too much emphasis on the evolving partnership between North Vietnam and China, VOA risked intensifying the 'dimensions of threat that looms from the North. . . . Since one of our propaganda objectives in South Vietnam has been to dispel the illusion that VC are 10 ft tall,' cautioned Murrow, 'unless very carefully handled the addition of the Chinese factor might prove counter-productive'.[81] In other words, Murrow was worried that because VOA broadcasts to North Vietnam could also be heard in the South, any undue emphasis on Chinese assistance might only have inflated the perception of the threat. This would then have had two possible effects: the South Vietnamese may have been more unwilling than ever to fight given the added Chinese factor and been induced to seek peace terms with North Vietnam; or they may have conceived it to be necessary to step up their demands for an increased American combat commitment, something that the United States was not prepared to do at this stage.

The second lesson of the Vietnam experience is that propaganda can only reflect the policies of the government it represents. If those policies are judged to be wrong – practically or morally – then no amount of propaganda will convince otherwise. The repressive nature of the Diem régime made propaganda designed to encourage support for it incredibly difficult. In 1961, for example, John Anspacher, the Public Affairs Officer attached to the American embassy in Saigon, told his seniors that it was impossible to 'do more' with the régime's image than it was doing itself. 'In other words,' he said, 'unless we rely on distortion, whatever we mirror will be a reflection of the face the [Government of South Vietnam] presents to the world.'[82]

Equally, it is essential that broadcasting and national policy correlate with each other. USIA clearly understood the importance of this and expressed a concern that 'we do not deceive ourselves into thinking we can play some role independent of basic national policy and actions. . . . Broadcasting', USIA continued, 'can make these policies and actions better and more widely known and understood – thus more effective. Broadcasting should not, certainly when it is attributed to the US or those whose actions we can influence, attempt to do anything else'.[83] This is certainly a powerful reminder of the limited power of propaganda, and reinforces the notion that propaganda itself is limited by policy objectives and the methods of fufilling them.

While America's propaganda failure can thus be explained away, one can still only partially account for the failure of America's radio *diplomacy* in persuading Hanoi not to continue supporting the Viet Cong. Effective diplomacy is often reinforced by propaganda which communicates a sense of credible (political or military) power. But this crucial element was lacking in America's diplomatic efforts towards Hanoi. In other words neither propaganda nor diplomacy were adequate substitutes for power.

The failures of American propaganda and radio diplomacy in Vietnam are best summarised by Thomas Sorenson. Writing about the massive surprise attacks launched by the Viet Cong in 1968, he believed that these could not have been successful if both the régime in Saigon and the American presence had enjoyed firmly-rooted popular support. This serves to demonstrate the 'hard lessons USIA learnt in Vietnam':

> In war, especially civil war, conventional propaganda and psychological warfare are only effective when victories are won on the field and morale-building political and economic reforms achieved behind the lines: There is no US government agency truly qualified

and staffed to conduct psychological operations in a war the size of Vietnam. USIA requires more men and money than available in peacetime to do the job properly. Propaganda cannot make bad policy palatable.[84]

Conclusion

A SUMMARY

In addition to offering a new and, it is hoped, exciting perspective from which to view the Cold War, this book has identified a strong relationship between diplomacy and international radio broadcasting by interweaving its subject on two levels. First, the study has described the activities of the BBC and Voice of America specifically. It has been an account of their often tortuous progression from enjoying little more than an indeterminate status after the Second World War to finally being fully accepted and integrated into the foreign policy process. Despite claims to the contrary, there was very little to differentiate between the BBC and VOA during the period under consideration. This is a bold statement, one which would surely raise many an eyebrow in Bush House! Yet this book does confirm that the two stations were in fact very similar in their objectives, application and approach: both have been used as agents of their government's propaganda and as the cardinal means by which their foreign policies have been projected. Ultimately the difference is essentially semantic; while the VOA is without question the voice of the American government (Vietnam notwithstanding), the BBC has tended to be regarded as the mouthpiece of the British government by its audiences throughout the world. The BBC's clear link with the Foreign Office Information Research Department is yet further verification of its propaganda objectives, while commentaries prepared by 'independent experts' convey a marked consistency with government policy. Together with Foreign Office control of its finances and broadcasting schedule, these make the BBC's claim of complete objectivity and independence questionable.

Second, the preceding chapters have isolated and examined in detail four case studies from the 1956–64 period – the Suez crisis, the Hungarian uprising, the Cuban missile crisis and the Vietnam war – to determine what insights about radio diplomacy and propaganda they can offer. But it is essential that the reader locate these events squarely within the context of the Cold War, which radio propaganda certainly helped to sustain as an endemic state by perpetuating tensions, attitudes and predispositions.

It is equally important to observe how the BBC and the Voice of

America maintained an often intricate relationship with their respective governments, foreign and intelligence services, and official propaganda agencies. In short, each event in the period represents a significant staging-post in the development of the BBC, the VOA, and their relationship to the shaping, implementation, and projection of foreign policy.

Broadcasting has certainly made an invaluable contribution to the diplomatic process by facilitating a state's relations with both its protagonists and allies – existing and potential. But it has also been necessary to illustrate how this is actually a two-way process. Hence the relationship forged by the BBC, VOA and government policy with incoming radio transmissions as monitored by the BBC and FBIS, has been scrutinised in detail. Their value to the diplomatic process has been inestimable. Given that one function of the diplomat is to obtain information in order that the prevailing and likely trends, intentions, responses, motivations etc. of a particular state might be identified and analysed, the monitoring of radio broadcasts is itself a technique of diplomacy. Monitored radio transmissions allow a state to gain a greater understanding of how its policies and intentions have been received in the target countries.[1] Furthermore, they have also acted as an important channel of diplomatic communication in their own right, as the events of the Cuban missile crisis dramatically confirm. Of course the problem associated with monitoring is that by relying too heavily on official sources the diplomat may be obtaining nothing more useful than a distorted version of reality.

At the same time it is imperative not to ascribe to broadcasting more influence than it warrants. As David Wade of *The Times* remarked in another context, 'in a comparative desert, a cup of water can get to look like a lake'.[2] The events examined in this study were, first and foremost, *diplomatic* events, motivated by political circumstances and shaped by politicians and statesmen who made their decisions independently of the media. These decisions were then reflected by the policies which governed broadcasts, as well as by the output itself.

This is most strikingly illustrated by reference to the Suez crisis. The motivation behind the Voice of the Arabs radio station was clearly political, based on Egypt's perception of its status in the Arab world. Its transmissions contributed to Jordan's decisions to dismiss General Glubb and not join the Baghdad Pact, but was not responsible for them. The British largely interpreted these actions as the consequence of Egyptian propaganda because it was easier than admitting to problems in the Anglo-Jordanian relationship and Britain's weakening status in the Middle East. Would General Glubb, the most vociferous opponent of Egyptian propaganda, have conceded that his dismissal was due more to personal animosity between himself and the King of Jordan? Similarly British policy was affected by the radio propaganda aligned against it. But ultimately, the decision taken by the British government to react to the nationalisation of the Suez crisis in the way it did was a political decision, made independently of the media.

Such considerations must also be applied to the other case studies. Since the onset of the Cold War, western broadcasters and Radio Free Europe in particular, had been encouraging (rather than demanding) revolutionary change in the Soviet satellite states. Other stations, such as the BBC, had accented the importance of achieving such change by 'peaceful methods'. Had the United States been basing foreign policy on its hardline crusading Cold War propaganda, then direct American involvement in the 1956 Hungarian uprising should have been forthcoming. But geographical, strategic and diplomatic considerations were paramount and, American propaganda notwithstanding, Hungarian insurgents faced the Soviet tanks alone. That many Hungarians had expected American military intervention on their behalf suggests that: (i) there was a breakdown in communication between American policy-makers and the propagandists; and (ii) if the mistakes of Hungary were to be avoided in the future, it was imperative that propagandists consider how the target audience would react to broadcasts.

Another function of the diplomat is to provide advice and contribute to policy. K.J. Holsti has written that this derives 'from their skill of interpretation and judgement about conditions in the country to which they are accredited. But even if diplomats are particularly useful in this capacity, it does not mean that their judgment will always be considered or that their advice or warnings will be heeded.'[3] This description can be most readily applied to the propagandist who has a similar role to play in the foreign policy process, and can be completely ignored by the politicians if their views clash. This is unfortunate; if nothing else propagandists are at least aware of how policies and decisions will be received in the target countries, and they understand the importance of public opinion to their ultimate success. All too often, this study has been the story of the failure to appreciate this. The Americans only finally recognised the necessity of involving VOA in the foreign policy process in the aftermath of the disastrous 1961 Bay of Pigs invasion, when the director of USIA was made a full member of the National Security Council.

However, the policy under consideration must be equally creditable. Again Britain's management of the Suez crisis is particularly instructive. The British government accepted that the question of the legality of the Canal's nationalisation was vague and largely indeterminate; Egypt promised that compensation would be paid to the shareholders and guaranteed that the passage of ships through the Canal would be unhindered. Nevertheless, in order that this perceived threat to their strategic interests might be reversed, Britain entered into collusion with France and Israel, bypassed the United Nations, and virtually ignored the protestations of its traditional ally, the United States. The military campaign against Egypt enjoyed little support throughout the world, and allowed Nasser to be observed as the injured party. No amount of propaganda or public relations skills could improve that situation; because the crisis was politically mishandled, it was also mishandled from a presentational point of view.

Coverage of the Hungarian uprising was more successful than Suez for two fundamental reasons. First, the issue was less vague; the Hungarian uprising could be viewed and thus presented from the black – or rather red – and white perspective favoured by Cold War propagandists, which enabled the Soviet Union to be depicted as the villain with little difficulty. In contrast attempts to demonise Nasser failed because he was never widely accepted as the true protagonist of the Suez crisis, especially among the increasingly influential non-aligned bloc of states.

Since the rationale behind the Cold War was a superpower confrontation based at least rhetorically on a collision of ideologies, and because this consumed most of the energy of politicians and propagandists alike, the BBC and VOA were relatively well prepared to combat what was regarded as the Soviet menace in Hungary. For the same reason, American propaganda and public diplomacy during the Cuban missile crisis was a resounding success.

In Vietnam, however, the Americans would certainly have preferred to observe the situation in stark Cold War terms, but could never quite see through the fog which enveloped their involvement. The US could never determine whether they were fighting against a Southern rebel force or Communists, fighting only Northern Communists, or if Vietnam was merely a war by proxy, fought at the instigation of red China and the Soviet Union; perhaps it was a combination of all three. In other words the Americans never really decided which war they were fighting, and confusion was added by their attempts to win 'hearts and minds' in the South. In such a complex situation, propaganda could never really make an impact for it had no clear identity, especially when it became entangled and ultimately conflicted with the aims of psychological warfare.

One further general conclusion can be drawn at this stage: international broadcasters and their governments or foreign services must work together. This has been very difficult to achieve, and the relationship between the British government and the BBC has suffered its consequences the most. The government consistently misunderstood the process by which the BBC overseas services operate; the politicians and their mandarins all too frequently assumed that language services could be introduced, or the times of their transmissions lengthened, as crisis circumstances dictated. Then once the crisis in question had reached a conclusion, the BBC was pressured to revert to its previous schedule, usually with the question of finance very much in mind. The Cold War is characterised, however, by various high-ranking BBC personnel trying to teach the politicians that broadcasting cannot shift quite so easily between long and short-term perspectives. In 1950, for example, Sir Ian Jacob perceptively wrote that 'broadcasting is not something that can be turned on and off like a tap'. It was necessary to fight, he said, 'a long-term campaign to get and maintain one's audience and to hold one's own in a highly competitive field'.[4] However, this book has suggested that the Voice of America was able to overcome this problem with little difficulty, managing to expand its operations as circumstances necessitated. This begs the question of how; what could the VOA do that the BBC quite clearly could not? One explanation seems to lie in the reputation of the two services. The BBC had established a solid and consistent reputation for accuracy and reliability among audiences since the inauguration of the Empire Service in 1932. It had considerable experience of operating in both times of peace and war, and realised that the most effective propaganda was based on accuracy, 'objectivity' and 'the truth' or at least the BBC's version of it. By frequently chopping and changing at the behest of the government or Foreign Office, the BBC would have been accused of being nothing more than a tool of British propaganda; its credibility would thereby have been eroded, and the success of its subtle form of propaganda based on facts would have been jeopardised. For this reason it could be said that the BBC's battle with the government during the Suez crisis was actually beneficial, for both the BBC and for British propaganda; accurately or not it could now be revered as editorially independent, its reputation and credibility therefore considerably enhanced.

On the other hand VOA was much more directly a tool of American foreign policy, with its editorials explaining and justifying the Administration's actions and policies. Moreover until the Hungarian uprising,

VOA adopted the hard-line crusading approach to world affairs that characterised American propaganda during the early years of the Cold War. In other words, its output was consistent with the prevailing American political perspective; it was overtly propagandistic (although the station would insist that its output was still accurate, truthful and objective), and so could alter its schedule with greater ease. It had more of a sense of its mission than the BBC, and less of a need to assert its own identity. And of course we must not overlook the fact that the State Department exerted considerably more control over the VOA – its staff and finance in particular – than the Foreign Office has ever enjoyed *vis-à-vis* the BBC.[5] The folly of such an approach was demonstrated by VOA's Cambodian (Khmer) language service. This was started in August 1955, but cancelled in July 1957. However, as the Vietnam war spilled over into Cambodia and the country was racked by its own political problems, Cambodian-language broadcasts were reinforced in May 1962. It is possible that had the VOA continued to broadcast directly into Cambodia, instead of succumbing to the complacency that seems to have characterised American policy towards that country in the late 1950s, American policy would at least have had a head-start. It is, of course, not being suggested that the Voice of America could have prevented Cambodia's slide towards chaos, but that American influence might have been greater. The question that cannot be answered with any degree of satisfaction, however, is whether this ability to rapidly change schedules as circumstances dictate has actually eroded the VOA's long-term influence and credibility.

To illustrate how the relationship between the VOA and foreign policy has been problematic, it is worthwhile jumping ahead a number of years to 1970. Superpower diplomacy was threatened when VOA broadcasts referred to Soviet 'duplicity' and 'deception' as Soviet anti-aircraft missiles were being introduced into Egypt; these broadcasts were transmitted just as intricate negotiations between the US and the USSR were showing signs of progress. They were the source of a bitter dispute between the State Department and the USIA, with the Secretary of State, William Rogers, having to remind the Director of USIA, Frank Shakespeare, that his agency was required by law to receive formal policy guidance from his Department.[6] This episode has echoes of an earlier dispute, also previously documented, when VOA broadcasts threatened South Vietnam with a severance of aid if the regime did not comply with the wishes of the State Department. Together these two episodes confirm that: (i) the integration of the USIA and VOA have not been completely integrated into the American foreign policy process; (ii) there was still a need for a closer working relationship between American propaganda and foreign policy élites, the consequences of the Bay of Pigs invasion notwithstanding; and (iii) the media's role in this same foreign policy process has, at times, threatened the delicate diplomacy pursued by the Administration and State Department.

The development of the mass media revolutionised the diplomatic process; not only were statesmen provided with an extra channel to quickly and efficiently communicate with their opposite numbers across the world, but they could also now address entire populations, thus consolidating the position of public opinion in foreign policy. The premise of this is that people-power can be a formidable force once it is harnessed. Individuals can act as an influence on their own governments, whether by writing a letter to *The Times*, or rising up in revolution to collectively confront their state system face to face. This book's introduction described how states have sought to control such externally-derived interference in their national affairs throughout the twentieth century through such initiatives as the 1936 League of Nations Convention, various United Nations Resolutions, ITU Declarations etc. However as the case studies have demonstrated such conventions have largely been ignored by states who operate an international radio broadcasting service for political ends and have often actively interfered in the internal affairs of another sovereign state.

In addition the media are used to present a favourable image of a nation's own policies, decisions, actions and positions to the wider world – to contribute to what K.J. Holsti termed 'substantive bargaining'.[7] This was a concern for all the principal actors in this study. Hence propaganda incorporates such terminology as 'democracy', 'justice', 'legality', and so on in order to create the illusion that right is on its side. By presenting a defence of policies and actions in this manner, it is hoped that confidence in the fight to maintain them will be sustained. At the same time such broadcast propaganda may raise the level of a population's awareness, obstructing the path to domestic unity and perhaps sow the seeds of disillusionment. Sir Hugh Greene applied this technique in BBC broadcasts over the Iron Curtain, and it was used to great effect during the Hungarian uprising. In addition British broadcast propaganda to Egypt during the Suez crisis practised this method and tried to separate the leaders from the people they led. Its success in each case was different. The satellite states were in effect an occupied region, with Communism imposed by an outside force. During the Cold War the hope of liberation was maintained among the intellectual classes in particular, who then formed the focus for a national resentment of the Soviet-imposed régime. Because there was no identifiable link between the state and the people it governed, western broadcasts could channel their energies into exacerbating that resentment.

In contrast Nasser was revered as a hero and a champion of anti-colonialism in Egypt and indeed throughout the entire Arab world, and western policies only served to reinforce that conviction. Gordon Waterfield's words, already elucidated in Chapter Two, can be restated. He said that 'once a foreign station starts to abuse anything Arab they close their ranks'.[8] For this reason, efforts to separate the régime from its people, vigorously pursued by the BBC during the Suez crisis, were unsuccessful.

There are a variety of problems associated with using the media in the diplomatic process. If each side presents its case and negotiating position in public, they are in danger of losing the flexibility that is so necessary to the successful conduct of diplomacy. Entire populations become aware should a government deviate from its stated position, and may therefore lose face and credibility in public opinion at home and abroad. While the possibility of such deviation may encourage more thoughtful diplomacy, the risks are actually much greater; and who can dispute the fact that in today's age of image managers and sound-bites, there is the added danger that moulding popular perception will take priority over long-term diplomatic considerations?

British propagandists during the Suez crisis appear to have recognised the importance of the media in combining traditional diplomacy with secret agendas. Many diplomatic exchanges occur at bilateral or multilateral conferences. According to K.J. Holsti these are often staged 'for the purpose of stalling or creating illusion that a government is seriously interested in bargaining, even though it really desires no agreement'.[9] This can be readily applied to the London Conferences of 1956 which historians now agree were used by the British government merely to stall for time until more aggressive action against Egypt could be prepared. In addition Britain could justifiably affirm that traditional multilateral diplomacy had been given an opportunity to work. The media, and the BBC in particular, were important in sustaining that illusion. Moreover, of course, coverage of such conferences also provides an excellent forum for propaganda.

Such flexibility and room for manoeuvre, the essential ingredients of any diplomatic exchange, also derive from the conveyance by a state of 'ominous warnings'.[10] These can be defined as deliberately vague threats which do not commit their source to any specific action, but which seek to induce the target state to undertake a particular course.

Thus the Voice of the Arabs described how the Arab world would unite in defence of Egypt and issued general threats without providing specifics. While during the Cuban missile crisis the threats were obvious to all the parties concerned, both American and Soviet broadcasts reiterated how the other 'must bear complete responsibility for its actions'. Such an approach serves to magnify the issue, attach symbolic importance to it, and prepares for escalation, again without firm commitment.

However the threats are framed they must be credible, that is, they must be supported by the capability and a willingness to carry them out. If a state perceives the threat against it as not credible, or perhaps as a bluff, then the influence and persuasive powers of the state which issued it are reduced. In short it is the perception of the threat, rather than the threat itself, which is most important to this process. It could even be reasonably argued on this premise that propaganda actually supports the deterrent effect of a state's weapons system; it is the presentation of the destructive capabilities of that weapons system, together with an announced willingness to use it, that may deter actions against the interests of the transmitting state.

However, most diplomatic communications are not this dramatic; principally, their functions are the exchange of views, identifying intentions, and engaging in persuasion without hard bargaining and threats. The period scrutinised in this study abounds with examples of how international radio was applied to such forms of substantive bargaining as part of the diplomatic process. Again during the Suez crisis, broadcasts from Cairo Radio and the Voice of the Arabs addressed western statesmen in person before presenting the Egyptian case to them. Jordan went to extreme lengths to affirm that the decision to dismiss General Glubb and not join the Baghdad Pact would not have adverse repercussions for Anglo-Jordanian relations. In other words, broadcasts not only presented diplomatic positions, but were involved in acts of persuasion, providing symbolic acts and signals, and affirming existing commitments.

The fact that English-language broadcasts, targeted at the Soviet Union by the BBC were never jammed, unlike their broadcasts in Russian, adds weight to the central thesis of this book, for it suggests that Russian statesmen relied on radio as a source of diplomatic news, intelligence and information. It also suggests that, given the low understanding of the language in the USSR, the authorities were not too worried by broadcasts in English. For this reason broadcasts in the native languages of the Soviet bloc were extremely important, many of which filtered through despite continuous efforts to jam them. For example by building on the success of their 'public diplomacy' during the Hungarian uprising, both the BBC and VOA established an enduring relationship with the people of Eastern Europe themselves, generating and sustaining hope and sympathy among them and affirming a commitment to their eventual liberation. The situation was made incredibly difficult from a presentational point of view by the coincidence of Hungary with Suez. Any attempt to portray the Soviet Union as aggressive or imperialist could now be denounced as hypocritical. Besides, the Soviet media presented the crisis as an internal matter to be settled as such by the Soviet Union and Hungary themselves; the outside powers which were accused of having helped generate the crisis in the first place were reduced to being passive bystanders. In such politically impotent circumstances the west could only maintain its propaganda offensive against the Soviet Union. Nevertheless, Soviet statesmen with a comprehensive knowledge of English could at least gather the latest western diplomatic communications from the BBC. The station therefore continued to play a pivotal role in the foreign policy process, despite the observed limitations. For the Voice of America the obstacles were formidable; the Soviet Union jammed broadcasts in both the Russian and English languages, thus reinforcing the notion that each station enjoyed substantially different reputations among their audiences.

Without a doubt the most dramatic example of international radio being used as a tool of diplomacy was during the Cuban missile crisis. Together American and Soviet broadcasts initially supplemented, but finally supplanted, the slow and cumbersome traditional diplomatic channels to resolve the crisis. The establishment of the so-called Hot-Line in the immediate aftermath of the crisis, linking the White House with the Kremlin, confirmed the acceptance of the need to combine speedy electronic communication with the privacy offered by traditional channels.

In the Suez and Hungarian crises, radio's involvement in finding a suitable resolution was minimal. This derived from the various ways the events had been perceived, presented and managed. This is not to suggest, however, that the BBC and VOA were impotent; both were able to build on the politically-generated resolutions to the crises. Hence as the Suez crisis reached its conclusion the BBC justified the decision to seek a military solution to it, while VOA and American propaganda turned towards projecting the ambitions and benefits of the Eisenhower Doctrine. In the case of Hungary, both stations were confined to limited objectives; they continued to encourage peaceful methods of change, express sympathy for the repressed people, and affirm to the Soviet Union their determination to support change in the satellite states. As we shall discover, such patient activity eventually paid off.

During the Cold War period therefore, the potential for what is often portrayed as a relatively stable situation to spiral out of control was always prevalent. The world was theoretically divided into three identifiable camps – east, west and the non-aligned. Security was a scarce commodity in the international system, making for an absence of certainty and predictability. In such circumstances one would expect that maintaining alliance relationships, and the forging of new ones, would be a priority. Yet these benefits of alliances were sacrificed in favour of fighting the Cold War both at the front and behind enemy lines. Both the BBC and VOA cut back, or curtailed altogether, broadcasts to western Europe and other 'friendly' regions. One frequently cited justification for this has been that these countries are able to obtain information from a variety of sources, so direct radio broadcasting was unnecessary. This, however, ignores two salient aspects of the process, both of which have been demonstrated: (i) there was a considerable amount of cross-listening, particularly behind the Iron Curtain. Here broadcasts in the native language were more or less continuously jammed, but the educated could still hear broadcasts in other languages originally intended for audiences elsewhere. In Hungary, for example, evidence has been supplied to show how there was an audience for BBC broadcasts in French and German, while Soviet citizens with a knowledge of English could listen to BBC broadcasts in that language. (ii) The credibility of a broadcasting station is eroded if it targets its output only at an ideological enemy. This was of course an inevitable hazard associated with broadcasting in the context of the Cold War.

The primary example of radio being used to maintain alliance relations lies within the context of the Cold War itself; by using international broadcasting, governments of both the east and west could portray themselves as protecting their sphere of influence against the expansionist tendencies of the other. In this way the suppression of revolution in Hungary could be presented by the Kremlin-controlled media as an act of alliance, with the paternal Soviet Union protecting Eastern Europe from its very own domino effect; the same reasoning could equally be applied to the US regarding Cuba and Latin America, while the domino theory has been most readily called upon to justify American involvement in Vietnam. Furthermore by maximising the ideological rhetoric that characterised the Cold War both sides could present themselves as the 'defenders of the faith', protecting threatened principles and a cherished way of life from the evil values propagated by their opponent. This was largely based on the premise that domestic and international support are easier to generate for principles rather than specific issues. For example, British propaganda could hope to achieve wider support by demonstrating the Suez crisis to be a matter of principle, rather than by presenting the vague and relatively unexciting details of the canal's nationalisation. If the value hierarchies of two nations are similar, then conflict can be avoided. However, international radio broadcasts are able to identify the differences in culture, value systems and hierarchies, which Cold War propaganda then projected, manipulated and used to fight its war of words. In this way the myths and misperceptions which helped create and sustain the Cold War, were perpetuated.

YESTERDAY, TODAY, TOMORROW

As technology advances, so the states continue to apply the electronic media to the diplomatic process. The role of international television, for example, is assuming an ever more dominant role, and the participation of CNN in the Gulf crisis of 1990–1 has entered media legend. Indeed, President Clinton used CNN to engage in diplomatic dialogue with the North Korean leadership during what he euphemistically referred to as a Global Press Conference.

The similarities between the events of the 1956–64 period and those of 1988–93 are quite remarkable. In 1956 France, Britain and Israel collectively waged war against Egypt; in 1991 western powers were challenged by a new belligerent power in the Middle East as they united to drive Iraq out of Kuwait. This can be accurately described as the first television war in terms of instantaneous pictures, enabling armchair strategists to fight it in 'real time'. Yet radio was still an important channel of communication, particularly in the Middle East itself,[11] and stories abound of Saudis and exiled Kuwaitis rushing to the shops to buy short-wave sets to hear the BBC and VOA. As if to prove the old axiom which affirms that, 'the more things change the more they stay the same', the BBC was accused of pro-Iraq bias, an allegation which was forcefully denied by Sam Younger, Head of the Arabic Service, who conducted his own investigation into the matter and brought in independent Arabic speakers to monitor programmes. The spirit of Paul F. Grey, by far the BBC's most vociferous critic during Suez, is definitely alive and well! The emotional pressure on the Arab staff was again a concern and, as in Hungary in 1956, a service was provided whereby messages could be relayed to family and friends unable to leave Kuwait and Iraq.[12] This time, however, there were no threats of cuts in the BBC's grant-in aid, no attempt to install a Liaison Officer, no extensive overhaul of language services. The relationship between the BBC and the government had been tested to the limit during the Suez crisis, and as a result was too well defined to allow a repeat performance.

Again in 1956, Hungarians rose in arms against their Soviet masters; in 1989 Eastern Europe was at last liberated as Communism collapsed. It cannot be denied that this was due more to the policies and individual perspective of world leaders, Mikhail Gorbachev in particular. Yet western broadcasters had, for decades, helped to sustain the hope of liberation behind the Iron Curtain, and together slowly ate away at the foundations of Communism. At the end of the old Hollywood westerns the hero, after saving the town from the villains, would always ride out to where he was needed next. This is a useful analogy that can be applied to Radio Free Europe and Radio Liberty. Their mission regarded as having been satisfactorily concluded, resources are now being diverted to Radio Free Asia, an area of the world where the Bamboo Curtain still stands, and Communism in North Korea, Vietnam and China appears to be as entrenched as ever. This decision has been subject to considerable criticism, especially by Czeslaw Milosz, professor emeritus at the University of California and a former Nobel prize winner. He has admitted to being ostracised by RFE/RL for what he calls his 'disagreement with their political orientation during some periods'. Milosz has, nevertheless, provided a forceful argument for the continuation of RFE/RL in a period when Eastern Europe, especially Yugoslavia, is in ferment:

> Unfortunately, large areas of the European-Asiatic continent are a caldron of war, and a major weapon in that spreading civil war is the distortion of news to suit the needs of local warlords. . . .
> . . . [RFE/RL] have gone through several reconstitutions and gathered experience that should not be squandered. To deprive ourselves of such a weapon at the moment when the situation in the Balkans alone threatens a major war would mean to fall victim to a dangerous provincialism and would justify a question about the sensitivity of the president to urgent tasks of foreign policy.[13]

Milosz is here serving a reminder that the halcyon days of the 'New

World Order', envisaged at the end of the Cold War, have simply not materialised. Certainly the world is no longer threatened by the possibility of a superpower confrontation spiralling out of control; but the absence of their overriding authority from the international system has not prevented smaller, yet more endurable wars and crises which appear to be intractable in the present circumstances, from erupting throughout the world. At the same time, we would be misguided if we failed to appreciate the shifting priorities of the international system, and international communications must also reflect this. Thus radio broadcasting, together with the ever onward march of television, will be pivotal in facilitating an interdependent global economic and trading system, and in promoting sustainable development and democratisation. One example of how these ideas can translate into practice was during the war in Afghanistan. The BBC began a Pashto service in 1981, just after the Soviet invasion, but its broadcasts were not directed exclusively to political ends; in response to requests by health agencies working in Afghanistan, BBC broadcasts included health advice, funded by agencies of the United Nations. This was a resounding success, and confirms that international radio broadcasting can have a positive and constructive, as well as a destructive and subversive role.[14] The wars in the former Yugoslavia, economic and political change in Russia and South Africa, the strengthening of the United Nations and, of course, the cohesion of the European Union are all now presenting their own unique challenges to international communications. Czeslaw Milosz seems not to have noticed such change; by focusing exclusively on Europe, he fails to concede that there is a need for a surrogate broadcasting station – Radio Free Asia – to 'encourage changes in China, Vietnam and elsewhere'.[15]

Only in China in 1989 was an anti-Communist revolution suppressed on the scale we had come to expect. Yet even here the authorities could not achieve the total blackout on news and information they would have liked. Television pictures again portrayed the full horror of the events of 4 June, but many still relied on the services of the international radio broadcasters. The demonstrators in Tiananmen Square demanded that the BBC stringer, Simon Long, 'Tell the world', and he did. But he also told the Chinese people themselves, as wallposters and loudspeakers relayed BBC reports. This became more important as the authorities began what the Head of the Chinese Service, Elizabeth Wright, described as 'one of the most complete disinformation campaigns in the history of the Chinese Communist party'.[16] Wright was here referring to attempts by the authorities to cover up the number of civilians killed in the clampdown of June 1989: 'With breathtaking cynicism,' she wrote, 'they had clearly decided that if they were going to lie, it might as well be a colossal lie.'[17]

In 1962 the United States and the Soviet Union came close to exchanging nuclear missiles over Cuba. Today there is no Soviet Union, and Cuba itself is on the brink of collapse. Yet the importance of international radio broadcasting remains. Not only does America's war of words with Cuba continue via Radio Marti,[18] but Mikhail Gorbachev listened to the BBC World Service for news and information as he was holed up in his Black Sea dacha and cut off from events during the attempted coup against him in 1991. 'The BBC knows everything already,' he later joked at a press conference.[19] And while the Vietnam syndrome haunted American politicians and military leaders throughout the 1970s and 1980s, the US has continued to assume the role of the world's policeman. There has even been talk of America facing its second Vietnam, first in the Gulf War against Iraq, and then in Somalia. Lessons learnt, or lessons forgone? Writing on the Gulf War, former managing director of the World Service, John Tusa, is not in any doubt:

> The next war will be covered more fully and with a greater concern for subtlety, for causal analysis as well as futuristic speculation, for the difference between what we have been told, what we know, what we do not know, and what is being deliberately withheld, and with a determination to report the bad news as well as the good. . . . The criteria of reporting should be the same when the subject is imminent defeat. That should be the lesson of the Gulf War.[20]

The full story of the Gulf War from the perspective of international radio has still to be told.[21] Yet it is actually a little surprising, if not unnerving, to discover that John Tusa felt the need to write these words. They could well have been written at the time of the Suez crisis; the ideas underpinning them were certainly expressed at that time – by the BBC, the government and the Foreign Office. It seems that 36 years later, the role of BBC overseas broadcasts during such crises is still the subject of excited debate.

The research applied in this book has encountered a number of difficulties. The first is one of definition. The arts and social sciences are far from being exact disciplines and so judgements, evaluations and conclusions are fluid and subject to heated questioning. For example, there is an absence of agreement on what constitutes propaganda, let alone diplomacy. The second difficulty lay within the research itself. Many of the relevant documents remain classified or are simply unavailable. Once we try to analyse the political decisions, policies and output of foreign stations, the obstacles become formidable in their capacity to obstruct scholarly research. Not only are there inevitable language difficulties, but many states – their foreign policies and their media – have so far not been studied to any satisfactory degree. The archives of the former Soviet Union are slowly being opened, but access to them remains difficult and thorough analysis a time-consuming effort. This is unfortunate; we know, via monitoring reports, what the Soviet propaganda line was at any particular time and what the Soviet media were saying, but we know virtually nothing of the decisions and reasoning which compelled this propaganda. Future researchers will undoubtedly benefit from the somewhat painstaking and often frustrating work of the scholars of today. Yet even in Britain and the US available information is, at best selective, at worst still confidential. Despite constant pressure from historians, an understanding of the IRD, for example, remains incomplete and unsatisfactory, a jigsaw puzzle assembled from the fragments of the story which are available.

There are also limitations to the analysis. The problem with a study of this nature is that one can identify individual policies – political and propaganda – and determine that the propaganda was disseminated. What is not easily quantified is the receptivity of the message. We must always contextualise the narrative, and remind ourselves of the conditions prevailing during the Cold War in order to understand the limits of radio propaganda reception. At its minimum, audience research provides statistics and numbers of listeners; at its best, there is possibly some selective feedback regarding content. But what must always linger at the back of the diligent propagandist's mind is that his message is simply not getting across, despite what audience research tells him. He may view a particular action or decision taken by a target government or population as a result of a successful propaganda campaign, but he has no real way of knowing for certain that the pressure of the propaganda was responsible or was even a contributory factor in the equation. Did radio propaganda *really* spark the Hungarian revolution in 1956, or would radio propagandists like to think it did merely to be confirmation of their power, despite the unfortunate outcome? In effect the propagandist is working blind. Newspapers are in a similar position: they take great delight in their sales figures, but they are meaningless if the newspapers are not read. After all, today's newspapers are tomorrow's fish and chips paper. The radio propagandist faces much the same problem, indeed more so, since a radio message is more immediate than the written word, lost to the ether as quickly as it was transmitted unless it is recorded on audio tape. The video recorder has become institutionalised as a method of preserving television images for future analysis and reflection. Unfortunately, historians of the radio have suffered in their research from a lack of available audio cassette recordings which have captured the radio message.[22]

The next stage is to advance the ideas and approach of this study and try to apply them to the contemporary events described in the previous few pages. For the next 30 years we will not know the decisions and policies of the BBC, the government or the Foreign Office today. A study of the kind attempted here will therefore have to wait. Yet the enormous amount of evidence that is available to the contemporary historian will yet again confirm that although we exist in an age of instant television pictures, direct satellite broadcasting and international television transmissions, international radio broadcasting will remain the preferred medium of global entertainment, news and information; and, of course, the public medium of international politics.

The principal discovery of this book is perhaps best summarised by an event that occurred in an even earlier period than the one covered here. In 1918 Edward L. Bernays of the US Foreign Press Bureau in New York suggested to Tomas Masaryk, then President of Czechoslovakia, that he proclaim his country's independence on a Sunday, rather than a Friday, to ensure better press coverage. Masaryk said: 'That, sir, is making history in the cables.' 'Sir,' replied Bernays, 'cables make history.'[23]

Notes

INTRODUCTION

1. Quoted in Robert W. Chandler, *War of Ideas: The US Propaganda Campaign in Vietnam* (Boulder: Westview Press, 1981), p. 3.
2. Quoted in Asa Briggs, *The Birth of Broadcasting* (Oxford: Oxford University Press, 1961), p. 309.
3. Notable exceptions include K.J. Holsti, *International Politics: A Framework for Analysis* 5th Edn (New Jersey: Prentice Hall, 1988); G.R. Berridge, *International Politics* (Brighton: Wheatsheaf, 1987); Richard Rosecrance, *International Relations* (New York: McGraw-Hill, 1973); Christer Jonsson, *Communication in International Bargaining* (London: Pinter Publishers, 1990); Alan James, 'Diplomacy and International Society', *International Relations*, 6 (1980), and Yoel Cohen, *Media Diplomacy* (London: Frank Cass, 1987).
4. It should be noted that the media will contribute to international relations in a different way in non-crisis conditions.
5. 'Wasting the Propaganda Dollar', *Foreign Policy* 56 (Autumn 1984).
6. However there is an English language service to Europe (launched in 1985) which can be received quite easily in the UK at night on medium-wave. In addition many continental Europeans can hear VOA on FM and cable, while VOA's world-wide English programme is easily accessible on short-wave.
7. Public Records Office FO953/2099/PEB1011/3118, June 1962.
8. Asa Briggs has noted that the Americans 'were not receptive to external short-wave broadcasting beamed directly at them.' *Sound and Vision* (London: Oxford University Press, 1979), p. 537.
9. Tusa does, however, derive comfort from the fact that the BBC can still be received in the US on short-wave, while programmes are relayed by seventy stations in the American Public Radio Network. *Conversations with the World* (London: BBC, 1990) p. 31.
10. White Paper on Overseas Information Services (1957), Cmnd. 225, 17 July 1957.
11. See US National Archives (USNA), RG306, 4/87/34/6, USIA Intelligence Bulletins, Memorandums and Summaries, IS-2-56.
12. Excluding China, total Communist output doubled between 1950–5 from 380 hours to 737 hours per week. Ibid.
13. Cord Meyer, *Facing Reality: From World Federalism to the CIA* (New York: Harper & Row, 1980), p. 360.
14. Robert Holt, *Radio Free Europe* (Minneapolis: University of Minneapolis Press, 1958), p. 5.
15. Ibid., p. 197.
16. In Wilbur Schramm (ed.), *The Process and Effects of Mass Communication* (Illinois: University of Illinois Press, 1965), pp. 433–5.

1   RADIO DIPLOMACY AND PROPAGANDA

1. W.J. West, *Truth Betrayed* (London: Duckworth, 1987), p. 79.
2. Ibid.
3. See Rosecrance (1973), pp. 122–3; 125–45.
4. West (1987), p. 22. This stimulated the first organised monitoring of international radio broadcasts, as Dalton suggested the Post Office make transcripts of these questionable transmissions.
5. Holland, the first to establish a regular international service, had begun transmitting broadcasts for expatriates in 1927. Germany followed in 1929, France in 1931. Then in 1934 Japan, with its own expanding empire in Asia, started a similar service.
6. Gerard Mansell has described the Munich crisis as the 'first major international crisis in which radio fully came into its own as a prime source of news.' *Let Truth Be Told* (London: BBC, 1982), p. 59.
7. West (1987), pp. 111–13.
8. Briggs (1979) has noted that broadcasting recorded all the major events of the early Cold War, 'and in many respects was influenced by them.' p. 508.
9. Robert Holt, 'A New Approach to Political Communication', in J.B. Whitton (ed.), *Propaganda and the Cold War* (Connecticut: Greenwood Press, 1963), p. 44.
10. Ibid.
11. Lester Markel, *New York Times Magazine,* 13 July 1958, p. 46.
12. He wrote that propaganda 'does not depend on the will of those who use it or on a doctrine, but is a result of the medium itself.' Jacques Ellul, *Propaganda: The Formation of Men's Attitudes* (New York: Vintage Books, 1965, reprint 1973), pp. 238–9.
13. Ibid., pp. 240–1.
14. Holsti (1988), pp. 196–7.
15. See for example Vladimir Artomov & Vladimir Semyonov, 'The BBC: History, Apparatus, Methods of Radio Propaganda', *Historical Journal of Film, Radio and Television* 4 (1984), pp. 73–89.
16. USNA, RG306, 4/87/30/4-5, USIA Special Reports, 1953–63, S-23-53, 30 November 1953.
17. Philip M. Taylor, *War and the Media* (Manchester: Manchester University Press, 1992), p. 19.
18. Quoted in Philip M. Taylor, *The Projection of Britain* (Cambridge: CUP, 1981), p. 190.
19. Quoted in Ibid., p. 190.
20. Charter of the United Nations, Article 2, Paragraph 4.
21. Resolution 290 (iv).
22. Cited in Erik Barnouw, *The Image Empire* (New York: OUP, 1970), p. 121.
23. For an excellent account of this see Maury Lisann, *Broadcasting to the Soviet Union* (New York: Praeger, 1975).
24. Terence H. Qualter, *Opinion Control in the Democracies* (London: Macmillan, 1985), pp. 218–19.
25. See Taylor (1981), Chapter 5.

26. Asa Briggs, *The BBC: The First Fifty Years* (Oxford: Oxford University Press, 1985), p. 143.
27. Of course independence refers to the BBC's declared freedom from editorial control by the Foreign Office.
28. D. Browne, *International Radio Broadcasting* (New York: Praeger, 1982), p. 173.
29. Quoted in K.L. Adelman, 'Speaking of America: Public Diplomacy in Our Time', *Foreign Affairs*, 59 (1981), p. 920.
30. Four objectives were integral to the Campaign of Truth: (i) generating confidence in American leadership; (ii) providing a fair representation of the US by countering misrepresentation and misconceptions about it; (iii) displaying American aspirations for peace, but determination to be prepared for war; (iv) undermining the confidence of Communists in the Soviet Union and encouraging non-Communist forces.
31. For an account of the effects of McCarthyism on the VOA and USIA, see Thomas Sorenson, *The Word War* (New York: Harper & Row, 1968), pp. 31–41.
32. NSC-68 was formulated in April 1950 and identified the fundamental objective of the Soviet Union as nothing less than world hegemony.
33. USIA Special Reports, S-23-53, June 1953.
34. Browne (1982), p. 104. 'VOA is careful to include news that will *interpret US policy,* which is apparently its main function.' [Emphasis added] USIA Intelligence Bulletins, Memorandums and Summaries, IM-1-154, 25 October 1954.
35. Laurien Alexandre, *The Voice of America* (New York: Ablex, 1988), p. 163.
36. See Michael McClintock, *Instruments of Statecraft* (New York: Pantheon, 1992).
37. Whitton (1963), p. 7.
38. Ibid.
39. Mansell (1982), p. 213, has described how the 1946 White Paper on Broadcasting 'set out in broad outline the Government's views on the scope of BBC broadcasting overseas in the post-war era,' and 'sought to define in precise terms the nature of the BBC external services and the Government. That definition remains operative to this day.'
40. See for example, CAB128/30, CM(56)43, 14 June 1956, and BBC Written Archives Centre (WAC), R1/1/24, Board of Governors Minutes, 19 July 1956.
41. For a discussion on the merits of the Charter see Sorenson (1968), pp. 235–6, and Browne (1982), pp. 108–11.

2 THE SUEZ CRISIS, 1956

1. Two volumes in particular were the direct result of this access to previously classified material: W. Scott Lucas, *Divided We Stand* (London: Hodder & Stoughton, 1991), and Keith Kyle *Suez* (London: Weidenfeld & Nicolson, 1991).
2. David Sanders, *Losing an Empire, Finding a Role* (London: Macmillan, 1990), p. 72.

3. Francis Williams, *A Prime Minister Remembers: The War and Post-War Memoirs of the Rt Hon. Earl Attlee* (London: William Heinemann, 1961), pp. 149–74.
4. Briggs (1979), p. 510.
5. Quoted in Mansell (1982), p. 223.
6. Quoted in Briggs (1979), p. 522.
7. Quoted in ibid., p. 222.
8. *Hansard* 484, Cols. 1268–72, 21 February 1951.
9. Quoted in Briggs (1979), p. 517.
10. Other proposals rejected by Drogheda include the curtailment of broadcasts to Western Europe and a reduction in the General Overseas Service in English.
11. The Arabic-language service was the responsibility of the Eastern Service until 1959, when a separate Arabic Service was established.
12. G. Waterfield, *The Listener*, 29 December 1956. Selwyn Lloyd commented that Nasser 'possessed a propaganda machine which even Dr. Goebbels would have envied.' *Suez* (New York: Mayflower, 1978), p. 34.
13. FO371/125455/JE1091/2, 24 December 1956.
14. In correspondence with the author, 30 December 1992.
15. FO953/1654/PB1041/129, 8 November 1956.
16. FO371/113608, 24 June 1955.
17. FO371/113608, 13–15 July 1955.
18. Anthony Nutting, *No End of a Lesson* (London: Constable, 1967), p. 101.
19. Some American officials also believed that propaganda directed at French North Africa exacerbated France's problems in the area. See *Foreign Relations of the United States (FRUS)* 1955–7, XV, p. 388.
20. *Summary of World Broadcasts* (SWB), IV, 21 December 1955.
21. *FRUS* XV, pp. 203–4. Since the details of this broadcast are unrecorded, the accuracy of Nasser's claim cannot be verified.
22. Ibid., pp. 28–36.
23. Lord Strang in his study of *The Foreign Office* (1955) described IRD as being responsible for 'research and provision of material on special subjects,' (pp. 211–12), while the 1973 *Diplomatic Service List* recorded how IRD provided the 'compilation of information reports for Her Majesty's Missions abroad.' Denis Healey recalled in his memoirs how IRD had been established to 'organise propaganda for Britain abroad, but in the end destroyed its usefulness by spreading disinformation.' *The Time of My Life* (London: Penguin, 1990), p. 106.
24. Owen said 'its style of operation got out of step with our more open democracy and reform was inevitable.' On the other hand, one former operative who wishes to remain anonymous has testified that 'it died because there was little top level interest in its potential and because from 1961 onwards, worse than average officials were appointed'. In correspondence with the author, 7 August 1992.
25. Former operative in correspondence with the author, 7 August 1992. He claimed that 'IRD was the *official* source for Bush House's East European services' (original emphasis). However Hamilton Duckworth

has said rather surprisingly: 'I personally have no knowledge of a relationship of the Arabic service with [IRD] and I have no reason to suppose such existed.' In correspondence with the author, 30 December 1992.

26. FO953/1630/P1041/17, 15 March 1956.
27. FO953/1633/P1041/75, 10 September 1956.
28. See for example WAC, Arabic Scripts, 'Political Question and Answer' (PQA), 14.
29. Peter Partner, *Arab Voices* (London: BBC, 1988), p. 72.
30. In 1958, however, Gordon Waterfield, then head of the Eastern Service, revealed the relevant SWB was read by the managers of the Arabic service each day. 'It is taken into account ... for ... selection of what political questions received from correspondents should be answered and in some cases influences the subject for one or more of the talks in the Arabic service'. WAC, E1/1854/1, 29 April 1958.
31. PQA 38, 4 January 1956.
32. PQA 92, 20 June 1956, and PQA 137, 30 November 1956.
33. Quoted in Kyle (1991), p. 86.
34. SWB IV, 23 December 1955.
35. See Kyle (1991), p. 92.
36. SWB IV, 9 January 1956.
37. FO953/1631/P1041/41, 24 April 1956.
38. Ibid.
39. CAB128/30, CM16(56), 22 February 1956.
40. SWB IV, 21 February 1956; also period 17–21 February 1956; FO371/118861/JE1053/7G, 22 February 1956, and FO371/12270/V1075/22, 20 January 1956.
41. King Hussein wrote in his memoirs that 'what most people do not realise ... is that General Glubb was a strictly Jordanian affair.' Quoted in Kennett Love, *Suez: The Twice Fought War* (London: Longman, 1969), p. 208.
42. Lloyd (1978), p. 48.
43. Nutting (1967), p. 17. Eden himself recorded in his memoirs that the root of the problem lay in the King's 'personal dislike of Glubb' and his intense paranoia about him assuming increasing control of Jordan's defence. *Full Circle* (London: Cassell, 1960), p. 347 fn.
44. SWB IV, 3 March 1956.
45. This was, however, balanced by the Tripartite Declaration and the obligation to defend Israel in the event of Arab attack. PQA 18, 16 November 1956.
46. 'World of Today', 22 January 1957, WAC Arabic Scripts.
47. 'Topic of Today', 29 November 1956, WAC Arabic Scripts.
48. CAB128/30, CM21(56), 9 March 1956.
49. *FRUS* XV, p. 375.
50. FO371/119220/JE1433/36B, 30 March 1956.
51. FO371/119228/JE1451/1, 30 January 1956.
52. Throughout the period Britain was concerned with the 'harsh anti-British propaganda on Saudi Radio and in Saudi papers.' The US made a representation to the Saudi government on this matter. *FRUS* XV, p. 606.

53. CAB128/30, CM(56)24, 21 March 1956. Similar had been US policy since 30 October 1955. See *FRUS* 1955–7, XIV, p. 384.
54. *FRUS* XIV, p. 414.
55. Love (1969), p. 207.
56. 'Now It's a War of Words', *Daily Mail*, 15 March 1956; 'This is a War We Must Win', *The Guardian*, 27 April 1956. Both were written by Glubb.
57. Waterfield (1956), p. 948. A Foreign Office memorandum reveals that Waterfield saw 'no alternative to Nasser,' and therefore believed it 'a mistake to attack him.' FO953/1643, 20 September 1956.
58. Waterfield (1956), p. 948.
59. Hamilton Duckworth, in correspondence with the author, 30 December 1992.
60. WAC, R34/1580/1, Suez 1, 18 September 1956.
61. FO953/1654/PB1041/122, 5 November 1956.
62. FO953/1654/PB1041/122, 6 November 1956.
63. Ibid.
64. Briggs (1979), p. 154. Briggs dedicated this fourth volume of his *History of Broadcasting in the United Kingdom* to Clark.
65. FO953/1654/PB1041/122, 6 November 1956.
66. FO953/1654/PB1041/122, 11 November 1956. The radio station in Bahrain experienced similar problems but were much more ruthlessly and efficiently dealt with. The Residency noted a 'pro-Egyptian bias,' especially by the news compositor. He was quickly dismissed and the Residency then recorded little anti-British bias. FO953/1690/PG11639/39, 4 September 1956.
67. Oren Stephens, *USIA Meets the Test* (1957), p. 14.
68. Ibid.
69. N. Newsome, *Tribune*, 14 December 1945, quoted in Briggs (1979), p. 147.
70. In 1954 Ralph White, Director of USIA's Broadcasting Services, recorded the widespread belief that 'the first hour of VOA programming in Arabic loses by not containing any music.' USIA Country Project Correspondence 1952–63, Egypt 1954, 7 April 1954.
71. Figg minuted, 'I had no sinister purposes in asking for this. I was only curious to know how the programmes were made ...' FO953/1652/PB1041/75, 25 July 1956.
72. FO953/1652/PB1041/75, 25 July 1956.
73. FO953/2098/PEB1001/13, 13 February 1962. Another minuted: 'Foreigners, especially in the new nations, do not understand that serious British newspapers are not necessarily reflecting HMG, still less that the BBC in relaying them is not doing so.' Ibid.
74. Hamilton Duckworth, in correspondence with the author, 30 December 1992.
75. FO953/1654/PB1041/124, 2 November 1956.
76. Stephens (1957), p. 37.
77. Robert W. Pirsein, *The Voice of America* (New York: Arno Press, 1979), p. 362.
78. Because of the so-called 'Geneva Spirit' in East–West relations at this time, Czechoslovakia was used as a front for the supply of these arms.

79. *FRUS* XIV, p. 355.
80. Ibid., p. 395.
81. FO800/669, Eg/17, 30 September 1955.
82. For example PQA 8, 19 September 1955.
83. 'Topic of Today', 22 November 1956, WAC Arabic Scripts.
84. FO371/118846/JE1024/15, 20 November 1956.
85. SWB IV, 27 February 1956. SWB IV, 24 January 1956, noted: 'Approximately since the conclusion of the arms deal... there has been a distinct increase in Cairo Radio's use of Soviet and Chinese material, particularly the former... chosen to demonstrate a Great Power's approval of Egyptian policy, especially as regards Baghdad Pact and the Egyptian–Czech arms agreement.'
86. According to Kyle (1991), p. 54, an 'occupation army in disguise.'
87. FO953/1651/PB1041/57, 12 June 1956.
88. FO371/11922/JE1433/70, 21 July 1956.
89. Hugh Thomas, *The Suez Affair* (Harmondsworth, Penguin: 1967), p. 18.
90. SWB IV, 9 June 1956.
91. SWB IV, 29 June 1956.
92. Lucas (1991), p. 133.
93. *FRUS* XV, pp. 538–40.
94. The State Department cited 'anti-US and anti-west propaganda' as having contributed to their decision. See ibid. pp. 583–4.
95. Ibid., pp. 813–14.
96. Ibid., pp. 949–53.
97. SWB IV, 21 July 1956.
98. Ibid.
99. Ibid.
100. Ibid.
101. *FRUS* XV, p. 825.
102. Love (1968), p. 335.
103. Quoted in Kyle (1991), p. 130.
104. SWB IV, 28 July 1956.
105. On 26 July a telegram was received by the State Department from its embassy in Egypt detailing the contents of the speech. *FRUS* XV, pp. 906–8. The source citation notes that this was received in Washington at 12:33 am on 27 July, 'Repeated niact [sic] to London and Paris. A translation of Nasser's speech was transmitted from Cairo, 3 July.'
106. Described as 'American and British conspiracies against Egypt'; this was no exaggeration given their activities to overthrow Nasser.
107. *FRUS* XV, pp. 906–8.
108. PQA 108, 8 August 1956.
109. *FRUS* 1955–7 XVI, p. 6.
110. Ibid., p. 36.
111. It was noted: 'From a narrow legal point, his action amounted to no more than a decision to buy out the shareholders.' CAB128/30, CM(56)54, 27 July 1956.
112. FO953/1692/PG11639/66, 28 September 1956.
113. WAC, R34/1580/1, Suez 1, 16 October 1956; September 1956.
114. WAC, R34/1580/2, Suez 2. It continued by saying that although negative

propaganda, portraying Nasser as a 'man of unmitigated evil' was avoided, 'attention has been drawn to the reckless megalomania revealed in his book, *The Philosophy of Revolution,* on which James Morris broadcast three important talks, and to the duplicity with which he has pursued his aims.'

115. *Topic of Today*, 16 August 1956.
116. It was noted that because goods travelling from America and Britain to be distributed throughout Asia would have to travel around the African Cape to reach India, an extra cost of £22 million per year would be added to import bills. Krishna Menon said, 'it is a question of India's survival. . . . We have to import grains, most of which go through the canal.' PQA 117, 12 September 1956.
117. *Topic of Today*, 27 September 1956.
118. PQA 163, 8 March 1957.
119. FO953/1692/PG11639/72, 10 October 1956.
120. Ibid.
121. WAC, E1/2,453/1, USSR Russian Broadcasts (2), 1955-, 17 October 1956. Communist radio propaganda to the Arab area tripled from c.80 hours per week in 1948 to 241 hours per week in 1956. During Suez many broadcasts were at dictation speed. USIA Special Reports, S-49-59.
122. USIA noted how 'Soviet output has used only Egyptian military communiqués in its reports on the fighting, and to Arabs even more than to other audiences, has presented an exaggerated picture of Egyptian strength.' USIA Special Reports, S-22-56, 3 December 1956.
123. FO371/118846/JE1024/1, 19 April 1956.
124. USIA Special Reports, S-5-62.
125. See Browne (1982), pp. 224–38, and G.D. Rawnsley, 'Crisis and Credibility of Radio Moscow,' *Shortwave Magazine* (September 1993), pp. 18–19.
126. *FRUS* XVI, p. 1125.
127. Carsten Holbraad, *Superpowers and International Conflict* (London: Macmillan, 1979), p. 33. Khrushchev claimed, however, that the threat of 'volunteers' was a decision made 'to give Egypt concrete assistance.' *Khrushchev Remembers* (London: André Deutsch, 1971), p. 436.
128. PRO, DEFE 4/92, JP(56)176(F), 14 November 1956.
129. SWB I, 5 November 1956.
130. Ibid.
131. SWB I, published 16 November 1956.
132. *FRUS* XVI, pp. 1003–4.
133. Frank D. Doney, USIA Information Officer in New Delhi, reported how the Egyptians 'generally believe that Russia forced England and France to withdraw from Suez and give no credit to the United States.' USIA Country Area Project Correspondence 1952–63, Egypt, 10 June 1956.
134. *Topic of Today*, 8 November 1956. That the Soviet Union really believed they had defused the crisis is implied by Khrushchev (1971) who wrote in his memoirs that 'it was a great victory for us when we ended the crisis.' p. 436.
135. USIA Special Reports, S-22-56, 3 December 1956.

136. This is not merely academic; the *News of the World* on 3 October 1993 carried a report that a bank-robber had successfully used a cucumber in a plastic bag!

137. For an interesting theoretical treatment of this question see Holbraad (1979), pp. 25–9.

138. Gabriel Partos, *The World That Came In From the Cold* (London: RIIA, 1993), p. 64.

139. Khrushchev (1971), p. 436. On the other hand, Walter Lacquer is of the opinion that the threats were made only after it was certain the Soviet Union would not have to support them with action, knowing the US was not prepared to intervene in the crisis. In the final analysis the Soviet Union could offer little more than psychological and moral support. Holbraad (1979), p. 25.

140. Eden (1960), p. 555.

141. Lloyd's broadcast was relayed live off the General Overseas Service in America, New Zealand and the colonies. It was also recorded for re-broadcasting in Australia and South Africa, and a Spanish version was recorded in Argentina.

142. WAC, R34/1580/1, Suez 1, 18 September 1956.

143. SWB IV, 22 August 1956.

144. SWB IV, 3 October 1956. Dulles must have been delighted at this broadcast which described him as 'leader of the western camp.'

145. *FRUS* XVI. pp. 95–6.

146. WAC, R34/1580/1, Suez 1, 18 September 1956.

147. SWB IV, 10 August 1956.

148. SWB IV, 11 August 1956.

149. WAC, R34/1580/1, Suez 1, 18 September 1956.

150. Ibid.

151. PQA 117, 12 September 1956.

152. *FRUS* XVI, p. 262.

153. Ibid., p. 327.

154. SWB IV, 13 September and 19 September 1956.

155. J.A.C. Brown believed the effectiveness of propaganda to be in inverse proportion to the size of the issue, i.e. the more important the issue, the less effective the propaganda. This implies that the globalisation of issues and threats of nuclear war are not effective. *Techniques of Persuasion* (Harmondsworth, Penguin, 1963), p. 55. We should therefore ask whether the purpose of such propaganda is merely to scaremonger, designed to reinforce other propaganda, or is it aimed at provoking action and/or change of opinion via scaremongering?

156. FO953/PG11639/15, 3 August 1956.

157. FO953/1690/PG11639/45, 6 September 1956.

158. Mohammed Heikal, *Cutting the Lion's Tail* (London: André Deutsch, 1986), p. 176.

159. SWB IV, 16 October 1956.

160. The movement of Iraqi troops towards the border with Jordan was, after all, designed as a smokescreen to mask the actual preparations for military intervention in Egypt.

161. FO371/121786, 3 November 1956.

162. PREM11/1149/171, 5 November 1956.
163. Ibid.
164. See FO371/118897/JE1091/138, 20 November 1956.
165. FO953/1648/PB1012/33, 8 October 1956.
166. Mansell (1982), p. 231.
167. Ibid.
168. J.B. Clark, 2 November 1956, quoted in WAC, R34/1580/3, Suez 3. See also *Manchester Guardian*, 17 November 1956: 'Inquiries today about the functions which this official has been asked to carry out were greeted with protestations of ignorance. It was not known what gap in the normally close contact that has always been maintained between the BBC External Services and the Foreign Office the new appointment was designed to fill. It was claimed, however, that the new appointment "in no way divagates from the degree of independence enjoyed by the BBC."'
169. 'The Suez Crisis and the BBC: A Study of Successful Resistance to Government Pressure,' an internal report prepared in case the Pilkington inquiry into broadcasting decided to inquire into the matter but never seen until the lapse of 30 years allowed the relevant file, WAC, R34/1580/3, Suez 3, to be opened.
170. Ibid.
171. FO953/1643/PB1011/44, 26 July 1956.
172. Quoted in Kyle (1991), p. 346.
173. PQA 151, 25 January 1957.
174. PQA 179, 26 April 1957.
175. FO953/1714/P1011/2, 4 January 1957.
176. *Topic of Today*, 15 February 1957. The Arabic press had followed the British debate with interest but chided such practice as a sign of weakness.
177. PQA 157, 15 February 1957.
178. Ibid.
179. FO953/1643/PB1011/54, 30 September 1956.
180. WAC, R34/1580/3, Suez Crisis 3.
181. Ibid.
182. FO953/1654/PB1041/124, 2 May 1956.
183. Hamilton Duckworth, in correspondence with the author, 30 December 1992.
184. John Drinkall, in correspondence with the author, 26 June 1993.
185. Stephens (1957), p. 8.
186. Kyle (1991), p. 383.
187. Similarly during the first sorties the Ministry of Defence advocated that a public warning should be issued by the BBC advising civilians to keep clear of Egyptian airfields. CAB128/30, (56)72, 31 October 1956.
188. Love (1986), p. 566.
189. Kyle (1991), p. 465.
190. PQA 137, 30 November 1956.
191. Partner (1988), p. 107.
192. Ibid., p. 108.
193. SWB IV, 2 November 1956 and 7 December 1956.
194. SWB IV, 22 and 23 November 1956.

195. CAB128/30, CC(56)87, 22 November 1956.
196. CAB128/30, CC(56)89, 27 November 1956.
197. SWB IV, 1 November 1956.
198. SWB IV, 1 and 2 January 1957.
199. PREM11/11741, 2 October 1956.
200. See the memoirs of his wartime exploits as a member of SOE, *Baker Street Irregular* (London: Methuen, 1965) finally published after being banned by the War Office for ten years.
201. FO953/1634/P1041/89, 8 December 1956.
202. Quoted by Kyle (1991), p. 527.
203. SWB IV, 19–22 January 1957.
204. Sorenson (1968), p. 89.
205. SWB IV, 24 November 1956.
206. *FRUS* XVI, pp. 1232–3.
207. FO953/1738/P1041/12, 11 January 1957.
208. USIA Area Project Correspondence 1954–63, Miscellaneous Domestic, Correspondence Near East and Africa, 1955–61. Also see Report on Trip to Africa by Henry Loomis 1959, for the limitations of these broadcasts.
209. CAB128/30, CM(56)67, 26 September 1956.
210. Partner (1988), p. 42.
211. Evelyn Shuckburgh in correspondence with the author, 22 August 1992.
212. See Taylor (1981), pp. 194–215.
213. The nearest dates available are 1951–4, found in WAC, E3/116, O/S Audience Research, Eastern Services, Arabic Broadcasts.
214. The Board of Governors concluded that the BBC had achieved a 'successful and creditable result during a period of great difficulty.' Briggs (1985), p. 318. The 'great difficulty' referred not only to Suez but to its coincidence with the Hungarian uprising.
215. While Paper on Overseas Information Services, Cmnd.225, 17 July 1957.
216. Charles Hill, *Both Sides of the Hill* (London: Houghton Mifflin, 1964), p. 188.
217. These services were Swahili, Somali and Burmese.
218. The Committee also recommended the abolition of the Swedish, Norwegian, Portuguese and Danish services (in addition to Dutch which the BBC itself had proposed), 'as well as certain vernacular services to the Commonwealth'; the contraction of French, the curtailment of Italian (and the North American service) and, given the 1955 Austrian settlement, the integration of the Austrian and German services. On the other hand the General Overseas Service was expanded, as were the services to Russia and the satellites; and depending on improved relay facilities, it was advocated that the Kuoyu and Cantonese services be increased.
219. Pirsein (1979), p. 361.
220. Cmnd.225.
221. Sorenson (1968), p. 89.

3 THE HUNGARIAN UPRISING, 1956

1. The last broadcast from the Hungarian Petofi transmitter before the revolution was crushed by Soviet troops. SWB II, 4 November 1956.
2. Dubrovnik Radio, Yugoslavia, quoted in *The Times*, 4 November 1991.
3. Miklos Molnár, *From Béla Kun to János Kádár* (London: George Allen & Unwin, 1990 English translation), p. 164.
4. Quoted in G. Barraclough (ed.), *Survey of International Affairs, 1955–58* (London: Oxford University Press, 1961), p. 72.
5. Holt (1958), p. 207. For a full description of how these balloons were used see Meyer (1980), and Allan Michie, *Voices Through the Iron Curtain* (New York: Dodd Mead, 1963).
6. In particular see Holt (1958) and Michie (1963).
7. David Wise and Thomas Ross, *The Invisible Government* (London: Jonathan Cape, 1965), p. 326. In its interviews with refugees, USIA found that almost 50 per cent of refugees said that western broadcasts gave the impression of impending military intervention. See USIA Special Reports 1955–9, SR-6, 28 December 1956.
8. Goldberg was a Russian who began his BBC career as a monitor of Spanish-language broadcasts during the war, and later established a tremendous following in the Soviet Union as the BBC's chief commentator on Soviet affairs. In 1979 Vladimir Artomov and Vladimir Semyonov described Goldberg, by then a 'political observer,' as 'a most experienced, skilled propagandist'. (1984), p. 79.
9. D. Wedgwood-Benn, in correspondence with the author, 14 April 1992.
10. On 30 November 1956 Budapest Radio described BBC broadcasts as being 'increasingly full of hatred.' 'In concocting alarmist rumours,' the station continued, 'they are . . . striving to outdo Free Europe Radio.' SWB Part IIb.
11. WAC, E1/2036/4, Hungary A–Z, 24 June 1956.
12. WAC, E2/812/1, Hungarian Revolution, 17 January 1957.
13. A 1956 USIA survey of Hungarian refugees found that 96 per cent listened to Western broadcasts regularly or occasionally. Of this figure, 79 per cent listened to RFE most, 30 per cent to BBC and only 29 per cent to VOA. USIA Special Reports, SR-6, 28 December 1956.
14. Andrew Felkay, *Hungary and the USSR, 1956–58* (Connecticut: Greenwood Press, 1989), p. 70.
15. H. Greene, *The Third Floor Front* (London: The Bodley Head, 1969), p. 32.
16. Ibid., p. 32.
17. See M. Tracey, *A Variety of Lives: A Biography of Sir Hugh Greene* (London: The Bodley Head, 1983).
18. RFE was the subject of vociferous criticism at the aforementioned Strasbourg meeting. Its Policy Adviser, Bill Griffith, told Tarjan that he knew RFE had 'committed many errors of judgment' during the uprising and attributed them to a 'lack of the sort of experience the BBC had built up over the years.' WAC, E2/812/1, 17 January 1957.
19. Ibid.

20. Marcel Fodor, *History of the Voice of America, 1960–61*, Chapter 23, p. 10.
21. WAC, E3/12/2, Audience Research, O/S, Central Europe, Hungary File 2, Report January–June 1956, 26 November 1956.
22. USIA Special Reports, S-7-53, October 1953. This documents the measures which the state took to discourage listening, ranging from setting high prices for receivers to infiltrating listener groups with spies and informers.
23. Ibid.
24. WAC, E3/12/2, 26 November 1956.
25. This is how Bruce Lockhart of the BBC ended his commentaries to the Eastern Bloc after World War Two.
26. In reference to the satellites Grey preferred 'publicity' to 'propaganda'.
27. FO371/122081/N1052/12, c.5 December 1956.
28. WAC, E35/1/1, Hungarian Section News (HSN), 27 October 1956.
29. Zorthian was later to make his mark during the Vietnam war as head of the Joint US Public Affairs Office in Saigon from 1965 onwards to co-ordinate the USIS and the Pentagon's psychological warfare.
30. USIA Special Reports, S-31-56. The BBC, he apparently said, had 'watered down its broadcasts' so that they were almost 'innocuous'.
31. The BBC could of course have quite justifiably encouraged the Hungarians to overthrow an oppressive gulag-ridden régime, but could not be responsible for pitting ordinary people against the might of the Soviet army.
32. HSN, 4 November 1956. It is quite ironic that only several hours later Budapest Radio should fall into Soviet hands and go dead in the middle of a transmission. A similar note of thanks was sent by Bucharest Radio to the BBC during the 1989 Romanian revolution.
33. WAC, E2/812/1, Hungarian Revolution, 4 November 1956.
34. Back in 1952 the BBC had told the USIA that they 'remind the East Germans that they are not forgotten, and that we share their problems and give sympathy.' USIA Special Reports, S-23-53, 30 November 1953.
35. See for example HSN, 31 October and 23 November 1956.
36. HSN, 4 November 1956. Then on 20 November, Andrew Martin described how public opinion in Britain was united over Hungary. He conceded that this was of little comfort for a nation 'fighting for freedom and survival,' but believed that it did reflect world opinion. HSN, 20 November 1956.
37. Quoted in Memo from IBs/PME – Robert A. Bauer – to IOP – Alfred V. Boerner, on Emergency Operations of European Division of VOA, 13 November 1956, USIA HC.
38. Ibid.
39. Pirsein (1979), p. 365.
40. Ibid.
41. Fodor, Chapter 23, p. 10.
42. HSN, 28 October 1956.
43. USIA Special Reports, S-7-53, October 1957.
44. Ibid.
45. Quoted in Howard Frederick, *Cuban–American Radio Wars* (Norwood: Ablex, 1986), p. 15.

46. One who did take advantage of the situation and entered Hungary with a BBC television crew was George Mikes of the BBC Hungarian service and author of *The Hungarian Revolution* (London: André Deutsch, 1957).
47. Broadcast 24 October 1956, quoted in Memo from Bauer to Boerner, 13 November 1956, USIA HC.
48. *FRUS* 1955–7, XXV, p. 275 fn.
49. Former IRD operative who wishes to remain anonymous, in correspondence with the author, 12 October 1992. D. Read does not mention this episode in his history of Reuters, *The Power of News* (Oxford: Oxford University Press, 1992).
50. 'Fighting Over in Budapest: A City of Silent Protest', *The Times*, 13 November 1956.
51. Greene (1969), pp. 29–31.
52. Ibid.
53. Andrew Walker, *A Skyful of Freedom* (London: Broadside, 1992), p. 128.
54. USIA Special Reports, 30 November 1953.
55. Whitton (1963), p. 3.
56. Quoted in Sorenson (1968), p. 44.
57. Ibid.
58. Pirsein (1979), p. 44.
59. Ibid.
60. USIA Special Reports, S-31-56.
61. *FRUS* XXV, p. 276.
62. Hungarian refugees expressed their appreciation of VOA's anti-Communism, but regretted the gap between words and deeds. VOA was considered an arm of government and a symbol of the US; the Hungarians said they therefore wanted confirmation that their hopes of liberation would be realised. A few however did feel that 'VOA broadcasts should not promise more than can actually be delivered by the West.' USIA Special Reports, S-7-53, October 1957.
63. USIA Special Reports, S-31-56.
64. *FRUS* XXV, p. 276.
65. Ibid.
66. USIA Special Reports, S-31-56.
67. Dwight D. Eisenhower, *The White House Years: Waging Peace, 1956–61* (London: Heinemann, 1966), p. 95. His biographer, Stephen Ambrose, said: 'There was no pressure . . . save the amorphous one of world public opinion, that Eisenhower could bring to bear on the Soviets in Hungary. He knew it, had known it all along, which made all the four years of Republican talk about "liberation" so essentially hypocritical.' *Eisenhower: Soldier and President* (New York: Simon & Schuster, 1990), p. 423.
68. USIA Special Reports, S-13-57, 29 November 1957.
69. FO371/122422/NH1051/2, 22 May 1956.
70. FO371/122422/NH1051/1, 13 January 1956.
71. Ibid. In May 1956 Ian Jacob, the Director of the Overseas Service, wrote to the Foreign Office listing similar themes which the BBC had

continuously pursued. 'It may be to some degree a coincidence.' he wrote, 'that the work of a decade on these themes by the BBC has been followed by major admissions and modifications... with a resultant loosening of the régime. ... The Soviet domination of East Europe must be further weakened and its recovery prevented.' FO953/1640/PB1011/ 3, 31 May 1956.
72. USIA Special Reports, S-31-56.
73. FO371/122422/NH1051/1, 13 January 1956.
74. Ibid.
75. Imre Nagy, 'Ethics and Morals in Hungarian Public Life,' in Béla Király and Paul Jones (eds), *The Hungarian Revolution of 1956 in Budapest* (Boulder: Colorado University Press, 1978), p. 11.
76. FO371/122081/N1052/5, 17 July 1956.
77. Ibid. Ward did not specify how this extension of influence was to be achieved.
78. FO371/122081/N1052/5a, 11 October 1956.
79. Ibid.
80. 'Subject–VOA Hungarian Programming, November 1954–November 1956', USIA HC, undated.
81. *FRUS* XXV, pp. 104–5.
82. Ibid.
83. Ibid.
84. Ibid.
85. For a full description see Mikes (1957), pp. 80–1.
86. Bill Lomax, *Hungary 1956* (London: Allison & Busby, 1976), pp. 120–3.
87. Eisenhower (1966), p. 64.
88. SWB IIb, 24 October 1956.
89. SWB I, 24 October 1956.
90. Mikes (1957), has written that Nagy's appointment was never formally announced, only that the radio began to refer to him as Premier from 7.30 am on 24 October. p. 87.
91. HSN, 27 October 1956.
92. SWB I, 24 October 1956.
93. Ibid.
94. HSN, 25 October 1956.
95. Ibid. It is apparent that the BBC assumed a similar role *vis-à-vis* Poland. On 6 November 1956, Polish radio said that 'voices of warning can be heard from everywhere.... "We think," said the London BBC... "that Poles should preserve calm. The opportunity won by Poland's determination and prudence should not be lost."' Polish radio added that they 'willingly listen to friendly voices from any sources.' FO953/1644/ PB1011/74.
96. HSN, 24 October 1956. Handwritten into this typed script was, 'Czechoslovak radio this evening mentioned the events in Hungary, briefly, for the first time.' The author is not specified.
97. Ibid.
98. Ibid.
99. However there is evidence that the Russian people were able to listen to the BBC and did accept it as the truth. Douglas Jay, a British MP

who visited Moscow during the Polish crisis when jamming had been
suspended, recorded how the 'ordinary Russian public heard the news
from the BBC's Russian Service broadcasts,' and that 'Moscow taxi
drivers were telling their passengers the Warsaw story heard over the
radio from London.' FO953/1644/PB1011/74, 12 December 1956.

100. This applied equally to Hungary. USIA found that despite heavy jam-
     ming, at least one wavelength would be free of interference to allow
     party leaders to listen. USIA Special Reports, S-7-53, October 1953.
101. USIA disagreed. 'The direct impact of Western broadcasts on the Soviet
     elite,' read one research report, 'is probably close to nil.' USIA Special
     Reports, S-5-59, March 1959. No adequate explanation is offered.
102. HSN, 24 October 1956.
103. USIA Special Reports, S-3-53, 30 September 1953.
104. Pirsein (1979), p. 367.
105. Fodor, Chapter 23, p. 10.
106. SWB IIb, 26 October 1956.
107. HSN, 30 October 1956. The BBC did not specify the source of these
     figures, only saying as a preface that 'reports have reached London
     from Budapest . . .'
108. Molnar (1990), p. 240.
109. SWB IIb, 26 October 1956.
110. SWB IIb, 27 October 1956.
111. Ibid.
112. HSN, 27 October 1956.
113. Ibid.
114. SWB IIb, 28 October 1956.
115. HSN, 28 October 1956.
116. HSN, 31 October 1956.
117. SWB I, 30 October 1956.
118. Eisenhower (1966), pp. 78–9. Ambrose's view was that 'Eisenhower
     feared it was too good to be true.' (1990), p. 426.
119. 'Yes,' replied the President, 'if [the broadcast] is honest.' Eisenhower
     (1966), p. 79.
120. SWB IIb, 1 November 1956.
121. Ibid.
122. SWB IIb, 2 November 1956.
123. Pirsein (1979), p. 365.
124. HSN, 3 November 1956.
125. Pirsein (1979), p. 365.
126. SWB IIb, 4 November 1956. In the English translation the word 'obvi-
     ous' was replaced by 'apparent', thus altering the shade and interpreta-
     tion of the broadcast.
127. HSN, 4 November 1956.
128. Ibid.
129. Pirsein (1979), p. 366.
130. *FRUS* XXV, p. 401 fn. See also p. 417.
131. HSN, 13 November 1956.
132. WAC, E12/713/1, Publicity – Foreign, Hungarian Revolution, 1956–7.
133. SWB IIb, 11 November 1956.

134. HSN, 11 November 1956.
135. Ibid.
136. Ibid.
137. Esslin, an Austrian by birth, moved from the monitoring service to Bush House's German Service during the war. He was a future Head of BBC Radio Drama.
138. HSN, 13 November 1956.
139. Ibid.
140. Ibid.
141. Lean is an impressive, yet underrated member of the BBC. He rose through the Bush House hierarchy from being a member of the European services during the Second World War, to being the director of the external services in the early 1960s. He was also the author of the magnificent *Voices in the Darkness* (London: Secker & Warburg, 1943), a vivid account of radio propaganda during the early years of the Second World War.
142. WAC, E/2/812/1, 16 November 1956.
143. Ibid.
144. For examples see Lean (1943), p. 88.
145. HSN, 13 November 1956.
146. HSN, 19 November 1956.
147. HSN, 17 November 1956.
148. Ibid.
149. FO371/122081/N1052/12, c.5 November 1956.
150. USIA Special Reports, S-7-54, 29 November 1956.
151. Ibid.
152. *BBC Handbook, 1958* p. 152.
153. HSN, 22 November 1956.
154. *Daily Telegraph*, 26 November 1956. Also FO953/1644/PB1011/74, 12 December 1956.
155. FO371/122081/N1052/12, c.5 December 1956.
156. SWB IIb, published 8 January 1957.
157. SWB IIb, 18 January 1957.
158. Ibid.
159. WAC, E2/812/1, 4 January 1957.
160. Molnar (1990), p. 199.
161. FO371/122404/NH1011/94, 12 December 1956.
162. FO371/122404/NH1011/94, 19 December 1956.
163. Ibid.
164. WAC, E1/2043/1, Hungary: Magyar Kozponti Hirado RT, 1955–7, 3 May 1957.
165. Ibid.
166. Ibid.
167. The official record did not make explicit that the actual difference was between Priority I and Priority II.
168. Sorenson (1968), p. 93. The author also documents how thousands of copies of books and films about Hungary were produced and distributed abroad by USIA.
169. Ibid.

170. 8th Review of Operations, 1 January–30 June 1957, p. 5, USIA HC.
171. Ibid.

4 THE CUBAN MISSILE CRISIS, 1962

1. Martin Walker *The Cold War* (London: Fourth Estate, 1993), p. 114.
2. Ibid.
3. Sorenson (1968), p. 197.
4. Ibid., p. 208.
5. USIA Area Project Correspondence 1954–63, Latin America (Multi-correspondence 1955), 12 January 1955. WRUL's personalities included Havana Rose, a Cuban exile by the name of Miss Pepita Rivera.
6. By June 1960, VOA material broadcast in this way amounted to an impressive 80 000 hours.
7. Figures are taken from Pirsein (1979), pp. 404, 422–5.
8. USIA Area Project Files 1952–63, Latin America 1958–61, ZP6002, 11 April 1961.
9. Cuba began regular broadcasts in mid-1960, by which time USIA concluded that its 'propaganda became indistinguishable from the Soviet Union's.' See USIA Research Reports, R-29-61, 7 June 1961. For a brief but excellent history of Cuban international radio propaganda, see R-62-61, 14 December 1961.
10. See *FRUS*, 1958–60, VI, pp. 599–600.
11. Ibid., p. 88. It was noted that 'Station WKWF in Key West, although only one-half KW in power, is heard clearly in the greater Habana area in the morning and at night. Several anti-Castro figures . . . are interested in buying the station or taking air-time in order to broadcast the type of program the US government could not engage in, but what they feel would have a profound effect on the Cuban people'.
12. Ibid., pp. 1147–8.
13. USIA Country Project Correspondence, 1952–63, Cuban Correspondence, 6 June 1960. USIA believed that both the State Department and the CIA would be interested in his findings.
14. USIA Area Project Correspondence, 1954–63, Latin America, 28 February 1962.
15. The *New York Times* and the *Washington Post* both knew of the Bay of Pigs invasion in advance, but refrained from publishing the story 'in the national interest.'
16. Sorenson (1968), pp. 140–1.
17. Quoted in Ibid., p. 141.
18. See L. Vandenbroucke, *Perilous Options* (Oxford: Oxford University Press, 1993), pp. 20–5.
19. USIA Special Reports, R-20-61, 27 April 1961. Khrushchev (1971) recounted in his memoirs that the Soviet leadership first learnt of the invasion from the radio. Which station is not specified. p. 491. Khrushchev also intimated that propaganda was no longer a sufficient method of fighting the Cold War. See. p. 493.
20. Kennedy's 1961 Statement of the USIA mission included 'advising the

President, his representatives abroad' and various departments, 'on the implications of foreign opinion for present and contemplated' American policies and programmes. Sorenson (1968), p. 142.

21. McClintock (1992), p. 205.
22. Ibid., p. 203.
23. Memo: R.C Salvateira to Henry Loomis, marked official limited use only, 28 June 1962, USIA HC. The conclusion of an opinion poll amongst Cuban exiles suggested formulating a 'positive programme ... which could be beamed to Cuba by the Voice of America.' See USIA Area Project Correspondence, 1954–63, Latin American, 28 February 1962.
24. R.C. Salvateira to Henry Loomis, 28 June 1962, USIA HC.
25. A. Schlesinger Jr., *A Thousand Days* (Boston: Houghton Mifflin, 1965), p. 612.
26. Ibid.
27. See SWB I, 26 August 1962.
28. SWB I, 11 October 1962.
29. See McClintock (1992), pp. 143–4, 148, 153–5.
30. SWB I, 2 September 1962.
31. SWB I, 10 September 1962.
32. SWB I, 11 September 1962.
33. Ibid.
34. Khrushchev confirmed in his memoirs (1971) that the idea was to install 'missiles with nuclear warheads in Cuba without letting the United States find out they were there until it was too late to do anything about them'. p. 493.
35. Walker (1993), pp. 170–1.
36. SWB I, 5 October 1962.
37. SWB I, 3 October 1962.
38. B.J. Bernstein, 'A Jupiter Swap?' in Robert A. Divine (ed.) *The Cuban Missile Crisis* (New York: Markus Wiener, 1988), p. 266.
39. SWB I, 17 October 1962.
40. 'My sympathetic feelings and my best wishes, said Washington, are on the side of any country I see as an oppressed nation which unfurls the banner of freedom. How times have changed,' remarked Radio Moscow's Alexsandre Yefstayev. SWB I, 8 October 1962.
41. SWB I, 17 October 1962.
42. D.C. Watt (ed.) *Documents on International Affairs, 1962* (London: Oxford University Press, 1971), pp. 203–4.
43. M. Beschloss, *Kennedy v. Khrushchev* (London: Faber & Faber, 1991), p. 423.
44. How this exercise was organised is described by David Detzer in *The Brink* (London: J.M. Dent & Sons, 1980), pp. 182–3.
45. Sorenson (1968), p. 202; Beschloss (1991), p. 483.
46. Memo to all media elements from Thomas Sorenson, Deputy Director (Policy and Planning), 22 October 1962, USIA (hereafter Memo to all media elements).
47. Ibid.
48. The British were unhappy about the use of the word 'quarantine' since

it laid the relevant UN Resolution open to 'unnecessary criticism and ridicule.' FO371/162375/AK1261/3, 22 October 1962. The Americans, however, rejected 'blockade' because this could be construed as an act of war.

49. FO371/162376/AK1261/23, 23 October 1962.
50. Memo to all media elements.
51. Raymond Garthoff, *Reflections on the Missile Crisis* (Washington, DC: The Brookings Institution, 1987), p. 36. The rejected passages can be found in Beschloss (1991), p. 484.
52. CAB 128/36, CC61(62), 23 October 1962.
53. The American Ambassador delivered a copy to the Director-General of the Ministry of Foreign Affairs who failed to return it. By 25 October the embassy reported that official Polish reaction had not yet been received. FO371/162380/AK1261/105, 25 October 1962.
54. FO371/162382/AK1261/159, 27 October 1962.
55. FO371/162394/AK1261/388, 4 November 1962.
56. Ibid. In his memoirs Khrushchev (1971) justified such news management: 'Our people were fully informed of the dangerous situation that had developed,' he wrote rather incredulously, but he conceded that the Soviet leadership 'took care not to cause panic by the way we presented the facts.' p. 497.
57. FO371/162390/AK1261/320, 24 October 1962.
58. Ibid.
59. FO371/162375/AK1261/19, 23 October 1962. This is a remarkable document in which Roberts accurately sets out the likely themes which would be part of the Soviet propaganda offensive.
60. Ibid.
61. USIA Research Reports, R-118-62(A), 23 October 1962.
62. SWB I, 23 October 1962.
63. Ibid.
64. SWB I, 27 October 1962.
65. SWB I, 23 October 1962.
66. Ibid.
67. Ibid.
68. Ibid.
69. Alec Douglas Home believed that the Soviets would use Cuba to 'exacerbate President Kennedy's difficulties and then offer a reduction of tension over Cuba in return for concessions over Berlin'. CAB 128/36, CC59(62), 9 October 1962.
70. FO371/162380/AK1261/119, 23 October 1962.
71. FO371/162375/AK1261/19, 23 October 1962.
72. Quoted by Beschloss (1991), p. 485, fn.
73. Both Charles Bohlen, former Ambassador to the Soviet Union, and Adlai Stevenson, Ambassador to the UN, recommended that the US enter into negotiations with the Soviet Union before any public announcement was made. See T.G. Paterson, 'Fixation with Cuba', in T.G. Paterson (ed.), *Kennedy's Quest for Victory* (Oxford: Oxford University Press, 1989), p. 150. As his explanation for why Kennedy rejected negotiation, Paterson states that there was nothing to negotiate, especially the Jupiter missiles

in Turkey. Paterson also places enormous emphasis on the psychological constraints which Kennedy was under.

74. That Kennedy hoped to publicly humiliate Khrushchev after the Bay of Pigs invasion is also suggested by the phrasing of the statement. Kennedy talked of 'our courage and our commitments'; that is, the speech included a strong personal element. This reinforces the notion that after the events of 1961, the President believed his own courage to be in question.

75. SWB I, 17 September 1962.

76. SWB I, 24 October 1962.

77. Ibid.

78. SWB I, 25 October 1962.

79. Ibid.

80. SWB I, 2 November 1962.

81. FO371/162382/AK1261. 26 October 1962.

82. FO371/162381/AK1261/134, 27 October 1962.

83. Walker (1993), p. 175.

84. SWB I, 27 October 1962.

85. A Soviet clandestine radio station broadcasting to Turkey had already tried to frighten Turkey into believing that it would be a 'legitimate target for retaliatory action if war broke out' because of the presence of NATO missiles there. USIA Research Reports, R-128-62(A), 28 October 1962.

86. SWB I, 27 October 1962.

87. S. Strange, 'Cuba and After', G.W. Keeton & G. Schwarzenburger (eds), *Year Book of World Affairs*, 1962 (London: Stevens & Sons, 1963), p. 2.

88. FO371/162382/AK1261/149, 28 October 1962.

89. FO371/162392/AK1261/346, 12 November 1962.

90. Russian officials have apparently admitted that Khrushchev's first message was drafted with the assistance of civilian advisers, all of whom feared imminent nuclear war. The second message was written in the presence of Khrushchev's generals. Walker (1993), p. 175.

91. Quoted in Beschloss (1991), p. 527.

92. A. Horelick, 'The Soviet Gamble', in Divine (1988), pp. 122–3.

93. Khrushchev even failed to mention this fact in his memoirs; the relevant passages should have been included in pp. 448–9.

94. FO371/162382/AK1261/144/G, 27 October 1962.

95. FO371/162388/AK1261/27/G, 28 October 1962.

96. See *Thirteen Days: A Memoir of the Cuban Missile Crisis* (New York: New American Library, 1969).

97. 'Homage to Plain Dumb Luck', in Divine (1988), p. 195.

98. USIA Potomac Cable 246, 24 October 1962, USIA HC.

99. FO371/162375/AK1261/13, 23 October 1962.

100. D. C. Watt (1971), pp. 226–7.

101. Ibid.

102. SWB I, 28 October 1962.

103. FO371/162382/AK1261/149, 28 October 1962.

104. Quoted in Beschloss (1991), pp. 541–2.

105. 'Cold War Model', in Divine (1988), p. 342.

106. SWB I, 31 October 1962.

107. H. Macmillan, *At the End of the Day 1961–63* (London: Macmillan, 1973), pp. 214–16.
108. CAB 128/36, CC63(62), 29 October 1962.
109. Beschloss (1991), p. 542.
110. Sorenson (1968), p. 238.
111. As the Soviet Union tried to bargain the Jupiters in Turkey for Cuba, Radio Moscow made frantic efforts to reassure Cubans of their unremitting support by increasing the length of its daily programmes to Cuba to ten hours and telling them that they would not be abandoned. USIA Research Reports, R-127-62(A), 27 October 1962.
112. 'Fidel Castro's Theatre of Now', *New York Times*, 20 January 1992.
113. 'Castro Anniversary', BBC General News talk, 2 January 1963, WAC.
114. FO371/162383/AK1261/166, 29 October 1962.
115. Ibid.
116. FO371/162391/AK1261/335, 1 November 1962.
117. It is not surprising that Marchant should so appreciate the power of radio. During the 1930s he contributed a number of talks to the BBC for a number of producers, including Guy Burgess. See West (1987), p. 49.
118. SWB III, 31 October 1962.
119. FO371/162386/AK1261/237, 31 October 1962.
120. FO371/162396/AK1261/436, 6 November 1962.
121. SWB I, 7 November 1962; II, 1 November 1962.
122. 'Cuba: Incident Closed', BBC General News Talk, 8 January 1963, WAC.
123. FO371/162427/AK1261/2, 31 October 1962.
124. Ibid.
125. FO371/162347/AK1051/11, 22 October 1962.
126. Sorenson (1968), p. 238.

5　THE AMERICAN COMMITMENT TO VIETNAM

1. Quoted in Sorenson (1968), p. 247.
2. See *FRUS* 1961–3, I Vietnam 1961 (*FRUS* I), p. 412.
3. USIA Research Reports, quoted in Sorenson (1968), p. 53.
4. 'Voice Policies Disturb Aides', *New York Times*, 6 June 1965.
5. See for example USIA Country Project Correspondence, Vietnam, 17 May 1958.
6. Hale (1975), p. 41.
7. In correspondence with the author, 29 March 1993.
8. Ibid.
9. FO953/2056/PEB1004/16, 12 October 1960.
10. *FRUS* 1958–60, I, Vietnam, p. 247.
11. FO953/2056/PEB1004/16, 12 October 1960. These neutralist countries are not identified.
12. FO953/2056/PEB1004/2, 6 February 1961.
13. FO953/2098/PEB1001/9, 2 April 1962. The BBC did nevertheless enjoy regular re-broadcasting by other stations in the region, including Radio Vietnam, until relay stations in Sarawak, the Maldives and Cyprus enhanced direct broadcasting to Asia.

14. *FRUS* 1961–3, IV, Vietnam August–December 1963 (*FRUS* IV), p. 165.
15. A.M. Sperber, *Murrow: His Life and Times* (New York: Freundlich Books, 1965), p. 680.
16. McClintock (1992), p. 270, recorded that General Edward Lansdale rejected the Malayan approach, considering it too colonial and more concerned with establishing order than with defending democracy.
17. Chandler (1981), p. 9.
18. Ibid., p. 6.
19. Quoted in Walker (1993), p. 160.
20. Ibid.
21. *FRUS* 1959–60, I Vietnam, pp. 269–70.
22. Radio Hanoi highlighted how a number of candidates' names had been deleted from the lists, and noted how several had lodged complaints against being 'arbitrarily ousted from elections.' Ibid., pp. 228–9.
23. *FRUS* I, pp. 9–10.
24. FO371/166701/DV1015/79, 20 March 1962.
25. *FRUS* 1961–3, II, Vietnam 1962 (*FRUS* II), p. 744.
26. In fact Peter Arnett, a correspondent with the AP News Agency, has recorded how the embassy's decision that a change of government was desirable was 'never officially placed on record but appeared to be inserted into the rumour mill intentionally.' *Live From the Battlefield* (London: Bloomsbury, 1994), p. 114.
27. *FRUS* IV, pp. 300–1.
28. Ibid., p. 301.
29. Ibid., p. 350.
30. Donald M. Wilson (Acting Director, USIA) to Roger Hilsman (Assistant Secretary for Far Eastern Affairs), 10 October 1963, USIA HC.
31. Sorenson (1968), p. 191.
32. Minute by Lowell Bennett (Director of Office of Public Information), 17 September 1963, USIA HC.
33. Sperber (1965), p. 68.
34. Malcolm Browne, AP Saigon Bureau Chief, quoted in Arnett (1994), p. 105.
35. However USIA reported that the people did not believe government propaganda on the crisis, relying instead on the 'bamboo telegraph' relaying rumours and VOA reports.
36. Arnett (1994), p. 101.
37. SWB III, 20 May 1963.
38. The US had made the same mistake regarding the Huks in the Philippines. See McClintock (1992), pp. 103–4.
39. FO371/166701/DV1015/64G, 28 February 1962. The Liberation Broadcasting Station began broadcasting in February 1962 in Vietnamese, Cambodian, Chaochow, English and French. Two transmitters at 'unannounced locations' were used, but still tried to give the impression of broadcasting from South Vietnam. See USIA Research Reports, R-87-62(C), 20 August 1962.
40. FO371/166704/DV1015/123, 30 April 1962.
41. Ibid.
42. Mecklin to Wilson, 3 March 1964, USIA HC.
43. Her father, the Ambassador to Washington, called her remarks 'imperti-

nent and disrespectful,' and his criticisms of his daughter were duly carried by VOA to Vietnam. *FRUS* III, Vietnam, January–August 1963 (*FRUS* III), p. 561 fn.

44. This episode confirms the power that such news photography can have: Ambassador Lodge described how Kennedy had a copy of the photograph in the White House and used it to justify his determination to 'shake things up' in South Vietnam. Arnett (1994), p. 108.
45. These emergency measures included strict news censorship, but many western correspondents continued to get their stories out of Vietnam via the American embassy.
46. *FRUS* III, pp. 618–19.
47. Ibid., p. 636.
48. Beschloss (1991), p. 635.
49. *FRUS* III, pp. 651–2.
50. Ibid., p. 640.
51. Weldon Brown, *Prelude to Disaster* (Washington: Kennikat Press, 1975), p. 204.
52. *FRUS* III, pp. 640, 649. Just what steps Hilsman was taking was not recorded.
53. *FRUS* IV, pp. 193–4.
54. SWB III, 20 and 21 September 1963.
55. *FRUS* IV, p. 465.
56. Ibid.
57. Beschloss (1991), p. 693.
58. In his address to the nation in 1964 Johnson drew parallels between Vietnam and the Cold War crises of Greece, Turkey, Berlin, Cuba and Lebanon. Martin Walker (1993), p. 196, has suggested that this revealed 'how thoroughly the US was misreading the political dynamics in South East Asia'.
59. Marylin B. Young, *The Vietnam Wars, 1945–1990* (New York: Harper Perennial, 1991), p. 113. This also involved blockading Haiphong harbour and bombing railways, roads, industry and training camps inside North Vietnam.
60. Mecklin to Wilson, 3 March 1964, USIA HC.
61. Ibid.
62. Ibid.
63. Ibid.
64. USIA Special Reports, S-9-61.
65. 'Increasing Broadcasts in Vietnamese', undated but c.late 1964, VOA Report, USIA HC.
66. Mecklin to Wilson, 3 March 1964, USIA HC.
67. Ibid.
68. Ibid.
69. Ibid.
70. Report entitled 'Radio Broadcasting', c.February 1964, USIA HC.
71. Mecklin to Wilson, 3 March 1964, USIA HC.
72. *FRUS* 1958–60, I, Vietnam, p. 206.
73. D.J. Duncanson, R.A. Yudkin & B. Zorthian, *Lessons of Vietnam: Three Interpretive Essays* (New York: American–Asian Education Exchange Inc., 1971), p. 46.

74. USIA Country Project Correspondence, 1951–61, Vietnam 1961, a series of files full of the details of such surveys and their findings.
75. Mecklin to Wilson, 3 March 1964, USIA HC.
76. Ibid.
77. USIA Country Project Correspondence, 1952–63, Vietnam 1958.
78. Mecklin to Wilson, 3 March 1964, USIA HC.
79. Ibid. However Ed Murrow pointed out that with over one million Chinese in South Vietnam, 'we must exercise caution in emphasising any traditional hostility between the two races per se, but rather concentrate on the present Chinese Communist régime.' *FRUS* III, p. 355.
80. Ibid., pp. 354–5.
81. Ibid.
82. *FRUS* I, p. 340.
83. Report on radio broadcasting, undated but believed to be 1964, USIA HC.
84. Sorenson (1968), pp. 291–2.

CONCLUSIONS

1. Gathering information from areas virtually cut-off from the outside world can be an immense problem. Chapter Three has illustrated how the monitoring service has a role to play in such circumstances. Yet we are constantly being reminded that other media of communication are also being used to such ends. Journalists in the besieged town of Gorazde, situated in the former Yugoslavia, used amateur radio to relay information to the outside world about the situation inside the town during April 1994. Earlier in Poland during the Communist crackdown against Solidarity in 1981, academics and students used a computer terminal connecting the Polish Academy of Sciences with the Mathematical Centre in Vienna to feed information exclusively to the BBC Polish service. See Walker (1992), p. 132.
2. Quoted in Kenneth Williams, *Just Williams* (London: 1985), p. 239.
3. Holsti (1988), p. 167.
4. Quoted in Briggs (1979), p. 521.
5. VOA transmissions still include editorials prepared by the State Department and acknowledged as such in broadcasts.
6. See D. Browne, *The Voice of America: Policies and Problems* (Kentucky: Lexington Association for Education in Journalism, 1976), p. 33.
7. Holsti (1988), p. 174.
8. *The Listener*, 29 December 1966, p. 948.
9. Holsti (1988), p. 170.
10. Ibid., p. 178.
11. On 31 July 1990, the American Assistant Secretary of State for Middle Eastern Affairs, John Kelly, announced that in the event of an invasion of Kuwait the US had no obligations or responsibilities to intervene. This was broadcast by the BBC World Service and was heard by Saddam Hussein in Baghdad. Did he interpret it as a green light to invade Kuwait only two days later? D. Kellner, *The Persian Gulf TV War* (Colorado: Westview Press, 1992), p. 14.

12. In the three months (September to December 1990) that the service, named 'Gulf-Link', was in operation, 6000 messages were sent.
13. 'Keep Radio Free Europe and Radio Liberty Going', *International Herald Tribune*, 4 March 1993.
14. This episode is best described by Walker (1992), pp. 124–5.
15. 'Economy Seen as Key to US Asia Policy', *International Herald Tribune*, 10 February 1993.
16. Quoted in Walker (1992), p. 140.
17. Ibid.
18. Beginning transmission in 1985, Marti is the Reagan-created successor to Radios Swan and Americas. Unlike its predecessors, however, Marti is overtly funded and operated by VOA from Florida.
19. J. Tusa, *A World In Your Ear* (London: Broadside, 1992), p. 18.
20. Ibid., pp. 40–1.
21. Two authors in particular have made a start to analysing the role of the BBC World Service during the Gulf War. See Tusa (1992), who was the managing director at the time, pp. 25–55, and Walker (1992), pp. 142–5 and *in passim*. For audience research see Graham Mytton and Mark Eggerman, 'The Role of International Radio as a Source of News in Some Middle Eastern Countries During the Gulf Crisis', in Graham Mytton (ed.), *Global Audiences: Research for Worldwide Broadcasting 1993*, (London: John Libbey, 1993).
22. One Barry Hill of Leeds, however, has been consistent, some would say eccentric, in his recording of radio programmes. His enormous archive, filling two houses, is now famous the world over. Unfortunately the archive moved to the USA in 1994.
23. Sorenson (1968), p. 6.

Select Bibliography

MEMOIRS, AUTOBIOGRAPHIES AND BIOGRAPHIES

Ambrose, Stephen, *Eisenhower: Soldier and President* (New York: Touchstone, 1990).

Arnett, Peter, *Live From the Battlefield* (London: Bloomsbury, 1994).

Boyle, Andrew, *Only the Wind Will Listen: Reith of the BBC* (London: Hutchinson, 1972).

Churchill, Randolph S., *The Rise and Fall of Sir Anthony Eden* (London: MacGibbon & Kee, 1959).

Cohen, Warren I. *The American Secretaries of State and Their Diplomacy, Vol. XIX: Dean Rusk* (New York: Cooper Square, 1980).

Eisenhower, Dwight D., *The White House Years: Waging Peace, 1956–1961* (London: Heinemann, 1966).

Fergusson, Bernard, *The Trumpet in the Hall, 1930–1958* (London: Collins, 1971).

Fisher, Nigel, *Harold Macmillan* (London: Weidenfeld & Nicolson, 1982).

Gerson, Louis L., *The American Secretaries of State and Their Diplomacy, Vol. XVII: John Foster Dulles* (New York: Cooper Publishers, 1980).

Goldie, Grace Wyndham, *Facing the Nation* (London: The Bodley Head, 1977).

Greene, Sir Hugh, *The Third Floor Front* (London: The Bodley Head, 1969).

Grisewood, Harman, *One Thing at a Time* (London: Hutchinson, 1968).

Healey, Denis, *The Time of my Life* (London: Penguin, 1990).

Hill, Charles, *Both Sides of the Hill* (London: Houghton Mufflin, 1972).

Horne, Alistair, *Macmillan* (2 vols.) (London: Macmillan, 1988 & 1989).

Kennedy, Robert F., *Thirteen Days: A Memoir of the Cuban Missile Crisis* (New York: W.W. Norton & Company, Inc., 1968).

Lacoutre, Jean, *Nasser* (English translation) (London: Secker & Warburg, 1973).

Lloyd, Selwyn, *Suez 1956: A Personal Account* (New York: Mayflower, 1978).

Macmillan, Harold, *Riding the Storm, 1956–1959* (London: Macmillan, 1971).

——, *Pointing the Way, 1959–1961* (London: Macmillan, 1972).

——, *At the End of the Day, 1961–1963* (London: Macmillan, 1973).

Marett, Sir Robert, *Through the Back Door: An Inside View of Britain's Overseas Information Services* (London: Pergamon Press, 1968).

Nutting, Anthony, *No End of a Lesson: The Story of Suez* (London: Constable, 1967).

Page, Tim, *Page After Page* (London: Paladin Grafton, 1990).

Renier, Olive & Vladimir Rubenstein, *Assigned to Listen: The Evesham Experience, 1939–43* (London: BBC, 1986).

Schlesinger Jr, Arthur M., *A Thousand Days: John F. Kennedy in the White House* (Boston: Houghton Mifflin, 1965).

Shuckburgh, Evelyn, *Descent to Suez: Diaries, 1951–56* (London: Weidenfeld & Nicolson, 1986).

Sperber, A.M., *Murrow: His Life and Times* (New York: Freundlich Books, 1986).

Sweet-Escott, Bickham, *Baker Street Irregular* (London: Methuen, 1965).

Talbot, Strobe (ed. & trans.), *Khrushchev Remembers* (London: André Deutsch, 1971).

Tracey, Michael, *A Variety of Lives: A Biography of Sir Hugh Greene* (London: The Bodley Head, 1983).

Williams, Francis, *A Prime Minister Remembers: The War and Post-War Memories of the Rt. Hon. Earl Attlee* (London: William Heinemann 1961).

BOOKS AND MONOGRAPHS

Alexandre, Laurien, *The Voice of America: From Détente to the Reagan Doctrine* (Ablex Publishing, 1988).

Ambrose, Stephen E., *Rise to Globalism: American Foreign Policy Since 1938* 5th edn. (London: Penguin, 1988).

Aster, Howard (ed.), *Challenges for International Broadcasting* (Lanham, USA: Mosaic Press, 1991).

Barber, Noel, *Seven Days of Freedom: The Hungarian Uprising, 1956* (London: Macmillan, 1974).

Barnouw, Erik, *The Image Empire: A History of Broadcasting in the United States* (New York: Oxford University Press, 1970).

Barraclough, Geoffrey, *Survey of International Affairs, 1955–6; 1956–58; 1959–60* (Royal Institute of International Affairs, London: Oxford University Press, 1960; 1961; 1964).

BBC, *The European Service of the BBC: Two Decades of Broadcasting to Europe, 1938–1959* (London: BBC Publications, 1959).

——, *Voice for the World* (London: BBC World Service Publications, 1988).

Berridge, G.R., *International Politics: States, Power and Conflict since 1945* (Brighton: Wheatsheaf, 1987).

Beschloss, Michael R., *Kennedy v. Khrushchev: The Crisis Years, 1960–1963* (London: Faber & Faber, 1991).

Black, John, *Organizing the Propaganda Instrument: The British Experience* (The Hague: Martinus Nijhoff, 1975).

Boardman, Robert (ed.), *The Management of Britain's External Relations* (London: Macmillan, 1973).

Briggs, Asa, *The History of Broadcasting in the United Kingdom* 4 Vols. (London: Oxford University Press, 1961–1979).

——, *Governing the BBC* (London: BBC Publications, 1979).

——, *The BBC: The First Fifty Years* (Oxford: Oxford University Press, 1985).

Brown, J.A.C., *Techniques of Persuasion: From Propaganda to Brainwashing* (Harmondsworth: Penguin, 1963).

Brown, Weldon A., *Prelude to Disaster: The American Role in Vietnam, 1940–1963* (Washington: Kennikat Press, 1975).

Browne, Donald R., *The Voice of America: Problems and Policies (Kentucky: Journalism Monograph (43), February 1976).

——, *International Radio Broadcasting: The Limits of the Limitless Medium* (New York: Praeger, 1982).

Brugioni, Dino A., *Eyeball to Eyeball: The Inside Story of the Cuban Missile Crisis* (New York: Random House, 1991).

Campbell, John, *Listening to the World*, BBC Lunchtime Lectures, 5th Series (4), (London: BBC, 1967).

Chandler, Robert W. *War of Ideas: The US Propaganda Campaign in Vietnam* (Boulder, Colorado: Westview Press, 1981).

Cockerell, Michael, Peter Hennessy and David Walker, *Sources Close to the Prime Minister: Inside the Hidden World of the News Manipulators* (London: Macmillan, 1984).

Cohen, Yoel, *Media Diplomacy: The Foreign Office in the Mass Communication Age* (London: Frank Cass, 1986).

Cruickshank, Charles, *The Fourth Arm: Psychological Warfare 1938–1945* London: Davies-Poynter, 1977).

Curran, Charles J., *Broadcasting from West of Suez*, BBC Lunchtime Lectures, 7th Series (2). (London: BBC, 1976).

Dennis, E., G. Gerbner and Y. Zasoursky (eds), *Beyond the Cold War: Soviet and American Media Images* (London: Sage Publications, 1991).

Dickie, John, *Inside the Foreign Office* (London: Chapman, 1992).

Dimbleby, David and David Reynolds, *An Ocean Apart: The Relationship Between Britain and America in the Twentieth Century* (London: Hodder & Stoughton, 1988).

Dinerstein, Herbert S., *The Making of a Missile Crisis: October 1962* (Baltimore, Johns Hopkins University Press, 1976).

Divine, Robert A. (ed.), *The Cuban Missile Crisis* (New York: Markus Wiener, 1988).

Dizzard, Wilson P., *The Strategy of Truth: The Story of the US Information Service* (Washington: Public Affairs Press, 1961).

Draper, Theodore, *Abuse of Power: US Foreign Policy from Cuba to Vietnam* (London: Pelican, 1969).

Duncanson, D.J., R.A. Yudkin and B. Zorthian, *Lessons of Vietnam: Three Interpretive Essays* (New York: American–Asian Education Exchange, 1971).

El Hussini, Mohrez Mahmoud, *Soviet–Egyptian Relations, 1945–85* (London: Macmillan Press, 1987).

Ellul, Jacques, *Propaganda: The Formation of Men's Attitudes* (New York: Vintage Books, 1965).

Felkay, Andrew, *Hungary and the USSR, 1956–1988: Kádár's Political Leadership* (Connecticut: Greenwood Press, 1989).

Frederick, Howard H., *Cuban–American Radio Wars: Ideology in International Telecommunications* (Norwood, New Jersey: Ablex, 1986).

Friedland, Lewis A., *Covering the World: International Television News Services* (New York: Twentieth Century Fund Press, 1992).

Garthoff, Raymond L., *Reflections on the Cuban Missile Crisis* (Washington, DC: The Brookings Institution, 1987).

Glahn, Gerhard von, *Law Among Nations: An Introduction to Public International Law* (5th edn.) (New York: Macmillan, 1986).

Hale, Julian, *Radio Power: Propaganda and International Broadcasting* (Philadelphia: Temple University Press, 1975).

Havighurst, Clark C. (ed.), *International Control of Propaganda* (New York: Oceana Publications, 1967).

Heikal, Mohammed, *Cutting the Lion's Tail* (London: André Deutsch, 1986).

Hoffman, Arthur S. (ed.), *International Communication and the New Diplomacy* (Indiana: Indiana University Press, 1968).

Holbraad, Carsten, *Superpowers and International Conflict* (London: Macmillan, 1979).

Holt, Robert T., *Radio Free Europe* (Minneapolis: University of Minnesota Press, 1958).

Holsti, K.J., *International Politics: A Framework for Analysis* (5th edn.) (New Jersey: Prentice Hall, 1988).

Howe, Ellice, *The Black Game* (London: Michael Joseph, 1982).

Jeffreys-Jones, Rhodri, *The CIA and American Democracy* (New Haven: Yale University Press, 1989).

Karnow, Stanley, *Vietnam: A History* (London: Guild Publishing, 1983).

Keeton, G.W. and G. Schwarzenberger (eds), *The Year Book of World Affairs 1957* (London: Tevens & Sons, 1957).

——, *The Year Book of World Affairs, 1963* (London: Stevens and Sons, 1963).

Kellner, Douglas, *The Persian Gulf TV War* (Boulder, Colorado: Westview Press, 1992).

Király, Béla and Paul Jones, *The Hungarian Revolution of 1956 in Retrospect* (Boulder, Colorado: Columbia University Press, 1978).

Kyle, Keith, *Suez* (London: Weidenfeld & Nicolson, 1991).

Latey, Maurice, *Broadcasting to the USSR and Eastern Europe*, BBC, Lunchtime Lectures, 3rd Series (2) (London: BBC, 1964).

Lean, Tangye, *Voices In the Darkness: The Story of the European Radio War* (London: Secker & Warburg, 1943).

Lisann, Maury, *Broadcasting to the Soviet Union: International Politics and Radio* (New York: Praeger; 1975).

Lomax, Bill, *Hungary 1956* (London: Allison & Busby, 1976).

Love, Kennett, *Suez: The Twice Fought War* (London: Longman, 1969).

Lucas, W. Scott, *Divided We Stand: Britain, the US and the Suez Crisis* (London: Hodder & Stoughton, 1991).

McClintock, Michael, *Instruments of Statecraft: US Guerrilla Warfare, Counter-Insurgency, Counter Terrorism, 1940–1990* (New York: Pantheon Books, 1992).

Mansell, Gerard, *Let Truth Be Told: 50 Years of BBC External Broadcasting* (London: BBC, 1982).

——, *Why External Broadcasting?* BBC Lunchtime Lectures, 10th Series (6) (London: BBC, 1976).

Meyer, Cord, *Facing Reality: From World Federalism to the CIA* (New York: Harper & Row, 1980).

Michie, Allan, *Voices Through the Iron Curtain: The Radio Free Europe Story* (New York: Dodd Mead, 1963).

Mikes, George, *The Hungarian Revolution* (London: André Deutsch, 1967).

Molnar, Miklos, *Budapest 1956: A History of the Hungarian Revolution* (London: George Allen & Unwin, 1971).

——, *From Bela Kun to Janos Kadar: Seventy Years of Hungarian Communism* (English translation) (Oxford: Berg Publishers, 1990).

Moncrieff, Anthony (ed.), *Suez Ten Years After* (London: BBC, 1967).

Mytton, Graham (ed.), *Global Audiences: Research for Worldwide Broadcasting, 1992* (London: John Libbey, 1993).

Partner, Peter, *Arab Voices: The BBC Arabic Service, 1938–1988* (London: BBC, 1988).

Partos, Gabriel, *The World That Came In From the Cold* (London: Royal Institute of International Affairs, 1993).

Pirsein, Robert W., *The Voice of America: An History of International Broadcasting Activities of the United States Government, 1940–1962* (New York: Arno Press, 1979).

Qualter, Terence H., *Opinion Control in the Democracies* (London: Macmillan, 1985).

Schram, Wilbur (ed.), *The Process and Effects of Mass Communication* (Urbana, Illinois: University of Illinois Press, 1965).

Short, K.R.M. (ed.), *Western Broadcasting Over the Iron Curtain* (New York: St. Martin's Press, 1986).

Sorenson, Thomas, *The Word War: The Story of American Propaganda* (New York: Harper & Row, 1968).

Swann, Sir Michael, *The BBC's External Services Under Threat? Address to the Royal Society of Arts* (London: BBC, 1978).

Taylor, Peter J., *Britain and the Cold War: 1945 as Geopolitical Transition* (London: Pinter Publishers, 1990).

Taylor, Philip M., *The Projection of Britain: British Overseas Publicity and Propaganda, 1919–1939* (Cambridge: Cambridge University Press, 1981).

——, *Munitions of the Mind: War Propaganda from the Ancient World to the Nuclear Age* (Northampton: Patrick Stephens, 1990).

——, *War and Media: Propaganda and Persuasion in the Gulf War* (Manchester: Manchester University Press, 1992).

Trethowan, Sir Ian, *The BBC and International Broadcasting* (London: BBC, 1981).

Tusa, John, *Conversations with the World* (London: BBC, 1990).

——, *A World in Your Ear* (London: Broadside, 1992).

Tyson, James, *US International Broadcasting and National Security* (New York: Rampo Press, 1983).

Urban, G.R. (ed.), *Talking to Eastern Europe: A Collection of the Best Readings from the Broadcasts and Background Papers of Radio Free Europe* (London: Eyre & Spottiswoode, 1964).

Walker, Andrew, *A Skyful of Freedom: 60 Years of the BBC World Service* (London: Broadside, 1992).

Walker, Martin, *The Cold War* (London: Fourth Estate, 1993).

West, W.J., *Truth Betrayed* (London: Duckworth, 1987).

Whitfield, Stephen J., *The Culture of the Cold War* (London: Johns Hopkins University Press, 1991).

Whitton, John B., *Propaganda and the Cold War: A Princeton University Symposium* (Connecticut: Public Affairs Press, 1963, 1984) (Reprint).

Wise, David and Thomas B. Ross, *The Invisible Government* (London: Jonathan Cape, 1965).

ARTICLES

Adelman, Kenneth, 'Speaking of America: Public Diplomacy in Our Time', *Foreign Affairs*, 59 (4), Spring 1981.

Artyomov, Vladimir and Vladimir Semyonov, 'The BBC: History, Apparatus, Methods of Radio Propaganda', *Historical Journal of Film, Radio and Television*, 4 (1), March 1984.

Boyd, Douglas A., 'Cross Cultural International Broadcasting in Arabic', *Gazette* (32), 1983.

—— 'International Broadcasting to the Arab World: Cultural, Economic and Political Motivations for Transnational Radio Communication', *Gazette* (44), 1989.

Browne, Donald R., 'The Media of the Arab World and Matters of Style', *Middle East Review*, 12, Summer 1980.

Davison, W. Phillips, 'News Media and International Negotiation', *Public Opinion Quarterly*, 38 (2), Summer 1974.

Dooley, Brian, 'The Cuban Missile Crisis: Thirty Years On', *History Today*, 42, October 1992.

Horelick, Arnold L., 'The Cuban Missile Crisis: An Analysis of Soviet Calculations and Behaviour', *World Politics*, 16 (3), April 1964.

MacKenzie, F.R., 'Eden, Suez and the BBC', *The Listener*, 82 (2125), 18 December 1969.

Markel, Lester, 'If We Are to Win the Colder War', *New York Times Magazine*, 13 July 1958.

Milosz, Czeslaw, 'Keep Radio Free Europe and Radio Liberty Going', *International Herald Tribune*, 4 March 1993.

Nason, James O.H., 'International Broadcasting as an Instrument of Foreign Policy', *Millennium* 6 (2), 1977.

Nicholls, John Spicer, 'Wasting the Propaganda Dollar', *Foreign Policy* 56, Autumn 1984.

'Radio in the Cold War', *World Today,* Vol. 10, 1954.

Rawnsley, Gary David, 'A Unique Archive', *History Today*, 43, July 1993.

——'Crisis and Credibility at Radio Moscow', *Shortwave Magazine*, 51 (9), September 1993.

Smith, Don D., 'Some Effects of Radio Moscow's North American Broadcasts', *Public Opinion Quarterly*, 34 (4), Winter 1970–71.

Smith, Lyn, 'Covert British Propaganda: The Information Research Department, 1947–1977', *Millennium: Journal of International Studies*, 9 (1), 1980.

Sulzberger, C.L., 'What's Wrong with American Propaganda?', *New York Times*, 14 May 1956, p. 24.

'U.S. Indictment of Russia Over Hungary', *The Times*, 21 June 1957, p. 14.

'VOA's Role in the Cuban Crisis', *Broadcasting*, 60, 1 May 1961, p. 74.

Wark, Wesley K., 'Coming in from the Cold: British Propaganda and Red Army Defectors, 1945–1952', *The International History Review*, 9 (1), February 1987.

Waterfield, Gordon, 'Suez and the Role of Broadcasting' *The Listener*, 29 December 1966.

Index